CAMBRIDGE LIBRARY COLLECTION

Books of enduring scholarly value

Religion

For centuries, scripture and theology were the focus of prodigious amounts of scholarship and publishing, dominated in the English-speaking world by the work of Protestant Christians. Enlightenment philosophy and science, anthropology, ethnology and the colonial experience all brought new perspectives, lively debates and heated controversies to the study of religion and its role in the world, many of which continue to this day. This series explores the editing and interpretation of religious texts, the history of religious ideas and institutions, and not least the encounter between religion and science.

A General View of Positivism

In A General View of Positivism French philosopher Auguste Comte (1798-1857) gives an overview of his social philosophy known as Positivism. Comte, credited with coining the term 'sociology' and one of the first to argue for it as a science, is concerned with reform, progress and the problem of social order in society. In this English edition of the work, published in 1865, he addresses the practical problems of implementing his philosophy or doctrine, as he also refers to Positivism, into society. He believes that society evolves through a series of stages that are ruled by social laws and culminate in a superior form of social life. During this reorganisation of society, which will find its greatest supporters among women and the working class, a new moral power will emerge. Under the motto Love, Order and Progress Comte wishes humanism to replace organised religion as the object of spiritual worship.

Cambridge University Press has long been a pioneer in the reissuing of out-of-print titles from its own backlist, producing digital reprints of books that are still sought after by scholars and students but could not be reprinted economically using traditional technology. The Cambridge Library Collection extends this activity to a wider range of books which are still of importance to researchers and professionals, either for the source material they contain, or as landmarks in the history of their academic discipline.

Drawing from the world-renowned collections in the Cambridge University Library, and guided by the advice of experts in each subject area, Cambridge University Press is using state-of-the-art scanning machines in its own Printing House to capture the content of each book selected for inclusion. The files are processed to give a consistently clear, crisp image, and the books finished to the high quality standard for which the Press is recognised around the world. The latest print-on-demand technology ensures that the books will remain available indefinitely, and that orders for single or multiple copies can quickly be supplied.

The Cambridge Library Collection will bring back to life books of enduring scholarly value across a wide range of disciplines in the humanities and social sciences and in science and technology.

A General View
of Positivism

Auguste Comte

CAMBRIDGE UNIVERSITY PRESS

Cambridge New York Melbourne Madrid Cape Town Singapore São Paolo Delhi

Published in the United States of America by Cambridge University Press, New York

www.cambridge.org
Information on this title: www.cambridge.org/9781108000642

This edition first published 1865
This digitally printed version 2009

ISBN 978-1-108-00064-2

A

GENERAL VIEW OF POSITIVISM.

TRANSLATED FROM THE FRENCH OF

AUGUSTE COMTE,

BY

J. H. BRIDGES,

Physician to the Bradford Infirmary ; late Fellow of Oriel College, Oxford.

LONDON:

TRÜBNER AND CO., 60, PATERNOSTER ROW.

1865.

REPUBLIC OF THE WEST—ORDER AND PROGRESS.

A

GENERAL VIEW OF POSITIVISM;

OR,

SUMMARY EXPOSITION

OF THE

SYSTEM OF THOUGHT AND LIFE,

ADAPTED TO THE

GREAT WESTERN REPUBLIC,

FORMED OF THE

FIVE ADVANCED NATIONS,

THE FRENCH, ITALIAN, SPANISH, BRITISH, AND GERMAN,

WHICH, SINCE THE TIME OF CHARLEMAGNE, HAVE ALWAYS CONSTITUTED
A POLITICAL WHOLE.

Réorganiser, sans dieu ni roi, par le culte systématique de l'Humanité.
Nul n'a droit qu'à faire son devoir.
L'esprit doit toujours être le ministre du cœur, et jamais son esclave.

Reorganization, irrespectively of God or king, by the worship of Humanity, systematically adopted.
Man's only right is to do his duty.
The Intellect should always be the servant of the Heart, and should never be its slave.

BY

AUGUSTE COMTE,

AUTHOR OF "SYSTEM OF POSITIVE PHILOSOPHY."

PARIS:
1848.

NOTICE.

THIS work was first published separately in 1848. The Second Edition, of which this is the Translation, was published in 1851, as part of the first volume of the Treatise on Positive Polity, to which it is the Introduction. The Table of Contents and Marginal Notes have been added by the Translator.

b

TABLE OF CONTENTS.

CHAPTER I.

INTELLECTUAL CHARACTER OF POSITIVISM.

CHAPTER II.

THE SOCIAL ASPECT OF POSITIVISM.

CHAPTER IV.

THE INFLUENCE OF POSITIVISM UPON WOMEN.

CHAPTER V.

THE RELATION OF POSITIVISM TO ART.

CHAPTER VI.

CONCLUSION. THE RELIGION OF HUMANITY.

A GENERAL VIEW OF POSITIVISM.

" We tire of thinking and even of acting ; we never tire of loving."

In the following series of systematic essays upon Positivism, the essential principles of the doctrine are first considered ; I then point out the agencies by which its propagation will be effected ; and I conclude by describing certain additional features indispensable to its completeness. My treatment of these questions will of course be summary : yet it will suffice, I hope, to overcome several excusable but unfounded prejudices. It will enable any competent reader to assure himself that the new general doctrine aims at something more than satisfying the Intellect ; that it is in reality quite as favourable to Feeling and even to Imagination.

INTRODUCTORY REMARKS.

Positivism consists essentially of a Philosophy and a Polity. These can never be dissevered ; the former being the basis, and the latter the end of one comprehensive system, in which our intellectual faculties and our social sympathies are brought into close correlation with each other. For, in the first place, the science of Society,

besides being more important than any other, supplies the
only logical and scientific link by which all our varied
observations of phenomena can be brought into one consistent whole.* Of this science it is even more true than
of any of the preceding sciences, that its real character
cannot be understood without explaining its exact relation
in all general features with the art corresponding to it.
Now here we find a coincidence which is assuredly not
fortuitous. At the very time when the theory of society
is being laid down, an immense sphere is opened for the
application of that theory ; the direction, namely, of the
social regeneration of Western Europe. For, if we take
another point of view, and look at the great crisis of
modern history, as its character is displayed in the natural
course of events, it becomes every day more evident how
hopeless is the task of reconstructing political institutions
without the previous remodelling of opinion and of life.
To form then a satisfactory synthesis of all human conceptions is the most urgent of our social wants : and it is
needed equally for the sake of Order and of Progress.
During the gradual accomplishment of this great philosophical work, a new moral power will arise spontaneously
throughout the West, which, as its influence increases,
will lay down a definite basis for the reorganization of
society. It will offer a general system of education for
the adoption of all civilized nations, and by this means
will supply in every department of public and private life
fixed principles of judgment and of conduct. Thus the
intellectual movement and the social crisis will be brought

---

* The establishment of this great principle is the most important result
of my " System of Positive Philosophy." This work was published 1830–1842,
with the title of " Course of Positive Philosophy," because it was based upon a
course of lectures delivered 1826–1829. But since that time I have always
given it the more appropriate name of System. Should the work reach a
second edition, the correction will be made formally : meanwhile, this will,
I hope, remove all misconception on the subject.

continually into close connection with each other. Both will combine to prepare the advanced portion of humanity for the acceptance of a true spiritual power, a power more coherent, as well as more progressive, than the noble but premature attempt of mediæval Catholicism.

The primary object, then, of Positivism is twofold: to generalize our scientific conceptions, and to systematize the art of social life. These are but two aspects of one and the same problem. They will form the subjects of the two first chapters of this work. I shall first explain the general spirit of the new philosophy. I shall then show its necessary connection with the whole course of that vast revolution which is now about to terminate under its guidance in social reconstruction.

This will lead us naturally to another question. The regenerating doctrine cannot do its work without adherents: in what quarter should we hope to find them? Now, with individual exceptions of great value, we cannot expect the adhesion of any of the upper classes in society. They are all more or less under the influence of baseless metaphysical theories, and of aristocratic self-seeking. They are absorbed in blind political agitation, and in disputes for the possession of the useless remnants of the old theological and military system. Their action only tends to prolong the revolutionary state indefinitely, and can never result in true social renovation.

Whether we regard its intellectual character or its social objects, it is certain that Positivism must look elsewhere for support. It will find a welcome in those classes only whose good sense has been left unimpaired by our vicious system of education, and whose generous sympathies are allowed to develope themselves freely. It is among Women, therefore, and among the Working classes that the heartiest supporters of the new doctrine will be found. It is intended, indeed, ultimately for all classes of society. But it will never gain much real influence over the higher ranks till it is forced upon their notice by these powerful patrons. When the work of spiritual reorganization is completed, it is on them that its maintenance will principally depend; and so too, their combined aid is necessary for its commencement. Having but little influence in political government, they are the more likely to appreciate the need of a moral government, the special object of which it will be to protect them against the oppressive action of the temporal power.

In the third chapter, therefore, I shall explain the mode in which philosophers and working men will co-operate. Both have been prepared for this coalition by the general course which modern history has taken, and it offers now the only hope we have of really decisive action. We shall find that the efforts of Positivism to regulate and develope the natural tendencies of the people, make it, even from the intellectual point of view, more coherent and complete.

But there is another and a more unexpected source from which Positivism will obtain support; and not till then will its true character and the full extent of its constructive power be appreciated. I shall show in the fourth chapter how eminently calculated is the Positive doctrine to raise and regulate the social condition of Women. It is from the feminine aspect only that human life, whether individually or collectively considered, can really be comprehended as a whole. For the only basis on which a system really embracing all the requirements of life can be formed, is the subordination of intellect to social feeling: a subordination which we find directly represented in the womanly type of character, whether regarded in its personal or social relations.

Although these questions cannot be treated fully in the present work, I hope to convince my readers that Positivism is more in accordance with the spontaneous tendencies of the people and of women than Catholicism, and is therefore better qualified to institute a spiritual power. It should be observed that the ground on which the support of both these classes is obtained is, that Positivism is the only system which can supersede the various subversive schemes that are growing every day more dangerous to all the relations of domestic and social life. Yet the tendency of the doctrine is to elevate the character of both of these classes; and it gives a most energetic sanction to all their legitimate aspirations.

Thus it is that a philosophy originating in speculations of the most abstract character, is found applicable not merely to every department of practical life, but also to the sphere of our moral nature. But to complete the proof of its universality I have still to speak of another very essential feature. I shall show, in spite of prejudices which exist very naturally on this point, that Positivism is eminently calculated to call the Imaginative faculties into exercise. It is by these faculties that the unity of human nature is most distinctly represented : they are themselves intellectual, but their field lies principally in our moral nature, and the result of their operation is to influence the active powers. The subject of women treated in the fourth chapter, will lead me by a natural transition to speak in the fifth of the Esthetic aspects of Positivism. I shall attempt to show that the new doctrine by the very fact of embracing the whole range of human relations in the spirit of reality, discloses the true theory of Art, which has hitherto been so great a deficiency in our speculative conceptions. The principle of the theory is that, in co-ordinating the primary functions of Humanity, Positivism places the Idealities of the poet midway between the Ideas of the philosopher and the Realities of the statesman. We see from this theory how it is that the poetical power of Positivism cannot be manifested at present. We must wait until moral and mental regeneration has advanced far enough to awaken the sympathies which naturally belong to it, and on which Art in its renewed state must depend for the future. The first mental and social shock once passed, Poetry will at last take her proper rank. She will lead Humanity onward towards a future which is now no longer vague and visionary, while at the same time she enables us to pay due honour to all phases of the past. The great object which Positivism sets before us individually and socially, is the endeavour to become more perfect. The highest importance is attached therefore to the imaginative faculties, because in every sphere with which they deal they stimulate the sense of perfection. Limited as my explanations in this work must be, I shall be able to show that Positivism, while opening out a new and wide field for art, supplies in the same spontaneous way new means of expression.

I shall thus have sketched with some detail the true character of the regenerating doctrine. All its principal aspects will have been considered. Beginning with its philosophical basis, I pass by natural transitions to its political purpose; thence to its action upon the people, its influence with women, and lastly, to its esthetic power. In concluding this work, which is but the introduction to a larger treatise, I have only to speak of the conception which unites all these various aspects. As summed up in the positivist motto, *Love, Order, Progress,* they lead us to the conception of Humanity, which implicitly involves and gives new force to each of them. Rightly interpreting this conception, we view Positivism at last as a complete and consistent whole. The subject will naturally lead us to speak in general terms of the future progress of social regeneration, as far as the history of the past enables us to foresee it. The movement originates in France, and is limited at first to the great family of Western nations. I shall show that it will afterwards extend, in accordance with definite laws, to the rest of the white race, and finally to the other two great races of man.

CHAPTER I.

THE INTELLECTUAL CHARACTER OF POSITIVISM.

The object of Philosophy is to present a systematic view of human life, as a basis for modifying its imperfections.

THE object of all true Philosophy is to frame a system which shall comprehend human life under every aspect, social as well as individual. It embraces, therefore, the three kinds of phenomena of which our life consists, Thoughts, Feelings, and Actions. Under all these aspects, the growth of Humanity is primarily spontaneous; and the basis upon which all wise attempts to modify it should proceed, can only be furnished by an exact acquaintance with the natural process. We are, however, able to modify this process systematically; and the importance of this is extreme, since we can thereby greatly diminish the partial deviations, the disastrous delays, and the grave inconsistencies to which so complex a growth would be liable were it left entirely to itself. To effect this necessary intervention is the proper sphere of politics. But a right conception cannot be formed of it without the aid of the philosopher, whose business it is to define and amend the principles on which it is conducted. With this object in view the philosopher endeavours to co-ordinate the various elements of man's existence, so that it may be conceived of theoretically as an integral whole. His synthesis can only be valid in so far as it is an exact and complete representation of the relations naturally existing. The first condition is therefore that these relations be carefully studied. When the philosopher, instead of forming such a synthesis, attempts to interfere more directly with the course of practical life, he commits the error of usurping the province of the statesman, to whom all practical measures exclusively belong. Philosophy and Politics are the two principal functions of the great social organism. Morality, systematically considered, forms the connecting link and at the same time the line of demarcation between them. It is the most important application of philosophy, and it gives a general direction to polity. Natural morality, that is to say the various emotions of our moral nature, will, as I have shown in my previous work, always govern the speculations of the one and the operations of the other. This I shall explain more fully.

But the synthesis, which it is the social function of Philosophy to construct, will neither be real nor permanent, unless it embraces every department of human nature, whether speculative, affective, or practical. These three orders of phenomena react upon each other so intimately, that any system which does not include all of them must inevitably be unreal and inadequate. Yet it is only in the present day, when Philosophy is reaching the positive stage, that this which is her highest and most essential mission can be fully apprehended.

The theological synthesis depended exclusively upon our affective nature; and to this is owing its original supremacy and its ultimate decline. For a long time its influence over all our highest speculations was paramount. This was especially the case during the Polytheistic period, when Imagination and Feeling still retained their sway under very slight restraint from the reasoning faculties. Yet even during the time of its highest development,

The Theological synthesis failed to include the practical side of human nature.

intellectually and socially, theology exercised no real control over practical life. It reacted, of course, upon it to some extent, but the effects of this were in most cases far more apparent than real. There was a natural antagonism between them, which though at first hardly perceived, went on increasing till at last it brought about the entire destruction of the theological fabric. A system so purely subjective could not harmonize with the necessarily objective tendencies and stubborn realities of practical life. Theology asserted all phenomena to be under the dominion of Wills more or less arbitrary : whereas in practical life men were led more and more clearly to the conception of invariable Laws. For without laws human action would have admitted of no rule or plan. In consequence of this utter inability of theology to deal with practical life, its treatment of speculative and even of moral problems was exceedingly imperfect, such problems being all more or less dependent on the practical necessities of life. To present a perfectly synthetic view of human nature was, then, impossible as long as the influence of theology lasted ; because the Intellect was impelled by Feeling and by the Active powers in two totally different directions. The failure of all metaphysical attempts to form a synthesis need not be dwelt upon here. Metaphysicians, in spite of their claims to absolute truth, have never been able to supersede theology in questions of feeling, and have proved still more inadequate in practical questions. Ontology, even when it was most triumphant in the schools, was always limited to subjects of a purely intellectual nature ; and even here its abstractions, useless in themselves, dealt only with the case of individual development, the metaphysical spirit being thoroughly incompatible with the social point of view. In my work on Positive Philosophy I have clearly proved that it constitutes only a transitory phase of mind, and is totally inadequate for any constructive purpose. For a time it was supreme; but its utility lay simply in its revolutionary tendencies. It aided the preliminary development of Humanity by its gradual inroads upon Theology, which, though in ancient times entrusted with the sole direction of society, had long since become in every respect utterly retrograde.

But all Positive speculations owe their first origin to the occupations of practical life; and, consequently, they have always given some indication of their capacity for regulating our active powers, which had been omitted from every former synthesis. Their value in this respect has been and still is materially impaired by their want of breadth, and their isolated and incoherent character; but it has always been instinctively felt. The importance that we attach to theories which teach the laws of phenomena, and give us the power of prevision, is chiefly due to the fact that they alone can regulate our otherwise blind action upon the external world. Hence it is that while the Positive spirit has been growing more and more theoretical, and has gradually extended to every department of speculation, it has never lost the practical tendencies which it derived from its source; and this even in the case of researches useless in themselves, and only to be justified as logical exercises. From its first origin in mathematics and astronomy, it has always shown its tendency to systematize the whole of our conceptions in every new subject which has been brought within the scope of its fundamental principle. It exercised for a long time a modifying influence upon theological and metaphysical principles, which has gone on increasing; and since the time of Descartes and Bacon it has become evident that it is destined to supersede them altogether. Positivism has gradually taken possession of the preliminary sciences of Physics and Biology, and in these the old system no longer prevails. All that remained was to complete the range of its influence by including the study of social phenomena. For this study metaphysics had proved incompetent; by theological thinkers it had only been pursued indirectly and empirically as a condition of government. I believe that my work on Positive Philosophy has so far supplied what was wanting. I think it must now be clear to all that the Positive spirit can embrace the entire range of thought without lessening, or rather with the effect of strengthening its original tendency to regulate practical life. And it is a further guarantee for the stability of the new intellectual synthesis that Social science, which is the final result of our researches, gives them that systematic character in which they had hitherto been wanting, by supplying the only connecting link of which they all admit.

This conception is already adopted by all true thinkers. All must now acknowledge that the Positive spirit tends necessarily towards the formation of a comprehensive and durable system, in which every practical as well as speculative subject shall be included. But such a system would still be far from realising that universal character without which Positivism would be incompetent to supersede Theology in the spiritual government of Humanity. For the element which really preponderates in every human being, that is to say, Affection, would still be left untouched. This element it is, and this only, which gives a stimulus and direction to the other two parts of our nature: without it the one would waste its force in ill-conceived, or, at least, useless studies, and the other in barren or even dangerous contention. With this immense deficiency the combination of our theoretical and active powers would be fruitless, because it would lack the only principle which could ensure its real and permanent stability. The failure would be even greater than the failure of Theology in dealing with practical questions; for the unity of human nature cannot really be made to depend either on the rational or the active faculties. In the life of the individual, and, still more, in the life of the race, the basis of unity, as I shall show in the fourth chapter, must always be feeling. It is to the fact that theology arose spontaneously from feeling that its influence is for the most part due. And although theology is now palpably on the decline, yet it will still retain, in principle at least, some legitimate claims to the direction of society so long as the new philosophy fails to occupy this important vantage-ground. We come then to the final conditions with which the modern synthesis must comply. Without neglecting the spheres of Thought and Action it must also comprehend the moral sphere; and the very principle on which its claim to universality rests must be derived from Feeling. Then, and not till then, can the claims of theology be finally set aside. For then the new system will have surpassed the old in that which is the one essential purpose of all general doctrines. It will have shown itself able to effect what no other doctrine has done, that is, to bring the three primary elements of our nature into harmony. If Positivism were to prove incapable of satisfying this condition, we must give up all hope of systematization of any kind. For while Positive principles are now sufficiently developed to neutralize those of Theology, yet, on the other hand, the influence of theology would continue to be far greater. Hence it is that many conscientious thinkers in the present day are so inclined to despair for the future of society. They see that the old principles on which society has been governed must finally become powerless. What they do not see is that a new basis for morality is being gradually laid down. Their theories are too imperfect and incoherent to show them the direction towards which the present time is ultimately tending. It must be owned, too, that their view seems borne out by the present character of the Positive method. While all allow its utility in the treatment of practical, and even of speculative, problems, it seems to most men, and very naturally, quite unfit to deal with questions of morality.

In human nature, and therefore in the Positive system, Affection is the preponderating element.   But on closer examination they will see reason to rectify their judgment. They will see that the hardness with which Positive science has been justly reproached, is due to the speciality and want of purpose with which it has hitherto been pursued, and is not at all inherent in its nature. Originating as it did in the necessities of our material nature, which for a long time restricted it to the study of the inorganic world, it has not till now become sufficiently complete or systematic to harmonize well with our moral nature. But now that it is brought to bear upon social questions, which for the future will form its most important field, it loses all the defects peculiar to its long period of infancy. The very attribute of reality which is claimed by the new philosophy, leads it to treat all subjects from the moral still more than from the intellectual side. The necessity of assigning with exact truth the place occupied by the intellect and by the heart in the organization of human nature and of society, leads to the decision that Affection must be the central point of the synthesis. In the treatment of social questions Positive science will be found utterly to discard those proud illusions of the supremacy of reason,

to which it had been liable during its preliminary stages.
Ratifying, in this respect, the common experience of men
even more forcibly than Catholicism, it teaches us that individual happiness and public welfare are far more dependent upon the heart than upon the intellect. But, independently of this, the question of co-ordinating the
faculties of our nature will convince us that the only
basis on which they can be brought into harmonious
union, is the preponderance of Affection over Reason,
and even over Activity.

The fact that intellect, as well as social sympathy, is
a distinctive attribute of our nature, might lead us to
suppose that either of these two might be supreme, and
therefore that there might be more than one method of
establishing unity. The fact, however, is that there is
only one; because these two elements are by no means
equal in their fitness for assuming the first place. Whether
we look at the distinctive qualities of each, or at the
degree of force which they possess, it is easy to see that
the only position for which the intellect is permanently
adapted is to be the servant of the social sympathies. If,
instead of being content with this honourable post, it
aspires to become supreme, its ambitious aims, which are
never realised, result simply in the most deplorable disorder.

Even with the individual, it is impossible to establish
permanent harmony between our various impulses, except
by giving complete supremacy to the feeling which
prompts the sincere and habitual desire of doing good.
This feeling is, no doubt, like the rest, in itself blind;
it has to learn from reason the right means of obtaining satisfaction; and our active faculties are then called
into requisition to apply those means. But common
experience proves that after all the principal condition

of right action is the benevolent impulse; with the ordinary amount of intellect and activity that is found in men this stimulus, if well sustained, is enough to direct our thoughts and energies to a good result. Without this habitual spring of action they would inevitably waste themselves in barren or incoherent efforts, and speedily relapse into their original torpor. Unity in our moral nature is, then, impossible, except so far as affection preponderates over intellect and activity.

The proper function of Intellect is the Service of the Social Sympathies.

True as this fundamental principle is for the individual, it is in public life that its necessity can be demonstrated most irrefutably. The problem is in reality the same, nor is any different solution of it required; only it assumes such increased dimensions, that less uncertainty is felt as to the method to be adopted. The various beings whom it is sought to harmonize have in this case each a separate existence; it is clear, therefore, that the first condition of co-operation must be sought in their own inherent tendency to universal love. No calculations of self-interest can rival this social instinct, whether in promptitude and breadth of intuition, or in boldness and tenacity of purpose. True it is that the benevolent emotions have in most cases less intrinsic energy than the selfish. But they have this beautiful quality, that social life not only permits their growth, but stimulates it to an almost unlimited extent, while it holds their antagonists in constant check. Indeed the increasing tendency in the former to prevail over the latter is the best measure by which to judge of the progress of Humanity. But the intellect may do much to confirm their influence. It may strengthen social feeling by diffusing juster views of the relations in which the various parts of society stand to each other; or it may guide its application by dwelling on the lessons which the past offers to the future. It is to this honourable service that the new philosophy would direct our intellectual powers. Here the highest sanction is given to their operations, and an exhaustless field is opened out for them, from which far deeper satisfaction may be gained than from the approbation of the learned societies, or from the puerile specialities with which they are at present occupied.

In fact, the ambitious claims which, ever since the hopeless decline of the theological synthesis, have been advanced by the intellect, never were or could be realized. Their only value lay in their solvent action on the theological system when it had become hostile to progress. The intellect is intended for service, not for empire; when it imagines itself supreme, it is really only obeying the personal instead of the social instincts. It never acts independently of feeling, be that feeling good or bad. The first condition of command is force; now reason has but light; the impulse that moves it must come from elsewhere. The metaphysical Utopias, in which a life of pure contemplation is held out as the highest ideal, attract the notice of our men of science; but are really nothing but illusions of pride, or veils for dishonest schemes. True there is a genuine satisfaction in the act of discovering truth; but it is not sufficiently intense to be an habitual guide of conduct. Indeed, so feeble is our intellect that the impulse of some passion is necessary to direct and sustain it in almost every effort. When the impulse comes from kindly feeling it attracts attention on account of its rarity or value; when it springs from the selfish motives of glory, ambition, or gain, it is too common to be remarked. This is usually the only difference between the two cases. It does indeed occasionally happen that the intellect is actuated by a sort of passion for

2

truth in itself, without any mixture of pride or vanity. Yet, in this case, as in every other, there is intense egotism in exercising the mental powers irrespectively of all social objects. Positivism, as I shall afterwards explain, is even more severe than Catholicism in its condemnation of this type of character, whether in metaphysicians or in men of science. The true philosopher would consider it a most culpable abuse of the opportunities which civilization affords him for the sake of the welfare of society, in leading a speculative life.

We have traced the Positive principle from its origin in the pursuits of active life, and have seen it extending successively to every department of speculation. We now find it, in its maturity, and that as a simple result of its strict adherence to fact, embracing the sphere of affection, and making that sphere the central point of its synthesis. It is henceforth a fundamental doctrine of Positivism, a doctrine of as great political as philosophical importance, that the Heart preponderates over the Intellect.

It is true that this doctrine, which is the only basis for establishing harmony in our nature, had been, as I before remarked, instinctively accepted by theological systems. But it *Under Theology the intellect was the slave of the heart; under Positivism, its servant.* was one of the fatalities of society in its preliminary phase, that the doctrine was coupled with an error which, after a time, destroyed all its value. In acknowledging the superiority of the heart the intellect was reduced to abject submission. Its only chance of growth lay in resistance to the established system. This course it followed with increasing effect, till after twenty centuries of insurrection, the system collapsed. The natural result of the process was to stimulate metaphysical and scientific pride, and to promote views subversive of all social order.

But Positivism, while systematically adopting the principle here spoken of as the foundation of individual and social discipline, interprets that principle in a different way. It teaches that while it is for the heart to suggest our problems, it is for the intellect to solve them. Now the intellect was at first quite inadequate to this task, for which a long and laborious training was needed. The heart, therefore, had to take its place, and in default of objective truth, to give free play to its subjective inspirations. But for these inspirations, all progress, as I showed in my "System of Positive Philosophy," would have been totally impossible. For a long time it was necessary that they should be believed absolutely; but as soon as our reason began to mould its conceptions upon observations, more or less accurate, of the external world, these supernatural dogmas became inevitably an obstacle to its growth. Here lies the chief source of the important modifications which theological belief has successively undergone. No further modifications are now possible without violating its essential principles; and since, meantime, Positive science is assuming every day larger proportions, the conflict between them is advancing with increasing vehemence and danger. The tendency on the one side is becoming more retrograde, on the other more revolutionary; because the impossibility of reconciling the two opposing forces is felt more and more strongly. Never was this position of affairs more manifest than now. The restoration of theology to its original power, supposing such a thing were possible, would have the most degrading influence on the intellect, and, consequently, on the character also; since it would involve the admission that our views of scientific truth were to be strained into accordance with our wishes and our wants. Therefore no important step in the progress of Humanity can now be made without totally abandoning the theological principle. The only service of any real value which it still renders, is that of forcing the attention of Western Europe, by the very fact of its reactionary tendencies, upon the greatest of all social questions. It is owing to its influence that the central point of the new synthesis is placed in our moral rather than our intellectual nature; and this in spite of every prejudice and habit of thought that has been formed during the revolutionary period of the last five centuries. And while in this, which is the primary condition of social organization, Positivism proves more efficient than Theology, it at the same time terminates the disunion which has existed so long between the intellect and the heart. For it follows logically from its principles, and also from the whole spirit of the system, that the intellect shall be free to exercise its full share of influence in every department of human life. When it is said that the intellect should be subordinate to the heart, what is meant is, that the intellect should devote itself exclusively to the problems which the heart suggests, the ultimate object being to find proper satisfaction for our various wants. Without this limitation, experience has shown too clearly that it would almost always follow its natural bent for useless or insoluble questions, which are the most plentiful and the easiest to deal with. But when any problem of a legitimate kind has been once proposed, it is the sole judge of the method to be pursued, and of the utility of the results obtained. Its province is to enquire into the present, in order to foresee the future, and to discover the means of improving it. In this province it is not to be interfered with. In a word the intellect is to be the servant of the heart, not its slave. Under these two correlative conditions the elements of our nature will at last be brought into harmony. The equilibrium of

these two elements, once established, is in little danger
of being disturbed.   For since it is equally favourable
to both of them, both will be interested in maintaining
it.   The fact that Reason in modern times has become
habituated to revolt, is no ground for supposing that it
will always retain its revolutionary character, even when
its legitimate claims have been fully satisfied.   Supposing
the case to arise, however, society, as I shall show afterwards, would not be without the means of repressing any
pretensions that were subversive of order.   There is another point of view which may assure us that the position
given to the heart under the new system will involve no
danger to the growth of intellect.   Love, when real, ever
desires light, in order to attain its ends.   The influence of
true feeling is as favourable to sound thought as to wise
activity.

Our doctrine, therefore, is one which ren- The subordi-
nation of the
ders hypocrisy and oppression alike impossible. intellect to the
heart is the *Sub-*
And it now stands forward as the result of all *jective Princi-*
ple of Positiv-
the efforts of the past, for the regeneration of ism.
order, which, whether considered individually or socially,
is so deeply compromised by the anarchy of the present
time.   It establishes a fundamental principle by which
true philosophy and sound polity are brought into correlation; a principle which can be felt as well as proved,
and which is at once the key-stone of a system and a basis
of government.   I shall show, moreover, in the fifth chapter that the doctrine is as rich in esthetic beauty as in
philosophical power and in social influence.   This will
complete the proof of its efficacy as the centre of a
universal system.   Viewed from the moral, scientific,
or poetical aspect, it is equally valuable; and it is the
only principle which can bring Humanity safely through
the most formidable crisis that she has ever yet under-

gone.   It will be now clear to all that the force of demonstration, a force peculiar to modern times, and which
still retains much of its destructive character, becomes
matured and elevated by Positivism.   It begins to develop
constructive tendencies, which will soon be developed more
largely.   It is not too much, then, to say that Positivism,
notwithstanding its speculative origin, offers as much
to natures of deep sympathy as to men of highly cultivated intellects, or of energetic character.

Objective ba-   The spirit and the principle of the synthesis
sis of the sys-
tem; External which all true philosophers should endeavour
Order of the
World, as re- to establish, have now been defined.   I pro-
vealed   by
Science.   ceed to explain the method that should be
followed in the task, and the peculiar difficulty with which
it is attended.

The object of the synthesis will not be secured until
it embraces the whole extent of its domain, the moral
and practical departments as well as the intellectual.   But
these three departments cannot be dealt with simultaneously.   They follow an order of succession which, so far
from dissevering them from the whole to which they
belong, is seen when carefully examined to be a natural
result of their mutual dependence.   The truth is, and it
is a truth of great importance, that Thoughts must be
systematised before Feelings, Feelings before Actions.   It
is, doubtless, owing to a confused apprehension of this
truth that philosophers hitherto, in framing their systems
of human nature, have dealt almost exclusively with our
intellectual faculties.

The necessity of commencing with the co-ordination of
ideas is not merely due to the fact that the relations of
these being more simple and more susceptible of demonstration, form a useful logical preparation for the re-
mainder of the task.   On closer examination we find a

more important, though less obvious reason. If this first portion of the work be once efficiently performed, it is the foundation of all the rest. In what remains no very serious difficulty will occur, provided always that we content ourselves with that degree of completeness which the ultimate purpose of the system requires.

To give such paramount importance to this portion of the subject may seem at first sight inconsistent with the proposition just laid down, that the strength of the intellectual faculties is far inferior to that of the other elements of our nature. It is quite certain that Feeling and Activity have much more to do with any practical step that we take than pure Reason. In attempting to explain this paradox, we come at last to the peculiar difficulty of this great problem of human Unity.

The first condition of unity is a subjective principle; and this principle in the Positive system is the subordination of the intellect to the heart. Without this the unity that we seek can never be placed on a permanent basis, whether individually or collectively. It is essential to have some influence sufficiently powerful to produce convergence amid the heterogeneous and often antagonistic tendencies of so complex an organism as ours. But this first condition, indispensable as it is, would be quite insufficient for the purpose, without some objective basis, existing independently of ourselves in the external world. That basis consists for us in the laws or Order of the phenomena by which Humanity is regulated. The subjection of human life to this order is incontestable : and as soon as the intellect has enabled us to comprehend it, it becomes possible for the feeling of love to exercise a controlling influence over our discordant tendencies. This, then, is the mission allotted to the intellect in the Positive synthesis ; in this sense it is that it should be consecrated to the service of the heart.

I have said that our conception of human unity must be totally inadequate, and, indeed, cannot deserve the name, so long as it does not embrace every element of our nature. But it would be equally fatal to the completeness of this great conception to think of human nature irrespectively of what lies outside it. A purely subjective unity, without any objective basis, would be simply impossible. In the first place any attempt to co-ordinate man's moral nature, without regard to the external world, supposing the attempt feasible, would have very little permanent influence on our happiness, whether collectively or individually; since happiness depends so largely upon our relations to all that exists around us. Besides this we have to consider the exceeding imperfection of our nature. Self-love is deeply implanted in it, and when left to itself is far stronger than Social Sympathy. The social instincts would never gain the mastery were they not sustained and called into constant exercise by the economy of the external world, an influence which at the same time checks the power of the selfish instincts.

By it the self-ish affections are controlled; the unselfish strengthened. To understand this economy aright, we must remember that it embraces not merely the inorganic world, but also the phenomena of our own existence. The phenomena of human life, though more modifiable than any others, are yet equally subject to invariable laws; laws which form the principal objects of Positive speculation. Now the benevolent affections, which themselves act in harmony with the laws of social development, incline us to submit to all other laws, as soon as the intellect has discovered their existence. The possibility of moral unity depends, therefore, even in the case of the individual, but still more in that of society, upon the necessity of recognizing our subjection to an external power. By this means our self-regarding instincts

are rendered susceptible of discipline. In themselves
they are strong enough to neutralize all sympathetic
tendencies, were it not for the support that the latter
find in this External Order. Its discovery is due to the
intellect; which is thus enlisted in the service of feeling,
with the ultimate purpose of regulating action.

Thus it is that an intellectual synthesis, or systematic
study of the laws of nature, is needed on far higher
grounds than those of satisfying our theoretical faculties,
which are, for the most part, very feeble, even in men
who devote themselves to a life of thought. It is needed,
because it solves at once the most difficult problem of
the moral synthesis. The higher impulses within us are
brought under the influence of a powerful stimulus from
without. By its means they are enabled to control our
discordant impulses, and to maintain a state of harmony
towards which they have always tended, but which, without such aid, could never be realised. Moreover, this conception of the order of nature evidently supplies the basis
for a synthesis of human action; for the efficacy of our
actions depends entirely upon their conformity to this
order. But this part of the subject has been fully explained in my previous work, and I need not enlarge
upon it further. As soon as the synthesis of mental conceptions enables us to form a synthesis of feelings, it is
clear that there will be no very serious difficulties in constructing a synthesis of actions. Unity of action depends
upon unity of impulse, and unity of design; and thus we
find that the co-ordination of human nature, as a whole,
depends ultimately upon the co-ordination of mental conceptions, a subject which seemed at first of comparatively
slight importance.

The subjective principle of Positivism, that is, the subordination of the intellect to the heart, is thus fortified by

an objective basis, the immutable Necessity of the external world; and by this means it becomes possible to bring human life within the influence of social sympathy. The superiority of the new synthesis to the old is even more evident under this second aspect than under the first. In theological systems the objective basis was supplied by spontaneous belief in a supernatural Will. Now, whatever the degree of reality attributed to these fictions, they all proceeded from a subjective source; and therefore their influence in most cases must have been very confused and fluctuating. In respect of moral discipline they cannot be compared either for precision, for force, or for stability, to the conception of an invariable Order, actually existing without us, and attested, whether we will or no, by every act of our existence.

Our conception of this External Order has been gradually growing from the earliest times, and is but just complete. This fundamental doctrine of Positivism is not to be attributed in the full breadth of its meanings to any single thinker. It is the slow result of a vast process carried out in separate departments, which began with the first use of our intellectual powers, and which is only just completed in those who exhibit those powers in their highest form. During the long period of her infancy Humanity has been preparing this the most precious of her intellectual attainments, as the basis for the only system of life which is permanently adapted to our nature. The doctrine has to be demonstrated in all the more essential cases from observation only, except so far as we admit argument from analogy. Deductive argument is not admissible, except in such cases as are evidently compounded of others in which the proof given has been sufficient. Thus, for instance, we are authorised by sound logic to assert the existence of laws of weather; though most of these are still, and, perhaps, always will be, unknown. For it is

clear that meteorological phenomena result from a combination of astronomical, physical, and chemical influences,
each of which has been proved to be subject to invariable
laws. But in all phenomena which are not thus reducible,
we must have recourse to inductive reasoning; for a principle which is the basis of all deduction cannot be itself
deduced. Hence it is that the doctrine, being so entirely
foreign as it is to our primitive mental state, requires such
a long course of preparation. Without such preparation
even the greatest thinkers could not anticipate it. It is
true that in some cases metaphysical conceptions of a law
have been formed before the proof really required had
been furnished. But they were never of much service,
except so far as they generalized in a more or less confused way the analogies naturally suggested by the laws
which had actually been discovered in simpler phenomena.
Besides, such assertions always remained very doubtful
and very barren in result, until they were based upon
some outline of a really Positive theory. Thus, in spite
of the apparent potency of this metaphysical method, to
which modern intellects are so addicted, the conception
of an External Order is still extremely imperfect in many
of the most cultivated minds, because they have not verified it sufficiently in the most intricate and important class
of phenomena, the phenomena of society. I am not, of
course, speaking of the few thinkers who accept my discovery of the principal laws of Sociology. Such uncertainty in a subject so closely related to all others, produces
great confusion in men's minds, and affects their percep-
tion of an invariable order, even in the simplest subjects.
A proof of this is the utter delusion into which most
geometricians of the present day have fallen with respect
to what they call the Calculus of Chances; a conception
which presupposes that the phenomena considered are not

subject to law. The doctrine, therefore, cannot be considered as firmly established in any one case, until it has been verified specially in every one of the primary categories in which phenomena may be classed. But now that this difficult condition has really been fulfilled by the few thinkers who have risen to the level of their age, we have at last a firm objective basis on which to establish the harmony of our moral nature. That basis is, that all events whatever, the events of our own personal and social life included, are always subject to natural relations of sequence and similitude, which in all essential respects lie beyond the reach of our interference.

Even where not modifiable, its influence on the character is of the greatest value. This, then, is the external basis of our synthesis, which includes the moral and practical faculties, as well as the speculative. It rests at every point upon the unchangeable Order of the world. The right understanding of this order is the principal subject of our thoughts : its preponderating influence determines the general course of our feelings ; its gradual improvement is the constant object of our actions. To form a more precise notion of its influence, let us imagine that for a moment it were really to cease. The result would be that our intellectual faculties, after wasting themselves in wild extravagances, would sink rapidly into incurable sloth ; our nobler feelings would be unable to prevent the ascendancy of the lower instincts ; and our active powers would abandon themselves to purposeless agitation. Men have, it is true, been for a long time ignorant of this Order. Nevertheless we have been always subject to it; and its influence has always tended, though without our knowledge, to control our whole being ; our actions first, and subsequently our thoughts, and even our affections. As we have advanced in our knowledge of it, our thoughts have become less vague, our desires less capricious, our conduct less arbitrary. And now that we are able to grasp the full meaning of the conception, its influence extends to every part of our conduct. For it teaches us that the object to be aimed at in the economy devised by man, is wise development of the irresistible economy of nature, which cannot be amended till it is first studied and obeyed. In some departments it has the character of fate; that is, it admits of no modification. But even here, in spite of the superficial objections to it which have arisen from intellectual pride, it is necessary for the proper regulation of human life. Suppose, for instance, that man were exempt from the necessity of living on the earth, and were free to pass at will from one planet to another, the very notion of society would be rendered impossible by the licence which each individual would have to give way to whatever unsettling and distracting impulses his nature might incline him. Our propensities are so heterogeneous and so deficient in elevation, that there would be no fixity or consistency in our conduct, but for these insurmountable conditions. Our feeble reason may fret at such restrictions, but without them all its deliberations would be confused and purposeless. We are powerless to create: all that we can do in bettering our condition is to modify an order in which we can produce no radical change. Supposing us in possession of that absolute independence to which metaphysical pride aspires, it is certain that so far from improving our condition, it would be a bar to all development, whether social or individual. The true path of human progress lies in the opposite direction; in diminishing the vacillation, inconsistency, and discordance of our designs by furnishing external motives for those operations of our intellectual, moral, and practical powers, of which the original source was purely internal. The ties by which our various diverging tendencies are held together would be quite inadequate for their purpose, without a basis of support in the external world, which is unaffected by the spontaneous variations of our nature.

But, however great the value of Positive doctrine in pointing out the unchangeable aspects of the universal Order, what we have principally to consider are the numerous departments in which that order admits of artificial modifications. Here lies the most important sphere of human activity. The only phenomena, indeed, which we are wholly unable to modify are the simplest of all, the phenomena of the Solar System which we inhabit. It is true that now that we know its laws we can easily conceive them improved in certain respects; but to whatever degree our power over nature may extend, we shall never be able to produce the slightest change in them. What we have to do is so to dispose our life as to submit to these resistless fatalities in the best way we can; and this is comparatively easy, because their greater simplicity enables us to foresee them with more precision and in a more distant future. Their interpretation by Positive science has had a most important influence on the gradual education of the human intellect; and it will always continue to be the source from which we obtain the clearest and most impressive sense of Immutability. Too exclusively studied they might even now lead to fatalism; but controlled as their influence will be henceforward by a more philosophic education, they may well become a means of moral improvement, by disposing us to submit with resignation to all evils which are absolutely insurmountable.

But in most cases we can modify it; and in these the knowledge of   In other parts of the external economy, invariability in all primary aspects is found compatible with modifications in points of

secondary importance. These modifications be- *it forms the systematic basis of human action.*
come more numerous and extensive as the phe-
nomena are more complex. The reason of this
is, that the causes from a combination of which the effects
proceed being more varied and more accessible, offer
greater facilities to our feeble powers to interfere with
advantage. But all this has been fully explained in my
"System of Positive Philosophy." The tendency of that
work was to show that our intervention became more
efficacious in proportion as the phenomena upon which
we acted had a closer relation to the life of man or
society. Indeed the extensive modifications of which
society admits, go far to keep up the common mistake
that social phenomena are not subject to any constant law.

At the same time we have to remember that this increased possibility of human intervention in certain parts
of the External Order necessarily coexists with increased
imperfection, for which it is a valuable but very inadequate compensation. Both features alike result from the
increase of complexity. Even the laws of the Solar System are very far from perfect, notwithstanding their
greater simplicity, which indeed makes their defects more
perceptible. The existence of these defects should be
taken into careful consideration ; not indeed with the
hope of amending them, but as a check upon unreasoning
admiration. Besides, they lead us to a clearer conception
of the true position of Humanity, a position of which the
most striking feature is the necessity of struggling against
difficulties of every kind. Lastly, by observing these
defects we are less likely to waste our time in seeking for
absolute perfection, and so neglecting the wiser course of
looking for such improvements as are really possible.

In all other phenomena, the increasing imperfection of
the economy of nature becomes a powerful stimulus to

all our faculties, whether moral, intellectual, or practical. Here we find sufferings which can really be alleviated to a large extent by wise and well-sustained combination of efforts. This consideration should give a firmness and dignity of bearing, to which Humanity could never attain during her period of infancy. Those who look wisely into the future of society will feel that the conception of man becoming, without fear or boast, the arbiter, within certain limits, of his own destiny, has in it something far more satisfying than the old belief in Providence, which implied our remaining passive. Social union will be strengthened by the conception, because every one will see that union forms our principal resource against the miseries of human life. And while it calls out our noblest sympathies, it impresses us more strongly with the importance of high intellectual culture, being itself the object for which such culture is required. These important results have been ever on the increase in modern times; yet hitherto they have been too limited and casual to be appreciated rightly, except so far as we could anticipate the future of society by the light of sound historical principles. Art, so far as it is yet organized, does not include that part of the economy of nature which, being the most modifiable, the most imperfect, and the most important of all, ought on every ground to be regarded as the principal object of human exertions. Even Medical Art, specially so called, is only just beginning to free itself from its primitive routine. And Social Art, whether moral or political, is plunged in routine so deeply that few statesmen admit the possibility of shaking it off. Yet of all the arts, it is the one which best admits of being reduced to a system; and until this is done it will be impossible to place on a rational basis all the rest of our practical life. All these narrow views are due simply to insufficient recognition of the fact, that the highest phenomena are as much subject to laws as others. When the conception of the Order of Nature has become generally accepted in its full extent, the ordinary definition of Art will become as comprehensive and as homogeneous as that of Science ; and it will then become obvious to all sound thinkers that the principal sphere of both Art and Science is the social life of man.

Thus the social services of the Intellect are not limited to revealing the existence of an external Economy, and the necessity of submission to its sway. If the theory is to have any influence upon our active powers, it should include an exact estimate of the imperfections of this economy and of the limits within which it varies, so as to indicate and define the boundaries of human intervention. Thus it will always be an important function of philosophy to criticize nature in a Positive spirit, although the antipathy to theology by which such criticism was formerly animated has ceased to have much interest, from the very fact of having done its work so effectually. The object of Positive criticism is not controversial. It aims simply at putting the great question of human life in a clearer light. It bears closely on what Positivism teaches to be the great end of life, namely, the struggle to become more perfect; which implies previous imperfection. This truth is strikingly apparent when applied to the case of our own nature, for true morality requires a deep and habitual consciousness of our natural defects.

I have now described the fundamental condition of the Positive Synthesis. Deriving its subjective principle from the affections, it is dependent ultimately on the intellect for its objective basis. This basis connects it with the Economy of the external world, the dominion of

The chief difficulty of the Positive Synthesis was to complete our conception of the External Order, by extending it to Social phenomena.

3

which Humanity accepts, and at the same time modifies. I have left many points unexplained; but enough has been said for the purpose of this work, which is only the introduction to a larger treatise. We now come to the essential difficulty that presented itself in the construction of the Synthesis. That difficulty was to discover the true Theory of human and social Development. The first decisive step in this discovery renders the conception of the Order of Nature complete. It stands out then as the fundamental doctrine of an universal system, for which the whole course of modern progress has been preparing the way. For three centuries men of science have been unconsciously co-operating in the work. They have left no gap of any importance, except in the region of Moral and Social phenomena. And now that man's history has been for the first time systematically considered as a whole, and has been found to be, like all other phenomena, subject to invariable laws, the preparatory labours of modern Science are ended. Her remaining task is to construct that synthesis which will place her at the only point of view from which every department of knowledge can be embraced.

In my "System of Positive Philosophy" both these objects were aimed at. I attempted, and in the opinion of the principal thinkers of our time successfully, to complete and at the same time co-ordinate Natural Philosophy, by establishing the general law of human development, social as well as intellectual. I shall not now enter into the discussion of this law, since its truth is no longer contested. Fuller consideration of it is reserved for the third volume of my new treatise. It lays down, as is generally known, that our speculations upon all subjects whatsoever, pass necessarily through three successive stages: the Theological stage, in which free play is given to spontaneous fictions admitting of no proof; the Metaphysical stage, characterised by the prevalence of personified abstractions or entities; lastly, the Positive stage, based upon an exact view of the real facts of the case. The first, though purely provisional, is invariably the point from which we start; the third is the only permanent or normal state; the second has but a modifying or rather a solvent influence, which qualifies it for regulating the transition from the first stage to the third. We begin with theological Imagination, thence we pass through metaphysical Discussion, and we end at last with positive Demonstration. Thus by means of this one general law we are enabled to take a comprehensive and simultaneous view of the past, present, and future of Humanity.

In my "System of Positive Philosophy," this law of Filiation has always been associated with the law of Classification, the application of which to Social Dynamics furnishes the second element requisite for the theory of development. It fixes the order in which our different conceptions pass through each of these phases. That order, as is generally known, is determined by the decreasing generality, or what comes to the same thing, by the increasing complexity of the phenomena; the more complex being naturally dependent upon those that are more simple and less special. Arranging the sciences according to this mutual relation, we find them grouped naturally in six primary divisions: Mathematics, Astronomy, Physics, Chemistry, Biology, and Sociology. Each passes through the three phases of development before the one succeeding it. Without continuous reference to this classification the theory of development would be confused and vague.

The theory thus derived from the combination of this second or statical law with the dynamical law of the three stages, seems at first sight to include nothing but the intellectual movement. But my previous remarks will have shown that this is enough to guarantee its applicability to social progress also; since social progress has invariably depended on the growth of our fundamental beliefs with regard to the economy that surrounds us. The historical portion of my "Positive Philosophy" has proved an unbroken connection between the development of Activity and that of Speculation; on the combined influence of these depends the development of Affection. The theory therefore requires no alteration : what is wanted is merely an additional statement explaining the phases of active, that is to say, of political development. Human activity, as I have long since shown, passes successively through the stages of Offensive warfare, Defensive warfare, and Industry. The respective connection of these states with the preponderance of the theological, the metaphysical, or the positive spirit leads at once to a complete explanation of history. It reproduces in a systematic form the only historical conception which has become adopted by universal consent ; the division, namely, of history into Ancient, Mediæval, and Modern.

Thus the foundation of social science depends simply upon establishing the truth of this theory of development. We do this by combining the dynamic law, which is its distinctive feature, with the statical principle which renders it coherent ; we then complete the theory by extending it to practical life. All knowledge is now brought within the sphere of Natural Philosophy ; and the provisional distinction by which, since Aristotle and Plato, it has been so sharply demarcated from Moral Philosophy, ceases to exist. The Positive spirit, so long confined to the simpler inorganic phenomena, has now passed through its difficult course of probation. It extends to a more important and more intricate class of speculations, and disengages them for ever from all theological or metaphysical influence. All our notions of truth are thus rendered homogeneous, and begin at once to converge towards a central principle. A firm objective basis is consequently laid down for that complete co-ordination of human existence towards which all sound Philosophy has ever tended, but which the want of adequate materials has hitherto made impossible.

It will be felt, I think, that the principal difficulty of the Positive Synthesis was met by my discovery of the laws of development, if we bear in mind that while that theory completes and co-ordinates the objective basis of the system, it at the same time holds it in subordination to the subjective principle. It *By the discovery of Sociological laws social questions are made paramount; and thus our subjective principle is satisfied without danger to free thought.* is under the influence of this moral principle that the whole philosophical construction should be carried on. The enquiry into the Order of the Universe is an indispensable task, and it comes necessarily within the province of the intellect; but the intellect is too apt to aim in its pride at something beyond its proper function, which consists in unremitting service of the social sympathies. It would willingly escape from all control and follow its own bent towards speculative digressions ; a tendency which is at present favoured by the undisciplined habits of thought naturally due to the first rise of Positivism in its special departments. The influence of the moral principle is necessary to recall it to its true function; since if its investigations were allowed to assume an absolute character, and to recognise no limit, we should only be repeating in a scientific form many of the worst results of theological and metaphysical belief. The Universe is to be studied not for its own sake, but for the sake of Man or rather of Humanity. To study it in any other spirit would not only be immoral, but also highly irrational. For, as statements of pure objective truth, our scientific theories can never be really satisfactory. They can only satisfy us from the subjective point of view; that is, by limiting themselves to the treatment of such questions as have some direct or indirect influence over human life. It is for social feeling to determine these limits; outside which our knowledge will always remain imperfect as well as useless, and this even in the case of the simplest phenomena; as astronomy testifies. Were the influence of social feeling to be slackened, the Positive spirit would soon fall back to the subjects which were preferred during the period of its infancy; subjects the most remote from human interest, and therefore also the easiest. While its probationary period lasted, it was natural to investigate all accessible problems without distinction; and this was often justified by the logical value of many problems that, scientifically speaking, were useless. But now that the Positive method has been sufficiently developed to be applied exclusively to the purpose for which it was intended, there is no use whatever in prolonging the period of probation by these idle exercises. Indeed the want of purpose and discipline in our researches is rapidly assuming a retrograde character. Its tendency is to undo the chief results obtained by the spirit of detail during the time when that spirit was really essential to progress.

Here, then, we are met by a serious difficulty. The construction of the objective basis for the Positive synthesis imposes two conditions which seem, at first sight, incompatible. On the one hand we must allow the intellect to be free, or else we shall not have the full benefit of its services; and, on the other, we must control its natural tendency to unlimited digressions. The problem was insoluble, so long as the study of the natural economy did not include Sociology. But so soon as the Positive spirit extends to the treatment of social questions, these at once take precedence of all others, and thus the moral point of view becomes paramount. Objective science, proceeding from without inwards, falls at last into natural harmony with the subjective or moral principle, the superiority of which it had for so long a time resisted. As a mere speculative question it may be considered as proved to the satisfaction of every true thinker, that the social point of view is logically and scientifically supreme over all others, being the only point from which all our scientific conceptions can be regarded as a whole. Yet its influence can never be injurious to the progress of other Positive studies ; for these, whether for the sake of their method or of their subject matter, will always continue to be necessary as an introduction to the final science. Indeed the Positive system gives the highest sanction and the most powerful stimulus to all preliminary sciences, by insisting on the relation which each of them bears to the great whole, Humanity.

Thus the foundation of social science bears out the statement made at the beginning of this work, that the intellect would, under Positivism, accept its proper position of subordination to the heart. The recognition of this, which is the subjective principle of Positivism, renders the construction of a complete system of human life possible. The antagonism which, since the close of the Middle Ages, has arisen between Reason and Feeling, was an anomalous though inevitable condition. It is now for ever at an end ; and the only system which can really satisfy the wants of our nature, individually or collectively, is therefore ready for our acceptance. As long as the antagonism existed, it was hopeless to expect that Social Sympathy could do much to modify the preponderance of self-love in the affairs of life.   But the case is different as soon as reason and sympathy are brought into active co-opera- tion.   Separately, their influence in our imperfect organ- ization is very feeble ; but combined it may extend inde- finitely.   It will never, indeed, be able to do away with the fact that practical life must, to a large extent, be regulated by interested motives ; yet it may introduce a standard of morality inconceivably higher than any that has existed in the past, before these two modifying forces could be made to combine their action upon our stronger and lower instincts.

Distinction between Ab- stract and Con- crete laws. It is the former only that we require for the purpose before us.   In order to give a more precise conception of the intellectual basis on which the system of Positive Polity should rest, I must explain the general principle by which it should be limited.   It should be confined to what is really indispensable to the construction of that Polity. Otherwise the intellect will be carried away, as it has been before, by its tendency to useless digressions.   It will endeavour to extend the limits of its province; thereby escaping from the discipline imposed by social motives, and putting off all attempts at moral and social regeneration for a longer time than the construction of the philosophic basis for action really demands.   Here we shall find a fresh proof of the importance of my theory of development.   By that discovery the intel- lectual synthesis may be considered as having already reached the point from which the synthesis of affections may be at once begun ; and even that of actions, at least in its highest and most difficult part, morality properly so called.

With the view of restricting the construction of the

objective basis within reasonable limits, there is this distinction to be borne in mind. In the Order of Nature, there are two classes of laws; those that are simple or Abstract, those that are compound or Concrete. In my work on "Positive Philosophy," the distinction has been thoroughly established, and frequent use has been made of it. It will be sufficient here to point out its origin and the method of applying it.

Positive science may deal either with objects themselves as they exist, or with the separate phenomena that the objects exhibit. Of course we can only judge of an object by the sum of its phenomena; but it is open to us either to examine a special class of phenomena abstracted from all the beings that exhibit it, or to take some special object, and examine the whole concrete group of phenomena. In the latter case we shall be studying different systems of existence; in the former, different modes of activity. As good an example of the distinction as can be given is that, already mentioned, of Meteorology. The facts of weather are evidently combinations of astronomical, physical, chemical, biological, and even social phenomena; each of these classes requiring its own separate theories. Were these abstract laws sufficiently well known to us, then the whole difficulty of the concrete problem would be so to combine them, as to deduce the order in which each composite effect would follow. This, however, is a process which seems to me so far beyond our feeble powers of deduction, that, even supposing our knowledge of the abstract laws perfect, we should still be obliged to have recourse to the inductive method.

Now the investigation of the economy of nature here contemplated is evidently of the abstract kind. We decompose that economy into its primary phenomena, that is to say, into those which are not reducible to others.

These we range in classes; each of which, notwithstanding the connection that exists between all, requires a separate inductive process; for the existence of laws cannot be proved in any one of them by pure deduction. It is only with these simpler and more abstract relations that our synthesis is directly concerned : when these are established, they afford a rational groundwork for the more composite and concrete researches. The great complexity of concrete relations makes it probable that we shall never be able to co-ordinate them perfectly. In that case the synthesis would always remain limited to abstract laws. But its true object, that of supplying an objective basis for the great synthesis of human life, will none the less be attained. For this groundwork of abstract knowledge would introduce harmony between all our mental conceptions, and thereby would make it possible to systematize our feelings and actions, which is the object of all sound philosophy. The abstract study of nature is therefore all that is absolutely indispensable for the establishment of unity in human life. It serves as the foundation of all wise action; as the *philosophia prima,* the necessity of which in the normal state of humanity was dimly foreseen by Bacon. When the abstract laws exhibiting the various modes of activity have been brought systematically before us, our practical knowledge of each special system of existence ceases to be purely empirical, though the greater number of concrete laws may still be unknown. We find the best example of this truth in the most difficult and important subject of all, Sociology. Knowledge of the principal statical and dynamical laws of social existence is evidently sufficient for the purpose of systematizing the various aspects of private or public life, and thereby of rendering our condition far more perfect. Should this knowledge be acquired, of which there is now

no doubt, we need not regret being unable to give a satisfactory explanation of every state of society that we find
existing throughout the world in all ages. The discipline
of social feeling will check any foolish indulgence of the
spirit of curiosity, and prevent the understanding from
wasting its powers in useless speculations; for feeble as
these powers are, it is from them that Humanity derives
her most efficient means of contending against the defects
of the External Order. The discovery of the principal concrete laws would no doubt be attended by the most beneficial results, moral as well as physical; and this is the field
in which the science of the future will reap its richest
harvest. But such knowledge is not indispensable for our
present purpose, which is to form a complete synthesis of
life, effecting for the final state of humanity what the
theological synthesis effected for its primitive state. For
this purpose Abstract philosophy is undoubtedly sufficient;
so that even supposing that Concrete philosophy should
never become so perfect as we desire, social regeneration
will still be possible.

Regarded under this more simple aspect, our *In my Theory of Develop-*
system of scientific knowledge is already so far *ment, the required Synthe-*
elaborated, that all thinkers whose nature is *sis of Abstract
conceptions al-*
sufficiently sympathetic may proceed without *ready exists.*
delay to the problem of moral regeneration; a problem
which must prepare the way for that of political reorganization. For we shall find that the theory of development of which we have been speaking, when looked at
from another point of view, condenses and systematizes
all our abstract conceptions of the order of nature.

This will be understood by regarding all departments
of our knowledge as being really component parts of one
and the same science; the science of Humanity. All
other sciences are but the prelude or the development of

this. Before we can enter upon it directly, there are two subjects which it is necessary to investigate; our external circumstances, and the organization of our own nature. Social life cannot be understood without first understanding the medium in which it is developed, and the beings who manifest it. We shall make no progress, therefore, in the final science until we have sufficient abstract knowledge of the outer world and of individual life to define the influence of these laws on the special laws of social phenomena. And this is necessary from the logical as well as from the scientific point of view. The feeble faculties of our intellect require to be trained for the more difficult speculations by practice in the easier. For the same reasons, the study of the inorganic world should take precedence of the organic. For, in the first place, the laws of the more universal mode of existence have a preponderating influence over those of the more special modes; and in the second place it is clearly incumbent on us to begin the study of the Positive method with its simplest and most characteristic applications. I need not dwell further upon principles so fully established in my former work.

Social Philosophy, therefore, ought on every ground to be preceded by Natural Philosophy in the ordinary sense of the word ; that is to say by the study of inorganic and organic nature. It is reserved for our own century to take in the whole scope of science ; but the commencement of these preparatory studies dates from the first astronomical discoveries of antiquity. Natural Philosophy was completed by the modern science of Biology, of which the ancients possessed nothing but a few statical principles. The dependence of biological conditions upon astronomical is very certain. But these two sciences differ too much from each other and are two indirectly connected to give us an adequate conception of Natural Philosophy as a whole. It would be pushing the principle of condensation too far to reduce it to these two terms. One connecting link was supplied by the science of Chemistry which arose in the middle ages. The natural succession of Astronomy, Chemistry, and Biology leading gradually up to the final science, Sociology, made it possible to conceive more or less imperfectly of an intellectual synthesis. But the interposition of Chemistry was not enough: because, though its relation to Biology was intimate, it was too remote from Astronomy. For want of understanding the mode in which astronomical conditions really affected us, the arbitrary and chimerical fancies of astrology were employed, though of course quite valueless except for this temporary purpose. In the seventeenth century, however, the science of Physics, specially so called, was founded; and a satisfactory arrangement of scientific conceptions began to be formed. Physics included a series of inorganic researches, the more general branch of which bordered on Astronomy, the more special on Chemistry. To complete our view of the scientific hierarchy we have now only to go back to its origin, Mathematics; a class of speculations so simple and so general, that they passed at once and without effort into the Positive stage. Without Mathematics, Astronomy was impossible: and they will always continue to be the starting point of Positive education for the individual as they have been for the race. Even under the most absolute theological influence they stimulate the Positive spirit to a certain degree of systematic growth. From them it extends step by step to the subjects from which at first it had been most rigidly excluded.

We see from these brief remarks that the series of the abstract sciences naturally arranges itself according to the decrease in generality and the increase in complication.

We see the reason for the introduction of each member
of the series, and the mutual connection between them.
The classification is evidently the same as that before
laid down in my theory of development. That theory
therefore may be regarded, from the statical point of
view, as furnishing a direct basis for the co-ordination
of Abstract conceptions, on which, as we have seen, the
whole synthesis of human life depends. That co-ordination at once establishes unity in our intellectual operations. It realizes the desire obscurely expressed by
Bacon for a *scala intellectûs*, a ladder of the understanding,
by the aid of which our thoughts may pass with ease from
the lowest subjects to the highest, or *vice versâ*, without
weakening the sense of their continuous connection in
nature. Each of the six terms of which our series is
composed is in its central portion quite distinct from the
two adjoining links; but it is closely related in its commencement to the preceding term, in its conclusion to the
term which follows. A further proof of the homogeneous-
ness and continuity of the system is that the same principle of classification, when applied more closely, enables
us to arrange the various theories of which each science
consists. For example, the three great orders of mathematical speculations, Arithmetic, Geometry, and Mechanics, follow the same law of classification as that by
which the entire scale is regulated. And I have shown
in my "Positive Philosophy" that the same holds good of
the other sciences. As a whole, therefore, the series is
the most concise summary that can be formed of the vast
range of Abstract truth; and conversely, all rational researches of a special kind result in some partial development of this series. Each term in it requires its own
special processes of induction; yet in each we reason
deductively from the preceding term, a method which will

always be as necessary for purposes of instruction, as it
was originally for the purpose of discovery. Thus it is
that all our other studies are but a preparation for the
final science of Humanity. By it their mode of culture
will always be influenced, and will gradually be imbued
with the true spirit of generality, which is so closely connected with social sympathy. Nor is there any danger of
such influence becoming oppressive, since the very principle of our system is to combine a due measure of independence with practical convergence. The fact that our
theory of classification, by the very terms of its composition, subordinates intellectual to social considerations, is
eminently calculated to secure its popular acceptance. It
brings the whole speculative system under the criticism,
and at the same time under the protection of the public,
which is usually not slow to check any abuse of those habits
of abstraction which are necessary to the philosopher.

The same theory then which explains the mental evolution of Humanity, lays down the true method by which
our abstract conceptions should be classified; thus reconciling the conditions of Order and Movement, hitherto
more or less at variance. Its historical clearness and its
philosophical force strengthen each other, for we cannot
understand the connection of our conceptions except by
studying the succession of the phases through which they
pass. And on the other hand, but for the existence of
such a connection, it would be impossible to explain the
historical phases. So we see that for all sound thinkers,
History and Philosophy are inseparable.

A theory which embraces the statical as well
as the dynamical aspects of the subject, and
which fulfils the conditions here spoken of, may
certainly be regarded as establishing the true
objective basis on which unity can be established in our

Therefore we are in a position to proceed at once with the work of social regeneration.

intellectual functions. And this unity will be developed
and consolidated as our knowledge of its basis becomes
more satisfactory. But the social application of the system will have far more influence on the result than any
overstrained attempts at exact scientific accuracy. The
object of our philosophy is to direct the spiritual reorganization of the civilized world. It is with a view to this
object that all attempts at fresh discovery or at improved
arrangement should be conducted. Moral and political
requirements will lead us to investigate new relations;
but the search should not be carried farther than is necessary for their application. Sufficient for our purpose, if
this incipient classification of our mental products be so
far worked out that the synthesis of Affection and of
Action may be at once attempted; that is, that we may
begin at once to construct that system of morality under
which the final regeneration of Humanity will proceed.
Those who have read my "Positive Philosophy" will, I
think, be convinced that the time for this attempt has
arrived. How urgently it is needed will appear in every
part of the present work.

Error of iden-
tifying Posi-
tivism with
Atheism, Mate-
rialism, Fatal-
ism, or Optim-
ism. Atheism,
like Theology,
discusses in-
soluble mys-
teries.
I have now described the general spirit of
Positivism. But there are two or three points
on which some further explanation is necessary, as they are the source of misapprehen-
sions too common and too serious to be disregarded. Of course I only concern myself
with such objections as are made in good faith.

The fact of entire freedom from theological belief
being necessary before the Positive state can be perfectly
attained, has induced superficial observers to confound
Positivism with a state of pure negation. Now this state
was at one time, and that even so recently as the last century, favourable to progress; but at present in those who

unfortunately still remain in it, it is a radical obstacle to all sound social and even intellectual organization. I have long ago repudiated all philosophical or historical connection between Positivism and what is called Atheism. But it is desirable to expose the error somewhat more clearly.

Atheism, even from the intellectual point of view, is a very imperfect form of emancipation; for its tendency is to prolong the metaphysical stage indefinitely, by continuing to seek for new solutions of Theological problems, instead of setting aside all inaccessible researches on the ground of their utter inutility. The true Positive spirit consists in substituting the study of the invariable Laws of phenomena, for that of their so-called Causes, whether proximate or primary; in a word, in studying the *How* instead of the *Why*. Now this is wholly incompatible with the ambitions and visionary attempts of Atheism to explain the formation of the Universe, the origin of animal life, etc. The Positivist comparing the various phases of human speculation, looks upon these scientific chimeras as far less valuable even from the intellectual point of view than the first spontaneous inspirations of primeval times. The principle of Theology is to explain everything by supernatural *Wills*. That principle can never be set aside until we acknowledge the search for *Causes* to be beyond our reach, and limit ourselves to the knowledge of *Laws*. As long as men persist in attempting to answer the insoluble questions which occupied the attention of the childhood of our race, by far the more rational plan is to do as was done then, that is, simply to give free play to the imagination. These spontaneous beliefs have gradually fallen into disuse, not because they have been disproved, but because mankind has become more enlightened as to its wants and the scope of its

4

powers, and has gradually given an entirely new direction
to its speculative efforts.   If we insist upon penetrating
the unattainable mystery of the essential Cause that produces phenomena, there is no hypothesis more satisfactory
than that they proceed from Wills dwelling in them or
outside them ; an hypothesis which assimilates them to
the effect produced by the desires which exist within ourselves.   Were it not for the pride induced by metaphysical
and scientific studies, it would be inconceivable that any
atheist, modern or ancient, should have believed that his
vague hypotheses on such a subject were preferable to this
direct mode of explanation.   And it was the only mode
which really satisfied the reason, until men began to see
the utter inanity and inutility of all search for absolute
truth.   The Order of Nature is doubtless very imperfect
in every respect ; but its production is far more compatible with the hypothesis of an intelligent Will than with
that of a blind mechanism.   Persistent atheists therefore
would seem to be the most illogical of theologists : because
they occupy themselves with theological problems, and
yet reject the only appropriate method of handling them.
But the fact is that pure Atheism even in the present day
is very rare.   What is called Atheism is usually a phase of
Pantheism, which is really nothing but a relapse disguised
under learned terms, into a vague and abstract form of
Fetichism.   And it is not impossible that it may lead to
the reproduction in one form or other of every theological
phase, as soon as the check which modern society still
imposes on metaphysical extravagance, has become somewhat weakened.   The adoption of such theories as a satisfactory system of belief, indicates a very exaggerated or
rather false view of intellectual requirements, and a very
insufficient recognition of moral and social wants.   It is
generally connected with the visionary but mischievous

tendencies of ambitious thinkers to uphold what they call the empire of Reason. In the moral sphere, it forms a sort of basis for the degrading fallacies of modern metaphysicians as to the absolute preponderance of self-interest. Politically, its tendency is to unlimited prolongation of the revolutionary position: its spirit is that of blind hatred to the past: and it resists all attempts to explain it on Positive principles, with the view of disclosing the future. Atheism, therefore, is not likely to lead to Positivism except in those who pass through it rapidly as the last and most short-lived of metaphysical phases. And the wide diffusion of the scientific spirit in the present day makes this passage so easy that to arrive at maturity without accomplishing it, is a symptom of a certain mental weakness, which is often connected with moral insufficiency, and is very incompatible with Positivism. Negation offers but a feeble and precarious basis for union: and disbelief in Monotheism is of itself no better proof of a mind fit to grapple with the questions of the day than disbelief in Polytheism or Fetichism, which no one would maintain to be an adequate ground for claiming intellectual sympathy. The atheistic phase indeed was not really necessary, except for the revolutionists of the last century who took the lead in the movement towards radical regeneration of society. The necessity has already ceased; for the decayed condition of the old system makes the need of regeneration palpable to all. Persistence in anarchy, and Atheism is the most characteristic symptom of anarchy, is a temper of mind more unfavourable to the organic spirit, which ought by this time to have established its influence, than sincere adhesion to the old forms. This latter is of course obstructive: but at least it does not hinder us from fixing our attention upon the great social problem. Indeed it helps us to do so: because it forces the new philo-

sophy to throw aside every weapon of attack against the
older faith except its own higher capacity of satisfying
our moral and social wants. But in the Atheism maintained by many metaphysicians and scientific men of the
present day, Positivism, instead of wholesome rivalry of
this kind, will meet with nothing but barren resistance.
Anti-theological as such men may be, they feel unmixed repugnance for any attempts at social regeneration, although
their efforts in the last century had to some extent prepared the way for it. Far, then, from counting upon their
support, Positivists must expect to find them hostile:
although from the incoherence of their opinions it will
not be difficult to reclaim those of them whose errors are
not essentially due to pride.

Materialism
is due to the
encroachment
of the lower
sciences on the
domain of the
higher: an
error which
Positivism
rectifies.
The charge of Materialism which is often
made against Positive philosophy is of more
importance. It originates in the course of
scientific study upon which the Positive System
is based. In answering the charge, I need not
enter into any discussion of impenetrable mysteries. Our theory of development will enable us to see
distinctly the real ground of the confusion that exists
upon the subject.

Positive science was for a long time limited to the
simplest subjects: it could not reach the highest except
by a natural series of intermediate steps. As each of
these steps is taken, the student is apt to be influenced too
strongly by the methods and results of the preceding stage.
Here, as it seems to me, lies the real source of that scientific error which men have instinctively blamed as *materialism.* The name is just, because the tendency indicated is one which degrades the higher subjects of thought
by confounding them with the lower. It was hardly possible that this usurpation by one science of the domain of

another should have been wholly avoided. For since the more special phenomena do really depend upon the more general, it is perfectly legitimate for each science to exercise a certain deductive influence upon that which follows it in the scale. By such influence the special inductions of that science were rendered more coherent. The result, however, is that each of the sciences has to undergo a long struggle against the encroachments of the one preceding it; a struggle which even in the case of the subjects which have been studied longest, is not yet over. Nor can it entirely cease until the controlling influence of sound philosophy be established over the whole scale, introducing juster views of the relations of its several parts, about which at present there is such irrational confusion. Thus it appears that Materialism is a danger inherent in the mode in which the scientific studies necessary as a preparation for Positivism were pursued. Each science tended to absorb the one next to it, on the ground of having reached the Positive stage earlier and more thoroughly. The evil then is really deeper and more extensive than is imagined by most of those who deplore it. It passes generally unnoticed except in the highest class of subjects. These doubtless are more seriously affected, inasmuch as they undergo the encroaching process from all the rest; but we find the same thing in different degrees, in every step of the scientific scale. Even the lowest step, Mathematics, is no exception, though its position would seem at first sight to exempt it. To a philosophic eye there is Materialism in the common tendency of mathematicians at the present day to absorb Geometry or Mechanics into the Calculus, as well as in the more evident encroachments of Mathematics upon Physics, of Physics upon Chemistry, of Chemistry, which is more frequent, upon Biology, or lastly in the common tendency of the best biologists to look upon Sociology as a mere corollary of their own science.   In all these cases it is the same fundamental error : that is, an exaggerated use of deductive reasoning ; and in all it is attended with the same result; that the higher studies are in constant danger of being disorganized by the indiscriminate application of the lower.   All scientific specialists at the present time are more or less materialists, according as the phenomena they study are more or less simple and general.   Geometricians, therefore, are more liable to the error than any others ; they all aim consciously or otherwise at a synthesis in which the most elementary studies, those of Number, Space, and Motion, are made to regulate all the rest.   But the biologists who resist this encroachment most energetically, are often guilty of the same mistake. They not unfrequently attempt, for instance, to explain all sociological facts by the influence of climate and race, which are purely secondary ; thus showing their ignorance of the fundamental laws of Sociology, which can only be discovered by a series of direct inductions from history.

This philosophical estimate of Materialism explains how it is that it has been brought as a charge against Positivism, and at the same time proves the deep injustice of the charge.   Positivism, far from countenancing so dangerous an error, is, as we have seen, the only philosophy which can completely remove it.   The error arises from certain tendencies which are in themselves legitimate, but which have been carried too far ; and Positivism satisfies these tendencies in their due measure.   Hitherto the evil has remained unchecked, except by the theologico-metaphysical spirit, which, by giving rise to what is called Spiritualism, has rendered a very valuable service.   But useful as it has been, it could not arrest the active growth of Materialism, which has assumed in the eyes of modern thinkers something of a progressive character, from having been so long connected with the cause of resistance to a retrograde system. Notwithstanding all the protests of the spiritualists, the lower sciences have encroached upon the higher to an extent that seriously impairs their independence and their value. But Positivism meets the difficulty far more effectually. It satisfies and reconciles all that is really tenable in the rival claims of both Materialism and Spiritualism; and, having done this, it discards them both. It holds the one to be as dangerous to Order as the other to Progress. This result is an immediate consequence of the establishment of the encyclopædic scale, in which each science retains its own proper sphere of induction, while deductively it remains subordinate to the science which precedes it. But what really decides the matter is the fact that such paramount importance, both logically and scientifically, is given by Positive Philosophy to social questions. For these are the questions in which the influence of Materialism is most mischievous, and also in which it is most easily introduced. A system therefore which gives them the precedence over all other questions must hold Materialism to be quite as obstructive as Spiritualism, since both are alike an obstacle to the progress of that science for the sake of which all other sciences are studied. Further advance in the work of social regeneration implies the elimination of both of them, because it cannot proceed without exact knowledge of the laws of moral and social phenomena. In the next chapter I shall have to speak of the mischievous effects of Materialism upon the Art or practice of social life. It leads to a misconception of the most fundamental principle of that Art, namely, the systematic separation of spiritual and temporal power. To maintain that separation, to carry out on a more satisfactory basis the admirable attempt made in the

Middle Ages by the Catholic Church, is the most important
of political questions. Thus the antagonism of Positivism
to Materialism rests upon political no less than upon philosophical grounds.

With the view of securing a dispassionate consideration
of this subject, and of avoiding all confusion, I have laid
no stress upon the charge of immorality that is so often
brought against Materialism. The reproach, even when
made sincerely, is constantly belied by experience. Indeed it is inconsistent with all that we know of human
nature. Our opinions, whether right or wrong, have not,
fortunately, the absolute power over our feelings and conduct which is commonly attributed to them. Materialism
has been provisionally connected with the whole movement of emancipation, and it has therefore often been
found in common with the noblest aspirations. That connection, however, has now ceased; and it must be owned
that even in the most favourable cases this error, purely
intellectual though it be, has to a certain extent always
checked the free play of our nobler instincts, by leading
men to ignore or misconceive moral phenomena, which
were left unexplained by its crude hypothesis. Cabanis
gave a striking example of this tendency in his unfortunate attack upon mediæval chivalry. Cabanis was a
philosopher whose moral nature was as pure and sympathetic as his intellect was elevated and enlarged. Yet the
materialism of his day had entirely blinded him to the
beneficial results of the attempts made by the most energetic of our ancestors to institute the Worship of Woman.

We have now examined the two principal charges
brought against the Positive system, and we have found
that they apply merely to the unsystematic state in which
Positive principles are first introduced. But the system
is also accused of Fatalism and of Optimism; charges on

which it will not be necessary to dwell at great length,
because, though frequently made, they are not difficult to
refute.

The charge of Fatalism has accompanied every
fresh extension of Positive science, from its
first beginnings. Nor is this surprising; for
when any series of phenomena passes from the
dominion of Wills, whether modified by metaphysical abstractions or not, to the dominion of Laws, the regularity
of the latter contrasts so strongly with the instability of
the former, as to present an appearance of fatality, which
nothing but a very careful examination of the real character of scientific truth can dissipate. And the error is
the more likely to occur from the fact that our first types
of natural laws are derived from the phenomena of the
heavenly bodies. These, being wholly beyond our interference, always suggest the notion of absolute necessity, a
notion which it is difficult to prevent from extending to
more complex phenomena, as soon as they are brought
within the reach of the Positive method. And it is quite
true that Positivism holds the Order of Nature to be in its
primary aspects strictly invariable. All variations, whether
spontaneous or artificial, are only transient and of secondary import. The conception of unlimited variations
would in fact be equivalent to the rejection of Law altogether. But while this accounts for the fact that every
new Positive theory is accused of Fatalism, it is equally
clear that blind persistence in the accusation shows a very
shallow conception of what Positivism really is. For unchangeable as the Order of Nature is in its main aspects,
yet all phenomena, except those of Astronomy, admit of
being modified in their secondary relations, and this the
more as they are more complicated. The Positive spirit,
when confined to the subjects of Mathematics and Astro-

*Nor is Posi-
tivism fatalist,
since it asserts
the External
Order to be
modifiable.*

nomy, was inevitably fatalist; but this ceased to be the case when it extended to Physics and Chemistry, and especially to Biology, where the margin of variation is very considerable. Now that it embraces Social phenomena, the reproach, however it may have been once deserved, should be heard no longer, since these phenomena, which will for the future form its principal field, admit of larger modification than any others, and that chiefly by our own intervention. It is obvious then that Positivism, far from encouraging indolence, stimulates us to action, especially to social action, far more energetically than any Theological doctrine. It removes all groundless scruples, and prevents us from having recourse to chimeras. It encourages our efforts everywhere, except where they are manifestly useless.

The charge of Optimism applies to Theology rather than to Positivism. The Positivist judges of all historical actions *relatively*, but does not justify them indiscriminately. For the charge of Optimism there is even less ground than for that of Fatalism. The latter was, to a certain extent, connected with the rise of the Positive spirit; but Optimism is simply a result of Theology; and its influence has always been decreasing with the growth of Positivism. Astronomical laws, it is true, suggest the idea of perfection as naturally as that of necessity. On the other hand, their great simplicity places the defects of the Order of Nature in so clear a light, that optimists would never have sought their arguments in astronomy, were it not that the first elements of the science had to be worked out under the influence of Monotheism, a system which involved the hypothesis of absolute wisdom. But by the theory of development on which the Positive synthesis is here made to rest, Optimism is discarded as well as Fatalism, in the direct proportion of the intricacy of the phenomena. It is in the most intricate that the defects of Nature, as well as the power of modifying them, become most manifest. With regard, therefore, to social phenomena, the most complex of all, both charges are utterly misplaced. Any optimistic tendencies that writers on social subjects may display, must be due to the fact that their education has not been such as to teach them the nature and conditions of the true scientific spirit. For want of sound logical training, great misuse has been made in our own time of a property peculiar to social phenomena. It is that we find in them a greater amount of spontaneous wisdom than might have been expected from their complexity. It would be a mistake, however, to suppose this wisdom perfect. The phenomena in question are those of intelligent beings who are always occupied in amending the defects of their economy. It is obvious, therefore, that they will show less imperfection than if, in a case equally complicated, the agents could have been blind. The standard by which to judge of action is always to be taken relatively to the social state in which the action takes place. Therefore all historical positions and changes must have at least some grounds of justification; otherwise they would be totally incomprehensible, because inconsistent with the nature of the agents and of the actions performed by them. Now this naturally fosters a dangerous tendency to Optimism in all thinkers, who, whatever their powers may be, have not passed through any strict scientific training, and have consequently never cast off metaphysical and theological modes of thought in the higher subjects. Because every government shows a certain adaptation to the civilization of its time, they make the loose assertion that the adaptation is perfect; a conception which is of course chimerical. But it is unjust to charge Positivism with errors which are evidently contrary to its true spirit, and merely due to the want of logical and scientific training in those who

have hitherto engaged in the study of social questions.
The object of Sociology is to explain all historical facts;
not to justify them indiscriminately, as is done by those
who are unable to distinguish the influence of the agent
from that of surrounding circumstances.

The word
Positive con-
notes all the
highest intel-
lectual attri-
butes, and will
ultimately
have a moral
significance.
On reviewing this brief sketch of the intellectual character of Positivism, it will be seen
that all its essential attributes are summed up
in the word *Positive*, which I applied to the
new philosophy at its outset. All the languages of Western Europe agree in understanding by this
word and its derivatives the two qualities of *reality* and
usefulness. Combining these, we get at once an adequate
definition of the true philosophic spirit, which, after all,
is nothing but good sense generalized and put into a systematic form. The term also implies in all European languages, *certainty* and *precision*, qualities by which the intellect of modern nations is markedly distinguished from
that of antiquity. Again, the ordinary acceptation of the
term implies a directly *organic* tendency. Now the metaphysical spirit is incapable of organizing; it can only
criticise. This distinguishes it from the Positive spirit,
although for a time they had a common sphere of action.
By speaking of Positivism as organic, we imply that it
has a social purpose; that purpose being to supersede Theology in the spiritual direction of the human race.

But the word will bear yet a further meaning. The
organic character of the system leads us naturally to
another of its attributes, namely its invariable *relativity*.
Modern thinkers will never rise above that critical position which they have hitherto taken up towards the past,
except by repudiating all absolute principles. This last
meaning is more latent than the others, but is really contained in the term. It will soon become generally ac-

cepted, and the word *Positive* will be understood to mean *relative* as much as it now means *organic, precise, certain, useful,* and *real*. Thus the highest attributes of human wisdom have, with one exception, been gradually condensed into a single expressive term. All that is now wanting is that the word should denote what at first could form no part of the meaning, the union of moral with intellectual qualities. At present, only the latter are included ; but the course of modern progress makes it certain that the conception implied by the word Positive, will ultimately have a more direct reference to the heart than to the understanding. For it will soon be felt by all that the tendency of Positivism, and that by virtue of its primary characteristic, reality, is to make Feeling systematically supreme over Reason as well as over Activity. After all, the change consists simply in realising the full etymological value of the word *Philosophy*. For it was impossible to realize it until moral and mental conditions had been reconciled ; and this has been now done by the foundation of a Positive science of society.

CHAPTER II.

THE SOCIAL ASPECT OF POSITIVISM, AS SHOWN BY ITS
CONNECTION WITH THE GENERAL REVOLUTIONARY MOVE-
MENT OF WESTERN EUROPE.

As the chief characteristic of Positive Philosophy is
the paramount importance that is given, and that on
speculative grounds, to social considerations, its efficiency
for the purposes of practical life is involved in the very
spirit of the system. When this spirit is rightly understood, we find that it leads at once to an object far higher
than that of satisfying our scientific curiosity; the object,
namely, of organizing human life. Conversely, this
practical aspect of Positive Philosophy exercises the most
salutary influence upon its speculative character. By
keeping constantly before us the necessity of concentrating all scientific efforts upon the social object which
constitutes their value, we take the best possible means of
checking the tendency inherent in all abstract enquiries
to degenerate into useless digressions. But this general
connection between theory and practice would not by
itself be sufficient for our purpose. It would be impossible to secure the acceptance of a mental discipline, so new
and so difficult, were it not for considerations derived from
the general conditions of modern society; considerations
calculated to impress philosophers with a more definite
sense of obligation to do their utmost towards satisfying
the wants of the time. By thus arousing public sympa-

thies and showing that the success of Positivism is a matter of permanent and general importance, the coherence of the system as well as the elevation of its aims will be placed beyond dispute. We have hitherto been regarding Positivism as the issue in which intellectual development necessarily results. We have now to view it from the social side; for until we have done this, it is impossible to form a true conception of it.

And to do this, all that is here necessary is to point out the close relation in which the new philosophy stands to the whole course of the French Revolution. This revolution has now been agitating Western nations for sixty years. It is the final issue of the vast transition through which we have been passing during the five previous centuries. *The relation of Positivism to the French Revolution.*

In this great crisis there are naturally two principal phases; of which only the first, or negative, phase has yet been accomplished. In it we gave the last blow to the old system, but without arriving at any fixed and distinct prospect of the new. In the second or positive phase, which is at last beginning, a basis for the new social state has to be constructed. The first phase led as its ultimate result to the formation of a sound philosophical system; and by this system the second phase will be directed. It is this twofold connection which we are now to consider.

The strong reaction which was exercised upon the intellect by the first great shock of revolution was absolutely necessary to rouse and sustain our mental efforts in the search for a new system. For the greatest thinkers of the eighteenth century had been blinded to the true character of the new state by the effete remnants of the old. And the shock was especially necessary for the foundation of social science. For the basis of that *The negative or destructive phase of the Revolution stimulated the desire of Progress, and consequently the study of social phenomena.*

science is the conception of human Progress, a conception
which nothing but the Revolution could have brought
forward into sufficient prominence.

Social Order was regarded by the ancients as stationary:
and its theory under this provisional aspect was admirably
sketched out by the great Aristotle.   In this respect the
case of Sociology resembles that of Biology.   In Biology
statical conceptions were attained without the least knowledge of dynamical laws.   Similarly, the social speculations
of antiquity are entirely devoid of the conception of Progress.   Their historical field was too narrow to indicate
any continuous movement of Humanity.   It was not till
the Middle Ages that this movement became sufficiently
manifest to inspire the feeling that we were tending towards a state of increased perfection.   It was then seen
by all that Catholicism was superior to Polytheism and
Judaism ; and this was afterwards confirmed by the corresponding political improvement produced by the substitution of Feudalism for Roman government.   Confused
as this first feeling of human Progress was, it was yet
very intense and very largely diffused ; though it lost
much of its vitality in the theological and metaphysical
discussions of later centuries.   It is here that we must
look if we would understand that ardour in the cause of
Progress which is peculiar to the Western family of
nations, and which has been strong enough to check many
sophistical delusions, especially in the countries where the
noble aspirations of the Middle Ages have been least impaired by the metaphysical theories of Protestantism or
Deism.

But whatever the importance of this nascent feeling, it
was very far from sufficient to establish the conviction of
Progress as a fundamental principle of human society.   To
demonstrate any kind of progression, at least three terms

are requisite. Now the absolute character of theological philosophy, by which the comparison between Polytheism and Catholicism was instituted, prevented men from conceiving the bare possibility of any further stage. The limits of perfection were supposed to have been reached by the mediæval system, and beyond it there was nothing but the Christian Utopia of a future life. The decline of mediæval theology soon set the imagination free from any such obstacles; but it led at the same time to a mental reaction which for a long time was unfavourable to the development of this first conception of Progress. It brought a feeling of blind antipathy to the Middle Ages. Almost all thinkers in their dislike of the Catholic dogmas were seized with such irrational admiration for Antiquity as entirely to ignore the social superiority of the mediæval system; and it was only among the untaught masses, especially in the countries preserved from Protestantism, that any real feeling of this superiority was retained. It was not till the middle of the seventeenth century that modern thinkers began to dwell on the conception of Progress. It re-appeared then under a new aspect. Conclusive evidence had by that time been furnished that the more civilised portion of our race had advanced in science and industry, and even, though not so unquestionably, in the fine arts. But these aspects were only partial: and though they were undoubtedly the source of the more systematic views held by our own century upon the subject, they were not enough to demonstrate the fact of a progression. And indeed, from the social point of view, so far more important than any other, Progress seemed more doubtful than it had been in the Middle Ages.

But this condition of opinion was changed by the revolutionary shock which impelled France, the normal centre of Western Europe, to apply itself to the task of social regeneration. A third term of comparison, that is to say the type on which modern society is being moulded, now presented itself; though it lay as yet in a distant and obscure future. Compared with the mediæval system it was seen to be an advance as great as that which justified our ancestors of chivalrous times in asserting superiority to their predecessors of antiquity. Until the destruction of Catholic Feudalism became an overt fact, its effete remnants had concealed the political future, and the fact of continuous progress in society had always remained uncertain. Social phenomena have this peculiarity, that the object observed undergoes a process of development as well as and simultaneously with the observer. Now up to the time of the Revolution, political development, on which the principal argument for the theory of Progress must always be based, corresponded in its imperfection to the incapacity of the scientific spirit to frame the theory of it. A century ago, thinkers of the greatest eminence were unable to conceive of a really continuous progression: and Humanity, as they thought, was destined to move in circles or in oscillations. But under the influence of the Revolution a real sense of human development has arisen spontaneously and with more or less result, in minds of the most ordinary cast; first in France, and subsequently throughout the whole of Western Europe. In this respect the crisis has been most salutary; it has given us that mental courage as well as force without which the conception could never have arisen. It is the basis of social science and therefore of all Positive Philosophy; since it is only from the social aspect that Positive Philosophy admits of being viewed as a connected whole. Without the theory of Progress, the theory of Order, even supposing that it could be formed, would be inadequate as a basis for Sociology. It is essential that the two should be com-

bined. The very fact that Progress, however viewed, is
nothing but the development of Order, shews that Order
cannot be fully manifested without Progress. The dependence of Positivism upon the French Revolution may
now be understood more clearly. Nor was it by a merely
fortuitous coincidence that by this time the introductory
course of scientific knowledge by which the mind is
prepared for Positivism should have been sufficiently
completed.

But we must here observe that, beneficial as the intellectual reaction of this great crisis undoubtedly was, its
effects could not be realised until the ardour of the revolutionary spirit had been to some extent weakened. The
dazzling light thrown upon the Future for some time
obscured our vision of the Past. It disclosed, though
obscurely, the third term of the social progression; but
it prevented us from fairly appreciating the second term.
It encouraged that blind aversion to the Middle Ages,
which had been inspired by the emancipating process of
modern times; a feeling which had once been necessary
to induce us to abandon the old system. The suppression
of this intermediate step would be as fatal to the conception of Progress as the absence of the last; because
this last differs too widely from the first to admit of any
direct comparison with it. Right views upon the subject
were impossible therefore until full justice had been rendered to the Middle Ages, which form at once the point of
union and of separation between ancient and modern history. Now it was quite impossible to do this as long as
the excitement of the first years of the revolution lasted.
In this respect the philosophical reaction, organised at the
beginning of our century by the great De Maistre, was of
material assistance in preparing the true theory of Progress. His school was of brief duration, and it was no

doubt animated by a retrograde spirit; but it will always be ranked among the necessary antecedents of the Positive system; although its works are now entirely superseded by the rise of the new philosophy, which in a more perfect form has embodied all their chief results.

What was required therefore for the discovery of Sociological laws, and for the establishment upon these laws of a sound philosophical system, was an intellect in the vigour of youth, imbued with all the ardour of the revolutionary spirit, and yet spontaneously assimilating all that was valuable in the attempts of the retrograde school to appreciate the historical importance of the Middle Ages. In this way and in no other could the true spirit of history arise. For that spirit consists in the sense of human continuity, which had hitherto been felt by no one, not even by my illustrious and unfortunate predecessor Condorcet. Meantime the genius of Gall was completing the recent attempts to systematize biology, by commencing the study of the internal functions of the brain; as far at least as these could be understood from the phenomena of individual as distinct from social development. And now I have explained the series of social and intellectual conditions by which the discovery of sociological laws, and consequently the foundation of Positivism, was fixed for the precise date at which I began my philosophical career: that is to say one generation after the progressive dictatorship of the Convention, and almost immediately after the fall of the retrograde tyranny of Bonaparte.

Thus it appears that the revolutionary movement, and the long period of reaction which succeeded it, were alike necessary, before the new general doctrine could be distinctly conceived of as a whole. And if this preparation was needed for the establishment of Positivism as a philosophical system, far more needful was it for the recognition of its social value. For it guaranteed free exposition and discussion of opinion: and it led the public to look to Positivism as the system which contained in germ the ultimate solution of social problems. This is a point so obvious that we need not dwell upon it further.

Having satisfied ourselves of the dependence of Positivism upon the first phase of the Revolution, we have now to consider it as the future guide of the second phase.

It is often supposed that the destruction of the old regime was brought about by the Revolution. But history when carefully examined points to a very different conclusion. It shows that the Revolution was not the cause *The constructive phase of the Revolution. The first attempts to construct failed, being based on destructive principles.* but the consequence of the utter decomposition of the mediæval system; a process which had been going on for five centuries throughout Western Europe, and especially in France; spontaneously at first, and afterwards in a more systematic way. The Revolution, far from protracting the negative movement of previous centuries, was a bar to its further extension. It was a final outbreak in which men showed their irrevocable purpose of abandoning the old system altogether, and of proceeding at once to the task of entire reconstruction. The most conclusive proof of this intention was given by the abolition of royalty; which had been the rallying point of all the decaying remnants of the old French constitution. But with this exception, which only occupied the Convention during its first sitting, the constructive tendencies of the movement were apparent from its outset; and they showed themselves still more clearly as soon as the republican spirit had become predominant. It is obvious, however, that strong as these tendencies may have been, the first period of the Revolution produced results of an extremely negative and destructive kind. In fact the movement was in this respect a failure. This is partly to be attributed to the pressing necessities of the hard struggle for national independence which France maintained so gloriously against the combined attacks of the retrograde nations of Europe. But it is far more largely owing to the purely critical character of the metaphysical doctrines by which the revolutionary spirit was at that time directed.

The negative and the positive movements which have been going on in Western Europe since the close of the Middle Ages, have been of course connected with each other. But the former has necessarily advanced with greater rapidity than the latter. The old system had so entirely declined, that a desire for social regeneration had become general, before the groundwork of the new system had been sufficiently completed for its true character to be understood. As we have just seen, the doctrine by which social regeneration is now to be directed, could not have arisen previously to the Revolution. The impulse which the Revolution gave to thought was indispensable to its formation. Here then was an insurmountable fatality by which men were forced to make use of the critical principles which had been found serviceable in former struggles, as the only available instruments of construction. As soon as the old order had once been fairly abandoned, there was of course no utility whatever in the negative philosophy. But its doctrines had become familiar to men's minds, and its motto of "Liberty and Equality," was at that time the one most compatible with social progress. Thus the first stage of the revolutionary movement was accomplished under the influence of principles that had become obsolete, and that were quite inadequate to the new task required of them.

For constructive purposes the revolutionary philosophy was valueless; except so far as it put forward a vague programme of the political future, founded on sentiment rather than conviction, and unaccompanied by any explanation of the right mode of realizing it. In default of organic principles the doctrines of the critical school were employed: and the result speedily showed their inherent tendency to anarchy; a tendency as perilous to the germs of the new order as to the ruins of the old. The experiment was tried once for all, and it left such ineffaceable memories that it is not probable that any serious attempt will be made to repeat it. The incapacity for construction of the doctrine in which the revolutionary spirit had embodied itself was placed beyond the reach of doubt. The result was to impress every one with the deep urgent necessity for social renovation; but the principles of that renovation were still left undetermined.

In this condition of philosophical and political opinion, the necessity of Order was felt to be paramount, and a long period of reaction ensued. Dating from the official Deism introduced by Robespierre, it reached its height under the aggressive system of Bonaparte, and it was feebly protracted, in spite of the peace of 1815, by his insignificant successors. The only permanent result of this period was the historical and doctrinal evidence brought forward by De Maistre and his school, of the social inutility of modern metaphysics, while at the same time their intellectual weakness was being proved by the successful attempts of Cabanis, and still more of Gall, to extend the Positive method to the highest biological questions. In all other respects this elaborate attempt to prevent the final emancipation of Humanity proved a complete failure; in fact, it led to a revival of the instinct of Progress. Strong antipathies were roused everywhere by

Counter-revolution from 1794 to 1830.

these fruitless efforts at reconstructing a system which had
become so entirely obsolete, that even those who were
labouring to rebuild it no longer understood its character
or the conditions of its existence.

A re-awakening of the revolutionary spirit was then inevitable; and it took place as soon as peace was established,
and the chief upholder of the retrograde system had been
removed. The doctrines of negation were called back to
life; but very little illusion now remained as to their
capacity for organizing. In want of something better,
men accepted them as a means of resisting retrograde
principles, just as these last had owed their apparent success to the necessity of checking the tendency to anarchy.
Amidst these fresh debates on worn-out subjects, the public soon became aware that a final solution of the question
had not yet arisen even in germ. It therefore concerned
itself for little except the maintenance of Order and
Liberty; conditions as indispensable for the free action
of philosophy as for material prosperity. The whole position was most favourable for the construction of a definite
solution; and it was, in fact, during the last phase of the
retrograde movement that the elementary principle of a
solution was furnished, by my discovery in 1822, of the
two-fold law of intellectual development.

Political stagnation be-tween 1830 and 1848. The apparent indifference of the public, to
whom all the existing parties seemed equally
devoid of insight into the political future, was
at last mistaken by a blind government for tacit consent
to its unwise schemes. The cause of Progress was in
danger. Then came the memorable crisis of 1830, by
which the system of reaction, introduced thirty-six years
previously, was brought to an end. The convictions which
that system inspired were indeed so superficial, that its
supporters came of their own accord to disavow them, and

uphold in their own fashion the chief revolutionary doctrines. These again were abandoned by their previous supporters on their accession to power. When the history of these times is written, nothing will give a clearer view of the revulsion of feeling on both sides, than the debates which took place on Liberty of Education. Within a period of twenty years, it was alternately demanded and refused by both ; and this in behalf of the same principles, as they were called, though it was in reality a question of interest rather than principle on either side.

All previous convictions being thus thoroughly upset, more room was left for the instinctive feeling of the public ; and the question of reconciling the spirit of Order with that of Progress now came into prominence. It was the most important of all problems, and it was now placed in its true light. But this only made the absence of a solution more manifest ; and the principle of the solution existed nowhere but in Positivism, which as yet was immature. All the opinions of the day had become alike utterly incompatible, both with Order and with Progress. The Conservative school undertook to reconcile the 'two ; but it had no constructive power ; and the only result of its doctrines was to give equal encouragement to anarchy and to reaction, so as to be able always to neutralize the one by the other. The establishment of Constitutional Monarchy was now put forward as the ultimate issue of the great Revolution. But no one could seriously place any real confidence in a system so alien to the whole character of French history, offering as it did nothing but a superficial and unwise imitation of a political anomaly essentially peculiar to England.

The period then between 1830 and 1848 may be regarded as a natural pause in the political movement. The reaction which succeeded the original crisis had exhausted itself; but the final or organic phase of the Revolution was still delayed for want of definite principles to guide it. No conception had been formed of it, except by a small number of philosophic minds who had taken their stand upon the recently established laws of social science, and had found themselves able, without recourse to any chimerical views, to gain some general insight into the political future, of which Condorcet, my principal predecessor, knew so little. But it was impossible for the regenerating doctrine to spread more widely and to be accepted as the peaceful solution of social problems, until a distinct refutation had been given of the false assertion so authoritatively made that the parliamentary system was the ultimate issue of the Revolution. This notion once destroyed, the work of spiritual reorganization should be left entirely to the free efforts of independent thinkers. In these respects our last political change (1848) will have accomplished all that is required.

The present position, 1848-1850. Republicanism involves the great principle of subordinating Politics to Morals. Thanks to the instinctive sense and vigour of our working classes, the reactionist leanings of the Orleanist government, which had become hostile to the purpose for which it was originally instituted, have at last brought about the final abolition of monarchy in France. The prestige of monarchy had long been lost, and it now only impeded Progress, without being of any real benefit to Order. By its fictitious supremacy it directly hindered the work of spiritual reformation, whilst the measure of real power which it possessed was insufficient to control the wretched political agitation maintained by animosities of a purely personal character.

Viewed negatively, the principle of Republicanism sums up the first phase of the Revolution. It precludes the possibility of recurrence to Royalism, which, ever since the

second half of the reign of Louis XIV., has been the rallying point of all reactionist tendencies. Interpreting the
principle in its positive sense, we may regard it as a direct
step towards the final regeneration of society. By consecrating all human forces of whatever kind to the general
service of the community, republicanism recognizes the
doctrine of subordinating Politics to Morals. Of course it
is as a feeling rather than as a principle that this doctrine
is at present adopted; but it could not obtain acceptance
in any other way; and even when put forward in a more
systematic shape, it is upon the aid of feeling that it will
principally rely, as I have shown in the previous chapter.
In this respect France has proved worthy of her position
as the leader of the great family of Western nations, and
has in reality already entered upon the normal state.
Without the intervention of any theological system, she
has asserted the true principle on which society should
rest, a principle which originated in the Middle Ages under
the impulse of Catholicism; but for the general acceptance
of which a sounder philosophy and more suitable circumstances were necessary. The direct tendency, then, of the
French Republic is to sanction the fundamental principle
of Positivism, the preponderance, namely, of Feeling over
Intellect and Activity. Starting from this point, public
opinion will soon be convinced that the work of organizing society on republican principles is one which can only
be performed by the new philosophy.

The whole position brings into fuller prominence the fundamental problem previously
proposed, of reconciling Order and Progress.
The urgent necessity of doing so is acknowledged by all;
but the utter incapacity of any of the existing schools of
opinion to realize it becomes increasingly evident. The
abolition of monarchy removes the most important obstacle

*It gives pro-
minence to the
problem of re-
concilingOrder
and Progress.*

to social Progress : but at the same time it deprives us of the only remaining guarantee for public Order. Thus the time is doubly favourable to constructive tendencies ; yet at present there are no opinions which possess more than the purely negative value of checking, and that very imperfectly, the error opposite to their own. In a position which guarantees Progress and compromises Order, it is naturally for the latter that the greatest anxiety is felt ; and we are still without any organ capable of systematically defending it. Yet experience should have taught us how extremely fragile every government must be which is purely material, that is, which is based solely upon self-interest, and is destitute of sympathies and convictions. On the other hand, spiritual order is not to be hoped for at present in the absence of any doctrine which commands general respect. Even the social instinct is a force on the political value of which we cannot always rely ; for when not based on some definite principle, it not unfrequently becomes a source of disturbance. Hence, we are driven back to the continuance of a material system of government, although its inadequacy is acknowledged by all. In a republic, however, such a government cannot employ its most efficient instrument, corruption. It has to resort instead to repressive measures of a more or less transitory kind, every time that the danger of anarchy becomes too threatening. These occasional measures, however, naturally proportion themselves to the necessities of the case. Thus, though Order is exposed to greater perils than Progress, it can count on more powerful resources for its defence. Shortly after the publication of the first edition of this work, the extraordinary outbreak of June, 1848, proved that the republic could call into play, and, indeed, could push to excess, in the cause of public Order, forces far greater than those of the monarchy. Thus royalty no longer possesses that monopoly of preserving Order, which has hitherto induced a few sincere and thinking men to continue to support it; and henceforth the sole political characteristic which it retains is that of obstructing Progress. And yet by another reaction of this contradictory position of affairs, the monarchical party seems at present to have become the organ of resistance in behalf of material Order. Retrograde as its doctrines are, yet from their still retaining a certain organic tendency, the conservative instincts rally round them. To this the progressive instincts offer no serious obstacle, their insufficiency for the present needs being more or less distinctly recognised. It is not to the monarchical party, however, that we must look for conservative principles; for in this quarter they are wholly abandoned, and unhesitating adoption of every revolutionary principle is resorted to as a means of retaining power; so that the doctrines of the Revolution would seem fated to close their existence in the retrograde camp. So urgent is the need of Order that we are driven to accept for the moment a party which has lost all its old convictions, and which had apparently become extinct before the Republic began. Positivism and Positivism alone can disentangle and terminate this anomalous position. The principle upon which it depends is manifestly this: As long as Progress tends towards anarchy, so long will Order continue to be retrograde. But the retrograde movement never really attains its object: indeed its principles are always neutralized by inconsistent concessions. Judged by the boastful language of its leaders, we might imagine that it was destroying republicanism; whereas the movement would not exist at all, but for the peculiar circumstances in which we are placed; circumstances which are forced into greater prominence by the foolish opposition of most of the authori-

ties.　As soon as the instinct of political improvement
has placed itself under systematic guidance, its growth
will bear down all resistance ; and then the reason of its
present stagnation will be patent to all.

It brings the
metaphysical
revolutionary
schools into
discredit.
　And for this Theology is, unawares, preparing the way.　Its apparent preponderance
places Positivism in precisely that position
which I wished for ten years ago.　The two organic
principles can now be brought side by side, and their
relative strength tested, without the complication of any
metaphysical considerations.　For the incoherence of metaphysical systems is now recognised, and they are finally
decaying under the very political system which seemed at
one time likely to promote their acceptance.　Construction
is seen by all to be the thing wanted : and men are rapidly
becoming aware of the utter hollowness of all schools which
confine themselves to protests against the institutions of
theology, while admitting its essential principles.　So de-
funct, indeed, have these schools become, that they can no
longer fulfil even their old office of destruction.　This has
fallen now as an accessory task upon Positivism, which
offers the only systematic guarantee against retrogression
as well as against anarchy.　Psychologists, strictly so
called, have already for the most part disappeared with
the fall of constitutional monarchy ; so close is the relation between these two importations from Protestantism.
It seemed likely therefore that the Ideologists, their natural
rivals, would regain their influence with the people.　But
even they cannot win back the confidence reposed in them
during the great Revolution, because the doctrines in
virtue of which it was then given are now so utterly
exploded.　The most advanced of their number, unworthy
successors of the school of Voltaire and Danton, have
shown themselves thoroughly incapable either morally or

intellectually of directing the second phase of the revolution, which they are hardly able to distinguish from the first phase. Formerly I had taken as their type a man of far superior merit, the noble Armand Carrel, whose death was such a grievous loss to the republican cause. But he was a complete exception to the general rule. True republican convictions were impossible with men who had been schooled in parliamentary intrigues, and who had directed or aided the pertinacious efforts of the French press to rehabilitate the name of Bonaparte. Their accession to power was futile; for they could only maintain material order by calling in the retrograde party; and they soon became mere auxiliaries of this party, disgracefully abjuring all their philosophical convictions. There is one proceeding which, though it is but an episode in the course of events, will always remain as a test of the true character of this unnatural alliance. I allude to the Roman expedition of 1849; a detestable and contemptible act, for which just penalties will speedily be imposed on all who were accessory to it; not to speak of the damnatory verdict of history. But precisely the same hypocritical opposition to progress has been exhibited by the other class of Deists, the disciples, that is, of Rousseau, who profess to adopt Robespierre's policy. Having had no share in the government, they have not so entirely lost their hold upon the people; but they are at the present time totally devoid of political coherence. Their wild anarchy is incompatible with the general tone of feeling maintained by the industrial activity, the scientific spirit, and the esthetic culture of modern life. These Professors of the Guillotine, as they may be called, whose superficial sophisms would reduce exceptional outbreaks of popular fury into a cold-blooded system, soon found themselves forced, for the sake of popularity, to sanction the law which very properly abolished capital punishment for political offences. In the same way they are now obliged to disown the only real meaning of the red flag which serves to distinguish their party, too vague as it is for any other name. Equally wrong have they shown themselves in interpreting the tendencies of the working classes, from being so entirely taken up with questions of abstract rights. The people have allowed these rights to be taken from them without a struggle whenever the cause of Order has seemed to require it; yet they still persist, mechanically, in maintaining that it is on questions of this sort that the solution of all our difficulties depends. Taking for their political ideal a short and anomalous period of our history which is never likely to recur, they are always attempting to suppress liberty for the sake of what they call progress. In a time of unchangeable peace they are the only real supporters of war. Their conception of the organization of labour is simply to destroy the industrial hierarchy of capitalist and workman established in the Middle Ages; and, in fact, in every respect these sophistical anarchists are utterly out of keeping with the century in which they live. There are some, it is true, who still retain a measure of influence with the working classes, incapable and unworthy though they are of their position. But their credit is rapidly declining; and it is not likely to become dangerous at a time when political enthusiasm is no longer to be won by metaphysical prejudices. The only effect really produced by this party of disorder, is to serve as a bugbear for the benefit of the retrograde party, who thus obtain official support from the middle class, in a way which is quite contrary to all the principles and habits of that class. It is very improbable that these foolish levellers will ever succeed to power. Should they do so, however, their reign will be short, and will soon result in their final extinction; because it will convince the people of their profound incapacity to direct the regeneration of Europe. The position of affairs, therefore, is now distinct and clear; and it is leading men to withdraw their confidence from all metaphysical schools, as they had already withdrawn it from theology. In this general discredit of all the old systems the way becomes clear for Positivism, the only school which harmonizes with the real tendencies as well as with the essential needs of the nineteenth century.

In this explanation of the recent position of French affairs one point yet remains to be insisted on. We have seen from the general course of the philosophical, and yet more of the political, movement, the urgent necessity for a universal doctrine capable of checking erroneous action, and of avoiding or moderating popular outbreaks. *And it proves to all the necessity of a true spiritual power; a body of thinkers whose business is to study and to teach principles, holding aloof from political action.* But there is another need equally manifest, the need of a spiritual power, without which it would be utterly impossible to bring our philosophy to bear upon practical life. Widely divergent as the various metaphysical sects are, there is one point in which they all spontaneously agree; that is, in repudiating the distinction between temporal and spiritual authority. This has been the great revolutionary principle ever since the fourteenth century, and more especially since the rise of Protestantism. It originated in repugnance to the mediæval system. The so-called philosophers of our time, whether psychologists or ideologists, have, like their Greek predecessors, always aimed at a complete concentration of all social powers; and they have even spread this delusion among the students of special sciences. At present there is no appreciation, except in the Positive system, of that instinctive sagacity which led all the great men of the

6

Middle Ages to institute for the first time, the separation of moral from political authority. It was a masterpiece of human wisdom; but it was premature, and could not be permanently successful at a time when men were still governed on theological principles, and practical life still retained its military character. This separation of powers, on which the final organization of society will principally depend, is understood and valued nowhere but in the new school of philosophy, if we except the unconscious and tacit admiration for it which still exists in the countries from which Protestantism has been excluded. From the outset of the Revolution, the pride of theorists has always made them wish to become socially despotic; a state of things to which they have ever looked forward as their political ideal. Public opinion has by this time grown far too enlightened to allow any practical realization of a notion at once so chimerical and so retrograde. But public opinion not being as yet sufficiently organized, efforts in this direction are constantly being made. The longing among metaphysical reformers for practical as well as theoretical supremacy is now greater than ever; because, from the changed state of affairs, their ambition is no longer limited to mere administrative functions. Their various views diverge so widely, and all find so little sympathy in the public, that there is not much fear of their ever being able to check free discussion to any serious extent, by giving legal sanction to their own particular doctrine. But quite enough has been attempted to convince every one how essentially despotic every theory of society must be which opposes this fundamental principle of modern polity, the permanent separation of spiritual from temporal power. The disturbances caused by metaphysical ambition corroborate, then, the view urged so conclusively by the adherents of the new school, that

this division of powers is equally essential to Order and
to Progress.   If Positivist thinkers continue to withstand all temptations to mix actively in politics, and go
on quietly with their own work amidst the unmeaning
agitation around them, they will ultimately make the
impartial portion of the public familiar with this great
conception.   It will henceforth be judged irrespectively
of the religious doctrines with which it was originally
connected.   Men will involuntarily contrast it with other
systems, and will see more and more clearly that Positive principles afford the only basis for true freedom
as well as for true union.   They alone can tolerate
full discussion, because they alone rest upon solid proof.
Men's practical wisdom, guided by the peculiar nature
of our political position, will react strongly upon philosophers, and keep them strictly to their sphere of moral
and intellectual influence.   The slightest tendency towards
the assumption of political power will be checked, and
the desire for it will be considered as a certain sign
of mental weakness, and indeed of moral deficiency.
Now that royalty is abolished, all true thinkers are
secure of perfect freedom of thought, and even of expression, as long as they abide by the necessary conditions
of public order.   Royalty was the last remnant of the
system of castes, which gave the monopoly of deciding
on important social questions to a special family; its abolition completes the process of theological emancipation.
Of course the magistrates of a republic may show despotic
tendencies; but they can never become very dangerous
where power is held on so brief a tenure, and where, even
when concentrated in a single person, it emanates from
suffrage, incompetent as that may be.   It is easy for the
Positivist to show that these functionaries know very little
more than their constituents of the logical and scientific

conditions necessary for the systematic working out of moral and social doctrines. Such authorities, though devoid of any spiritual sanction, may, however, command obedience in the name of Order. But they can never be really respected, unless they adhere scrupulously to their temporal functions, without claiming the least authority over thought. Even before the central power falls into the hands of men really fit to wield it, the republican character of our government will have forced this conviction upon a nation that has now got rid of all political fanaticism, whether of a retrograde or anarchical kind. And the conviction is the more certain to arise, because practical authorities will become more and more absorbed in the maintenance of material order, and will therefore leave the question of spiritual order to the unrestricted efforts of thinkers. It is neither by accident nor by personal influence that I have myself always enjoyed so large a measure of freedom in writing, and subsequently in public lectures, and this under governments all of which were more or less oppressive. Every true philosopher will receive the same licence, if, like myself, he offers the intellectual and moral guarantees which the public and the civil power are fairly entitled to expect from the systematic organs of Humanity. The necessity of controlling levellers may lead to occasional acts of unwise violence. But I am convinced that respect will always be shown to constructive thinkers, and that they will soon be called in to the assistance of public order. For order will not be able to exist much longer without the sanction of some rational principle.

The need of a spiritual power is common to the whole Republic of Western Europe. The result, then, of the important political changes which have recently taken place is this. The second phase of the Revolution, which hitherto has been restricted to a few advanced minds, is now entered by the public, and men are rapidly forming juster views of its true character. It is becoming recognized that the only firm basis for a reform of our political institutions, is a complete reorganization of opinion and of life; and the way is open for the new religious doctrine to direct this work. I have thus explained the way in which the social mission of Positivism connects itself with the spontaneous changes which are taking place in France, the centre of the revolutionary movement. But it would be a mistake to suppose that France will be the only scene of these reorganizing efforts. Judging on sound historical principles, we cannot doubt that they will embrace the whole extent of Western Europe.

During the five centuries of revolutionary transition which have elapsed since the Middle Ages, we have lost sight of the fact that in all fundamental questions the Western nations form one political system. It was under Catholic Feudalism that they were first united; a union for which their incorporation into the Roman empire had prepared them, and which was finally organized by the incomparable genius of Charlemagne. In spite of national differences, embittered as they were afterwards by theological discord, this great Republic has in modern times shown intellectual and social growth both in the positive and negative direction, to which other portions of the human race, even in Europe, can show no parallel. The rupture of Catholicism, and the decline of Chivalry, at first seriously impaired this feeling of relationship. But it soon began to show itself again under new forms. It rests now, though the basis is inadequate, upon the feeling of community in industrial development, in esthetic culture, and in scientific discovery. Amidst the disorganized state of political affairs, which have obviously been tending towards some radical change, this similarity in civilization has produced a growing conviction that we are all participating in one and the same social movement; a movement limited as yet to our own family of nations. The first step in the great crisis was necessarily taken by the French nation, because it was better prepared than any other. It was there that the old order of things had been most thoroughly uprooted, and that most had been done in working out the materials of the new. But the strong sympathies which the outbreak of our revolution aroused in every part of Western Europe, showed that our sister-nations were only granting us the honorable post of danger in a movement in which all the nobler portion of Humanity was to participate. And this was the feeling proclaimed by the great republican assembly in the midst of their war of defence. The military extravagances which followed, and which form the distinguishing feature of the counter-revolution, of course checked the feeling of union on both sides. But so deeply was it rooted in all the antecedents of modern history that peace soon restored it to life, in spite of the pertinacious efforts of all parties interested in maintaining unnatural separation between France and other countries. What greatly facilitates this tendency is the decline of every form of theology, which removes the chief source of former disagreement. During the last phase of the counter-revolution, and still more during the long pause in the political movement which followed, each member of the group entered upon a series of revolutionary efforts more or less resembling those of the central nation. And our recent political changes cannot but strengthen this tendency; though of course with nations less fully prepared the results of these efforts have at present been less important than in France. Meanwhile it is evident that this uniform condition of internal agitation gives increased security for peace, by which its extension had been originally facilitated. And thus, although there is no organized international union as was the case in the Middle Ages, yet the pacific habits and intellectual culture of modern life have already been sufficiently diffused to call out an instinct of fraternity stronger than any that has ever existed before. It is strong enough to prevent the subject of social regeneration from being ever regarded as a merely national question.

And this is the point of view which displays the character of the second phase of the Revolution in its truest light. The first phase, although in its results advantageous to the other nations, was necessarily conducted as if peculiar to France, because no other country was ripe for the original outbreak. Indeed French nationality was stimulated by the necessity of resisting the counter revolutionary coalition. But the final and constructive phase which has begun now that the national limits of the crisis have been reached, should always be regarded as common to the whole of Western Europe. For it consists essentially in spiritual reorganization; and the need of this in one shape or other presses already with almost equal force upon each of the five nations who make up the great Western family. Conversely, the more occidental the character of the reforming movement, the greater will be the prominence given to intellectual and moral regeneration as compared with mere modifications of government, in which of course there must be very considerable national differences. The first social need of Western Europe is community in belief and in habits of life; and this must be based upon a uniform system of education controlled and applied by a spiritual power that shall be accepted by all. This want satisfied, the reconstruction of governments may be carried out in accordance with the special requirements of each nation. Difference in this respéct is legitimate : it will not affect the essential unity of the Positivist Republic, which will be bound together by more complete and durable ties than the Catholic Republic of the Middle Ages.

Not only then do we find from the whole condition of Western Europe that the movement of opinion transcends in importance all political agitation ; but we find that everything points to the necessity of establishing a spiritual power, as the sole means of directing this extension and systematic reform of opinion and of life with the requisite consistency and largeness of view. We now see that the old revolutionary prejudice of confounding temporal and spiritual power is directly antagonistic to social regeneration, although it once aided the preparation for it. In the first place it stimulates the sense of nationality, which ought to be subordinate to larger feelings of international fraternity. And at the same time, with the view of satisfying the conditions of uniformity which are so obviously required for the solution of the common problem, it induces efforts at forcible incorporation of all the nations into one, efforts as dangerous as they are fruitless.

This Republic consists of the Italian, Spanish, British, and German populations, grouped round France as their centre. My work on Positive Philosophy contains a detailed historical explanation of what I mean by the expression, Western Europe. But the conception is one of such importance in relation to the questions of our time, that I shall now proceed to enumerate and arrange in their order the elements of which this great family of nations consists.

Since the fall of the Roman empire, and more especially from the time of Charlemagne, France has always been the centre, socially as well as geographically, of this Western region which may be called the nucleus of

Humanity.   On the one great occasion of united political
action on the part of Western Europe, that is, in the
crusades of the 11th and 12th century, it was evidently
France that took the initiative.   It is true that when the
decomposition of Catholicism began to assume a systematic
form, the centre of the movement for two centuries shifted
its position.   It was Germany that gave birth to the
metaphysical principles of negation.   Their first political
application was in the Dutch and English revolutions,
which, incomplete as they were, owing to insufficient intellectual preparation, yet served as preludes to the great
final crisis.   These preludes were most important, as
showing the real social tendency of the critical doctrines.
But it was reserved for France to co-ordinate these doctrines into a consistent system and to propagate them
successfully.   France then resumed her position as the
principal centre in which the great moral and political
questions were to be worked out.   And this position she
will in all probability retain, as in fact it is only a recurrence to the normal organization of the Western Republic, which had been temporarily modified to meet
special conditions.   A fresh displacement of the centre of
the social movement is not to be expected, unless in a
future too distant to engage our attention.   It can indeed
only be the result of wide extension of our advanced
civilization beyond European limits, as will be explained
in the conclusion of this work.

North and south of this natural centre, we find two
pairs of nations, between which France will always form
an intermediate link, partly from her geographical position, and also from her language and manners.   The first
pair is for the most part, Protestant.   It comprises, first,
the great Germanic body, with the numerous nations that
may be regarded as its offshoots ; especially Holland,

which, since the Middle Ages, has been in every respect
the most advanced portion of Germany.   Secondly, Great
Britain, with which may be classed the United States,
notwithstanding their present attitude of rivalry.   The
second pair is exclusively Catholic.   It consists of the
great Italian nationality, which in spite of political divisions has always maintained its distinct character; and of
the population of the Spanish peninsula, (for Portugal,
sociologically considered, is not to be separated from
Spain,) which has so largely increased the Western
family by its colonies.   To complete the conception of
this group of advanced nations, we must add two accessory members, Greece and Poland, countries which,
though situated in Eastern Europe, are connected with
the West, the one by ancient history, the other by modern.
Besides these, there are various intermediate nationalities
which I need not now enumerate, connecting or demar-
cating the more important branches of the family.

In this vast Republic it is that the new philosophy is to
find its sphere of intellectual and moral action.   It will
endeavour so to modify the initiative of the central nation,
by the reacting influences of the other four, as to give
increased efficiency to the general movement.   It is a task
eminently calculated to test the social capabilities of
Positivism, and for which no other system is qualified.
The metaphysical spirit is as unfit for it as the theological.
The rupture of the mediæval system is due to the deca-
dence of theology : but the direct agency in the rupture
was the solvent force of the metaphysical spirit.   Neither
the one nor the other then is likely to recombine elements
the separation of which is principally due to their own
conceptions.   It is entirely to the spontaneous action of
the Positive spirit that we owe those new though insufficient links of union, whether industrial, artistic, or

scientific, which, since the close of the Middle Ages, have been leading us more and more decidedly to a reconstruction of the Western alliance. And now that Positivism has assumed its matured and systematic form, its competence for the work is even more unquestionable. It alone can effectually remove the national antipathies which still exist. But it will do this without impairing the natural qualities of any of them. Its object is by a wise combination of these qualities, to develop under a new form the feeling of a common Occidentality.

By extending the social movement to its proper limits, we thus exhibit on a larger scale the same features that were noticed when France alone was being considered. Abroad or at home, every great social problem that arises proves that the object of the second revolutionary phase is a reorganization of principles and of life. By this means a body of public opinion will be formed of sufficient force to lead gradually to the growth of new political institutions. These will be adapted to the special requirements of each nation, under the general superintendence of the spiritual power, from whom our fundamental principles will have proceeded. The general spirit of these principles is essentially historical, whereas the tendency of the negative phase of the revolution was anti-historical. Without blind hatred of the past, men would never have had sufficient energy to abandon the old system. But henceforth the best evidence of having attained complete emancipation will be the rendering full justice to the past in all its phases. This is the most characteristic feature of that relative spirit which distinguishes Positivism. The surest sign of superiority, whether in persons or systems, is fair appreciation of opponents. And this must always be the tendency of

Relation of Positivism to the mediæval system, to which we owe the first attempt to separate spiritual from temporal power.

social science when rightly understood, since its prevision
of the future is avowedly based upon systematic examination of the past.   It is the only way in which the free
and yet universal adoption of general principles of
social reconstruction can ever be possible.   Such reconstruction, viewed by the light of Sociology, will be
regarded as a necessary link in the series of human development; and thus many confused and incoherent notions
suggested by the arbitrary beliefs hitherto prevalent will
finally disappear.   The growth of public opinion in this
respect is aided by the increasing strength of social feeling.   Both combine to encourage the historical spirit
which distinguishes the second period of the Revolution, as
we see indicated already in so many of the popular sympathies of the day.

Acting on this principle, Positivists will always acknowledge the close relation between their own system and the
memorable effort of mediæval Catholicism.   In offering
for the acceptance of Humanity a new organization of life,
we would not dissociate it with all that has gone before.
On the contrary, it is our boast that we are but proposing for
her maturity the accomplishment of the noble effort of her
youth, an effort made when intellectual and social conditions precluded the possibility of success.   We are too full
of the future to fear any serious charge of retrogression
towards the past.   It would be strange were such a charge
to proceed from those of our opponents whose political
ideal is that amalgamation of temporal and spiritual power
which was adopted by the theocratic or military systems
of antiquity.

The separation of these powers in the Middle Ages is
the greatest advance ever yet made in the theory of social
Order.   It was imperfectly effected, because the time was
not ripe for it; but enough was done to show the object

of the separation, and some of its principal results were
partially arrived at. It originated the fundamental doctrine of modern social life, the subordination of Politics to
Morals; a doctrine which in spite of the most obstinate
resistance has survived the decline of the religion which
first proclaimed it. We see it now sanctioned by a republican government which has shaken off the fetters of
that religion more completely than any other. A further
result of the separation is the keen sense of personal
honour, combined with general fraternity, which distinguishes Western nations, especially those who have been
preserved from Protestantism. To the same source is due
the general feeling that men should be judged by their
intellectual and moral worth, irrespectively of social position, yet without upsetting that subordination of classes
which is rendered necessary by the requirements of practical life. And this has accustomed all classes to free
discussion of moral and even of political questions; since
every one feels it a right and a duty to judge actions and
persons by the general principles which a common system
of education has inculcated alike on all. I need not enlarge on the value of the mediæval church in organising the
political system of Western Europe, in which there was
no other recognised principle of union. All these social
results are usually attributed to the excellence of the
Christian doctrine; but history when fairly examined
shows that the source from which they are principally
derived is the Catholic principle of separating the two
powers. For these effects are nowhere visible except in
the countries where this separation has been effected,
although a similar code of morals and indeed a faith
identically the same has been received elsewhere. Besides, although sanctioned by the general tone of modern
life they have been neutralised to a considerable extent by

the decline of the Catholic organization, and this especially in the countries where the greatest efforts have been made to restore the doctrine to its original purity and power.

In these respects Positivism has already appreciated Catholicism more fully than any of its own defenders, not even excepting De Maistre himself, as indeed some of the more candid organs of the retrograde school have allowed. But the merit of Catholicism does not merely depend on the fact that it forms a most important link in the series of human development. What adds to the glory of its efforts is that, as history clearly proves, they were in advance of their time. The political failure of Catholicism resulted from the imperfection of its doctrines, and the resistance of the social medium in which it worked. It is true that Monotheism is far more compatible with the separation of powers than Polytheism. But from the absolute character of every kind of theology, there was always a tendency in the mediæval system to degenerate into mere theocracy. In fact, the proximate cause of its decline was the increased development of this tendency in the fourteenth century, and the resistance which it provoked among the kings, who stood forward to represent the general voice of condemnation. Again, though separation of powers was less difficult in the defensive system of mediæval warfare than in the aggressive system of antiquity, yet it is thoroughly repugnant to the military spirit in all its phases, because adverse to the concentration of authority which is requisite in war. And thus it was never thoroughly realised, except in the conceptions of a few leading men among both the spiritual and temporal class. Its brief success was principally caused by a temporary combination of circumstances. It was for the most part a condition of very unstable equilibrium, oscillating between theocracy and empire.

But Positive civilization will accomplish what in the Middle Ages could only be attempted. We are aided, not merely by the example of the Middle Ages, but by the preparatory labours of the last five centuries. New modes of thought have arisen, and practical life has assumed new phases; and all are alike tending towards the separation of powers. What in the Middle Ages was but dimly foreseen by a few ardent and aspiring minds, becomes now an inevitable and obvious result, instinctively felt and formally recognised by all. From the intellectual point of view, it is nothing more than the distinction between theory and practice; a distinction which is already admitted more or less formally throughout civilized Europe in subjects of less importance; which therefore it would be unreasonable to abandon in the most difficult of all arts and sciences. Viewed socially, it implies the separation of education from action; or of morals from politics; and few would deny that the maintenance of this separation is one of the greatest blessings of our progressive civilization. The distinction is of equal importance to morality and to liberty. It is the only way of bringing opinion and conduct under the control of principle : for the most obvious application of a principle has little weight when it is merely an act of obedience to a special command. Taking the more general question of bringing our political forces into harmony, it seems clear that theoretical and practical power are so totally distinct in origin and operation, whether in relation to the heart, intellect, or character, that the functions of counsel and of command ought never to belong to the same organs. All attempts to unite them are at once retrograde and visionary, and if successful would lead to the intolerable government of mediocrities equally unfit for either kind of power. But

But the mediæval attempt was premature; and Positivism will renew and complete it.

as I shall show in the following chapters this principle of separation will soon find increasing support among women and the working classes; the two elements of society in which we find the greatest amount of good sense and right feeling.

Modern society is, in fact, already ripe for the adoption of this fundamental principle of polity; and the opposition to it proceeds almost entirely from its connection with the doctrines of the mediæval church which have now become deservedly obsolete. But there will be an end of these revolutionary prejudices among all impartial observers as soon as the principle is seen embodied in Positivism, the only doctrine which is wholly disconnected with Theology. All human conceptions, all social improvements originated under theological influence, as we see proved clearly in many of the humblest details of life. But this has never prevented Humanity from finally appropriating to herself the results of the creeds which she has outgrown. And so it will be with this great political principle; it has already become obsolete except for the Positive school, which has verified inductively all the minor truths implied in it. The only direct attacks against it come from the metaphysicians, whose ambitious aspirations for absolute authority would be thwarted by it. It is they who attempt to fasten on Positivism the stigma of theocracy: a strange and in most cases disingenuous reproach, seeing that Positivists are distinguished from their opponents by discarding all beliefs which supersede the necessity for discussion. The fact is that serious disturbances will soon be caused by the pertinacious efforts of these adherents of pedantocracy to regulate by law what ought to be left to moral influences; and then the public will become more alive to the necessity of the Positivist doctrine of systematically separating political from moral government.   The latter should be understood to rely exclusively on the forces of conviction and persuasion; its influence on action being simply that of counsel; whereas the former employs direct compulsion, based upon superiority of physical force.

We now understand what is meant by the constructive character of the second revolutionary phase.   It implies a union of the social aspirations of the Middle Ages with the wise political instincts of the Convention.   In the interval of these two periods the more advanced nations were without any systematic organization, and were abandoned to the two-fold process of transition, which was decomposing the old order and preparing the new.   Both these preliminary steps are now sufficiently accomplished.   The desire for social regeneration has become too strong to be resisted, and a philosophical system capable of directing it has already arisen.   We may, therefore, recommence on a better intellectual and social basis the great effort of Catholicism, to bring Western Europe to a social system of peaceful activity and intellectual culture, in which Thought and Action should be subordinated to universal Love.   Reconstruction will begin at the points where demolition begun previously.   The dissolution of the old organism began in the fourteenth century by the destruction of its international character.   Conversely, reorganization begins by satisfying the intellectual and moral wants common to the five Western nations.

And here, since the object of this chapter is The Ethical system of Positivism. to explain the social value of Positivism, I may show briefly that it leads necessarily to the formation of a definite system of universal Morality; this being the ultimate object of all Philosophy, and the starting point of all Polity.   Since it is by its moral code that every spiritual power must be principally tested, this will be the

7

best mode of judging of the relative merits of Positivism and Catholicism.

Subjection of Self-love to Social love is the great ethical problem. The Social state of itself favours this result; but it may be hastened by organized and conscious effort.

To the Positivist the object of Morals is to make our sympathetic instincts preponderate as far as possible over the selfish instincts; social feelings over personal feelings. This way of viewing the subject is peculiar to the new philosophy, for no other system has included the more recent additions to the theory of human nature, of which Catholicism gave so imperfect a representation.

It is one of the first principles of Biology that organic life always preponderates over animal life. By this principle the Sociologist explains the superior strength of the self-regarding instincts, since these are all connected more or less closely with the instinct of self-preservation. But although there is no evading this fact, Sociology shows that it is compatible with the existence of benevolent affections, affections which Catholicism had asserted to be altogether alien to our nature, and to be entirely dependent on superhuman Grace derived from a sphere beyond the reach of Law. The great problem, then, is to raise social feeling by artificial effort to the position which, in the natural condition, is held by selfish feeling. The solution is to be found in another biological principle, namely, that functions and organs are developed by constant exercise, and atrophied by prolonged inaction. Now the effect of the Social state is, that while our sympathetic instincts are constantly stimulated, the selfish propensities are restricted; since, if free play were given to them, human intercourse would very shortly become impossible. Thus it compensates to some extent the natural weakness of the Sympathies that they are capable of almost indefinite extension, whilst Self-love meets inevitably with a

more or less efficient check.   Both these tendencies naturally increase with the progress of Humanity, and their
increase is the best measure of the degree of perfection
that we have attained.   Their growth, though spontaneous,
may be materially hastened by organized intervention,
both of individuals and of society, the object being to
increase all favourable influences and diminish the unfavourable.   This is the object of the art of Morals.   Like
every other art, it is restricted within certain limits.   But
in this case the limits are less narrow, because the phenomena, being more complex, are also more modifiable.

Positive morality differs therefore from that of theological as well as of metaphysical systems.   Its primary
principle is the preponderance of Social Sympathy.   Full
and free expansion of the benevolent emotions is made the
first condition of individual and social well being, since
these emotions are at once the sweetest to experience, and
are the only feelings which can find expression simultaneously in all.   The doctrine is as deep and pure as it is
simple and true.   It is eminently characteristic of a philosophy which, by virtue of its attribute of reality, subordinates all scientific conceptions to the social point of view,
as the sole point from which they can be co-ordinated into
a whole.   The intuitive methods of metaphysics could
never advance with any consistency beyond the sphere of
the individual.   Theology, especially Christian theology,
could only rise to social conceptions by an indirect process,
forced upon it, not by its principles, but by its practical
functions.   Intrinsically, its spirit was altogether personal;
the highest object placed before each individual was the
attainment of his own salvation, and all human affections
were made subordinate to the love of God.   It is true that
the first training of our higher feelings is due to theological systems; but their moral value depended mainly on

the wisdom of the priesthood. They compensated the defects of their doctrine, and at that time no better doctrine was available, by taking advantage of the antagonism which naturally presented itself between the interests of the imaginary and those of the real world. The moral value of Positivism, on the contrary, is inherent in its doctrine, and can be largely developed, independently of any spiritual discipline, though not so far as to dispense with the necessity for such discipline. Thus, while Morality as a science is made far more consistent by being placed in its true connection with the rest of our knowledge, the sphere of natural morality is widened by bringing human life, individually and collectively, under the direct and continuous influence of Social Feeling.

Intermediate between self-love and universal benevolence are the domestic affections: filial, fraternal, conjugal, paternal. I have stated that Positive morality is brought into a coherent and systematic form by its principle of universal love. This principle must now be examined first in its application to the separate aspects of the subject, and subsequently as the means by which the various parts may be co-ordinated.

There are three successive states of morality answering to the three principal stages of human life ; the personal, the domestic, and the social stage. The succession represents the gradual training of the sympathetic principle; it is drawn out step by step by a series of affections which, as it diminishes in intensity, increases in dignity. This series forms our best resource in attempting as far as possible to reach the normal state; subordination of self-love to social feeling. These are the two extremes in the scale of human affections; but between them there is an intermediate degree, namely, domestic attachment, and it is on this that the solution of the great moral problem depends. The love of his family leads Man out of his original state of Self-love and enables him to attain finally a sufficient measure of Social love.   Every attempt on the part of the moral educator to call this last into immediate action, regardless of the intermediate stage, is to be condemned as utterly chimerical and profoundly injurious.   Such attempts are regarded in the present day with far too favourable an eye.   Far from being a sign of social progress, they would, if successful, be an immense step backwards; since the feeling which inspires them is one of perverted admiration for antiquity.

Since the importance of domestic life is so great as a transition from selfish to social feeling, a systematic view of its relations will be the best mode of explaining the spirit of Positive morality, which is in every respect based upon the order found in nature.

The first germ of social feeling is seen in the affection of the child for its parents.   Filial love is the starting-point of our moral education : from it springs the instinct of Continuity, and consequently of reverence for our ancestors.   It is the first tie by which the new being feels himself bound to the whole past history of Man.   Brotherly love comes next, implanting the instinct of Solidarity, that is to say of union with our contemporaries; and thus we have already a sort of outline of social existence.   With maturity new phases of feeling are developed.   Relationships are formed of an entirely voluntary nature ; which have therefore a still more social character than the involuntary ties of earlier years.   This second stage in moral education begins with conjugal affection, the most important of all, in which perfect fullness of devotion is secured by the reciprocity and indissolubility of the bond.   It is the highest type of all sympathetic instincts, and has appropriated to itself in a special sense the name of Love.   From this most perfect of unions proceeds the last in the series of domestic sympathies, parental love. It completes the training by which Nature prepares us for universal sympathy : for it teaches us to care for our successors ; and thus it binds us to the Future, as filial love had bound us to the Past.

I placed the voluntary class of domestic sympathies after the involuntary, because it was the natural order of individual development, and it thus bore out my statement of the necessity of family life as an intermediate stage between personal and social life. But in treating more directly of the theory of the Family as the constituent element of the body politic, the inverse order should be followed. In that case conjugal attachment would come first, as being the feeling through which the family comes into existence as a new social unit, which in many cases consists simply of the original pair. Domestic sympathy, when once formed by marriage, is perpetuated first by parental then by filial affection ; it may afterwards be developed by the tie of brotherhood, the only relation by which different families can be brought into direct contact. The order followed here is that of decrease in intensity, and increase in extension. The feeling of fraternity, which I place last, because it is usually least powerful, will be seen to be of primary importance when regarded as the transition from domestic to social affections; it is, indeed, the natural type to which all social sympathies conform. But there is yet another intermediate relation, without which this brief exposition of the theory of the family would be incomplete ; I mean the relation of household servitude, which may be called indifferently domestic or social. It is a relation which at the present time is not properly appreciated on account of our dislike to all subjection ; and yet the word *domestic* is enough to remind us that in every normal state of Humanity, it supplies what would otherwise be a want in household relations. Its value lies in completing the education of the social instinct, by a special apprenticeship in obedience and command, both being subordinated to the universal principle of mutual sympathy.

The object of the preceding remarks was to show the efficacy of the Positive method in moral questions by applying it to the most important of all moral theories, the theory of the Family. For more detailed proof, I must refer to my treatise on "Positive Polity," to which this work is introductory. I would call attention, however, to the beneficial influence of Positivism on personal morality. Actions which hitherto had always been referred even by Catholic philosophers to personal interests, are now brought under the great principle of Love on which the whole Positive doctrine is based.

Feelings are only to be developed by constant exercise; and exercise is most necessary when the intrinsic energy of the feeling is least. *Personal virtues placed upon a social basis.* It is therefore quite contrary to the true spirit of moral education to degrade duty in questions of personal morality to a mere calculation of self-interest. Of course, in this elementary part of Ethics, it is easier to estimate the consequences of actions, and to show the personal utility of the rules enjoined. But this method of procedure inevitably stimulates the self-regarding propensities, which are already too preponderant, and the exercise of which ought as far as possible to be discouraged. Besides, it often results in practical failure. To leave the decision of such questions to the judgment of the individual, is to give a formal sanction to all the natural differences in men's inclinations. When the only motive urged is consideration for personal consequences, every one feels himself to be the best judge of these, and modifies the rule at his plea-

sure. Positivism, guided by a truer estimate of the facts,
entirely remodels this elementary part of .Ethics. Its
appeal is to social feeling, and not to personal, since the
actions in question are of a kind in which the individual
is far from being the only person interested. For example,
such virtues as temperance and chastity are inculcated by
the Positivist on other grounds than those of their personal
advantages. He will not of course be blind to their individual value ; but this is an aspect on which he will not
dwell too much, for fear of concentrating attention on self-
interest. At all events, he will never make it the basis of
his precepts, but will invariably rest them upon their
social value. There are cases in which men are preserved
by an unusually strong constitution from the injurious
effects of intemperance or libertinage ; but such men are
bound to sobriety and continence as rigorously as the rest,
because without these virtues they cannot perform their
social duties rightly. Even in the commonest of personal
virtues, cleanliness, this alteration in the point of view
may be made with advantage. A simple sanitary regulation is thus ennobled by knowing that the object of it is to
make each one of us more fit for the service of others. In
this way, and in no other, can moral education assume its
true character at the very outset. We shall become habituated to the feeling of subordination to Humanity, even
in our smallest actions. It is in these that we should be
trained to gain the mastery over the lower propensities;
and the more so that, in these simple cases, it is less difficult to appreciate their consequences.

The influence of Positivism on personal morality is in
itself a proof of its superiority to other systems. Its superiority in domestic morality we have already seen, and yet
this was the best aspect of Catholicism, forming indeed the
principal basis of its admirable moral code. On social

morality strictly so called, I need not dwell at length.
Here the value of the new philosophy will be more direct
and obvious, the fact of its standing at the social point of
view being the very feature which distinguishes it from
all other systems.   In defining the mutual duties arising
from the various relations of life, or again in giving soli-
dity and extension to the instinct of our common fraternity, neither theological nor metaphysical morality can
bear comparison with Positivism.   Its precepts are adapted
without difficulty to the special requirements of each case,
because they are ever in harmony with the general laws
of society and of human nature.   But on these obvious
characteristics of Positivism I need not farther enlarge, as
I shall have other occasions for referring to them.

After this brief exposition of Positive morality I must
allude with equal brevity to the means by which it will be
established and applied.   These are of two kinds.   The
first lay down the foundations of moral training for each
individual: they furnish principles, and they regulate
feelings.   The second carry out the work begun, and
ensure the application of the principles inculcated to practical life.   Both these functions are in the first instance
performed spontaneously, under the influence of the doctrine and of the sympathies evoked by it.   But for their
adequate performance a spiritual power specially devoted
to the purpose is necessary.

The moral education of the Positivist is based *Moral edu-cation consists* both upon Reason and on Feeling, the latter *partly of sci-entific demon-* having always the preponderance, in accordance *stration of ethical truth,* with the primary principle of the system. *but still more of culture of*

The result of the rational basis is to bring *the higher sympathies.* moral precepts to the test of rigorous demonstration, and to secure them against all danger from dis-
cussion, by showing that they rest upon the laws of our

individual and social nature. By knowing these laws, we are enabled to form a judgment of the influence of each affection, thought, action, or habit, be that influence direct or indirect, special or general, in private life or in public. Convictions based upon such knowledge will be as deep as any that are formed in the present day from the strictest scientific evidence, with that excess of intensity due to their higher importance and their close connection with our noblest feelings. Nor will such convictions be limited to those who are able to appreciate the logical value of the arguments. We see constantly in other departments of Positive science that men will adopt notions upon trust, and carry them out with the same zeal and confidence, as if they were thoroughly acquainted with all the grounds for their belief. All that is necessary is, that they should feel satisfied that their confidence is well bestowed, the fact being, in spite of all that is said of the independence of modern thought, that it is often given too readily. The most willing assent is yielded every day to the rules which mathematicians, astronomers, physicists, chemists, or biologists, have laid down in their respective arts, even in cases where the greatest interests are at stake. And similar assent will certainly be accorded to moral rules when they, like the rest, shall be acknowledged to be susceptible of scientific proof.

But while using the force of demonstration to an extent hitherto impossible, Positivists will take care not to exaggerate its importance. Moral education, even in its more systematic parts, should rest principally upon Feeling, as the mere statement of the great human problem indicates. The study of moral questions, intellectually speaking, is most valuable ; but the effect it leaves is not directly moral, since the analysis will refer, not to our own actions, but to those of others ; for all scientific investigations, to be impartial and free from confusion, must be objective, not subjective. Now to judge others without immediate reference to self, is a process which may possibly result in strong convictions; but so far from calling out right feelings, it will, if carried too far, interfere with or check their natural development. However, the new school of moralists is the less likely to err in this direction, that it would be totally inconsistent with that profound knowledge of human nature in which Positivism has already shown itself so far superior to Catholicism. No one knows so well as the Positivist that the principal source of real morality lies in direct exercise of our social sympathies, whether systematic or spontaneous. He will spare no efforts to develop these sympathies from the earliest years by every method which sound philosophy can indicate. It is in this that moral education, whether private or public, principally consists; and to it mental education is always to be held subordinate. I shall revert to these remarks in the next chapter, when I come to the general question of educating the People.

But however efficient the training received in youth, it will not be enough to regulate our conduct in after years, amidst all the distracting influences of practical life, unless the same spiritual power which provides the education prolong its influence over our maturity. Part of its task will be to recall individuals, classes, and even nations, when the case requires it, to principles which they have forgotten or misinterpreted, and to instruct them in the means of applying them wisely. And here, even more than in the work of education strictly so called, the appeal will be to Feeling rather than to pure Reason. Its force will be derived from Public Opinion strongly organized. If the spiritual power awards its praise and blame justly, public opinion, as I shall show in the next chapter, will lend it the most irresistible support. This moral action of Humanity upon each of her members has always existed whenever there was any real community of principles and feelings. But its strength will be far greater under the Positive system. The reality of the doctrine and the social character of modern civilization give advantages to the new spiritual power which were denied to Catholicism.

Commemoration of great men.
And these advantages are brought forward very prominently by the Positive system of commemoration. Commemoration, when regularly instituted, is a most valuable instrument in the hands of a spiritual power for continuing the work of moral education. It was the absolute character of Catholicism, even more than the defective state of mediæval society, that caused the failure of its noble aspirations to become the universal religion. In spite of all its efforts, its system of commemoration has always been restricted to very narrow limits, both in time and space. Outside these limits, Catholicism has always shown the same blindness and injustice that it now complains of receiving from its own opponents. Positivism, on the contrary, can yield the full measure of praise to all times and all countries, without either weakness or inconsistency. Possessing the true theory of human development, every mode and phase of that development will be celebrated. Thus every moral precept will be supported by the influence of posterity; and this in private life as well as in public, for the system of commemoration will be applied in the same spirit to the humblest services as well as to the highest.

While reserving special details for the treatise to which this work is introductory, I may yet give one illustration of this important aspect of Positivism; an illustration which probably will be the first step in the practical application of the system. I would propose to institute in Western Europe on any days that may be thought suitable, the yearly celebration of the three greatest of our predecessors, Cæsar, St. Paul, and Charlemagne, who are respectively the highest types of Greco-Roman civilization, of Mediæval Feudalism, and of Catholicism which forms the link between the two period. The services of these illustrious men have never yet been adequately recognised, for want of a sound historical theory enabling us to explain the prominent part which they played in the development of our race. Even in St. Paul's case the omission is noticeable. Positivism gives him a still higher place than has been given him by Theology; for it looks upon him as historically the founder of the religion which bears the inappropriate name of Christianity. In the other two cases the influence of Positive principles is even more necessary. For Cæsar has been almost equally misjudged by theological and by metaphysical writers; and Catholicism has done very little for the appreciation of Charlemagne. However, notwithstanding the absence of any systematic appreciation of these great men, yet from the reverence with which they are generally regarded, we can hardly doubt that the celebration here proposed would meet with ready acceptance throughout Western Europe.

To illustrate my meaning still further, I may observe that history presents cases where exactly the opposite course is called for, and which should be held up not for approbation but for infamy. Blame, it is true, should not be carried to the same extent as praise, because it stimulates the destructive instincts to a degree which is always painful and sometimes injurious. Yet strong condemnation is occasionally desirable. It strengthens social feelings and principles, if only by giving more significance to our approval. Thus I would suggest that after doing honour to the three great men who have done so much to promote the development of our race, there should be a solemn reprobation of the two principal oppponents of progress, Julian and Bonaparte; the latter being the more criminal of the two, the former the more insensate. Their influence has been sufficiently extensive to allow of all the Western nations joining in this damnatory verdict.*

The principal function of the spiritual power is to direct the future of society by means of education; and, as a supplementary part of education, to pronounce judgment upon the past in the mode here indicated. But there are functions of another kind, relating more immediately to the present; and these too, result naturally from its position as an educating body. If the educators are men worthy of their position, it will give them an influence over the whole course of practical life, whether private or public. Of course it will merely be the influence of council, and practical men will be free to accept or reject it; but its weight may be very considerable when given prudently, and when the authority from which it proceeds is recognized as competent. The questions on which its advice is most needed are the relations between different classes. Its action will be coextensive with the diffusion of Positive principles; for nations professing the same faith, and sharing in the same education, will naturally accept the same intellectual and moral directors. In the next chapter I shall treat this subject more in detail. I merely mention it here as one among the list of functions belonging to the new spiritual power.

The political motto of Positivism: Order and Progress. It will now not be difficult to show that all the characteristics of Positivism are summed up in its motto, *Order and Progress*, a motto which

* On reconsideration, Comte saw fit to withdraw this proposal. Politique Positive, vol. iv. ch. 5.

has a philosophical as well as political bearing, and which I shall always feel glad to have put forward.

Positivism is the only school which has given a definite significance to these two conceptions, whether regarded from their scientific or their social aspect. With regard to Progress, the assertion will hardly be disputed, no definition of it but the Positive ever having yet been given. In the case of Order, it is less apparent; but, as I have shown in the first chapter, it is no less profoundly true. All previous philosophies had regarded Order as stationary, a conception which rendered it wholly inapplicable to modern politics. But Positivism, by rejecting the absolute, and yet not introducing the arbitrary, represents Order in a totally new light, and adapts it to our progressive civilization. It places it on the firmest possible foundation, that is, on the doctrine of the invariability of the laws of nature, which defends it against all danger from subjective chimeras. The Positivist regards artificial Order in Social phenomena, as in all others, as resting necessarily upon the Order of nature, in other words, upon the whole series of natural laws.

But Order has to be reconciled with Progress: and here Positivism is still more obviously without a rival. Necessary as the reconciliation is, no other system has even attempted it. But the facility with which we are now enabled, by the encyclopædic scale, to pass from the simplest mathematical phenomena to the most complicated phenomena of political life, leads at once to a solution of the problem. Viewed scientifically, it is an instance of that necessary correlation of existence and movement, which we find indicated in the inorganic world, and which becomes still more distinct in Biology. Finding it in all the lower sciences, we are prepared for its appearance in a still more definite shape in Sociology.

Progress, the development of Order.

Here its practical importance becomes more obvious, though it had been implicitly involved before. In Sociology the correlation assumes this form: Order is the condition of all Progress; Progress is always the object of Order. Or, to penetrate the question still more deeply, Progress may be regarded simply as the development of Order; for the order of nature necessarily contains within itself the germ of all possible progress. The rational view of human affairs is to look on all their changes, not as new Creations, but as new Evolutions. And we find this principle fully borne out in history. Every social innovation has its roots in the past; and the rudest phases of savage life show the primitive trace of all subsequent improvement.

Analysis of Progress: material, physical, intellectual, and moral.

Progress then is in its essence identical with Order, and may be looked upon as Order made manifest. Therefore, in explaining this double conception on which the Science and Art of society depend, we may at present limit ourselves to the analysis of Progress. Thus simplified it is more easy to grasp, especially now that the novelty and importance of the question of Progress are attracting so much attention. For the public is becoming instinctively alive to its real significance, as the basis on which all sound moral and political teaching must henceforth rest.

Taking, then, this point of view, we may say that the one great object of life, personal or social, is to become more perfect in every way; in our external condition first, but also, and more especially, in our own nature. The first kind of progress we share in common with the higher animals; all of which make some efforts to improve their material position. It is of course the least elevated stage of progress, but being the easiest, it is the point from which we start towards the higher stages. A nation that has made no efforts to improve itself materially, will take but little interest in moral or mental improvement. This is the only ground on which enlightened men can feel much pleasure in the material progress of our own times. It stirs up influences that tend to the nobler kinds of Progress; influences which would meet with even greater opposition than they do, were not the temptations presented to the coarser natures by material prosperity so irresistible. Owing to the mental and moral anarchy in which we live, systematic efforts to gain the higher degrees of Progress are as yet impossible; and this explains, though it does not justify, the exaggerated importance attributed nowadays to material improvements. But the only kinds of improvement really characteristic of Humanity are those which concern our own nature; and even here we are not quite alone; for several of the higher animals show some slight tendencies to improve themselves physically.

Progress in the higher sense includes improvements of three sorts; that is to say, it may be Physical, Intellectual, or Moral progress; the difficulty of each class being in proportion to its value and the extent of its sphere. Physical progress, which again might be divided on the same principle, seems under some of its aspects almost the same thing as material. But regarded as a whole it is far more important and far more difficult: its influence on the well-being of Man is also much greater. We gain more, for instance, by the smallest addition to length of life, or by any increased security for health, than by the most elaborate improvements in our modes of travelling by land or water, in which birds will probably always have a great advantage over us. However, as I said before, physical progress is not exclusively confined to Man. Some of the animals, for instance, advance as

far as cleanliness, which is the first step in the progressive
scale.

Intellectual and Moral progress, then, is the only kind
really distinctive of our race. Individual animals sometimes show it, but never a whole species, except as a consequence of prolonged intervention on the part of Man.
Between these two highest grades, as between the two
lower, we shall find a difference of value, extent, and difficulty ; always supposing the standard to be the manner
in which they affect Man's well-being, collectively or individually. To strengthen the intellectual powers, whether for art or for science, whether it be the powers of
observation or those of induction and deduction, is, when
circumstances allow of their being made available for
social purposes, of greater and more extensive importance,
than all physical, and, *a fortiori* than all material improvements. But we know from the fundamental principle
laid down in the first chapter of this work, that moral
progress has even more to do with our well-being than
intellectual progress. The moral faculties are more modifiable, although the effort required to modify them is
greater. If the benevolence or courage of the human
race were increased, it would bring more real happiness
than any addition to our intellectual powers. Therefore,
to the question, What is the true object of human life,
whether looked at collectively or individually ? the simplest
and most precise answer would be, the perfection of our
moral nature ; since it has a more immediate and certain
influence on our well-being than perfection of any other
kind. All the other kinds are necessary, if for no other
reason than to prepare the way for this ; but from the
very fact of this connection, it may be regarded as their
representative ; since it involves them all implicitly and
stimulates them to increased activity. Keeping then to

the question of moral perfection, we find two qualities standing above the rest in practical importance, namely, Sympathy and Energy. Both these qualities are included in the word *Heart*, which in all European languages has a different meaning for the two sexes. Both will be developed by Positivism, more directly, more continuously, and with greater result, than under any former system. The whole tendency of Positivism is to encourage sympathy; since it subordinates every thought, desire, and action to social feeling. Energy is also presupposed, and at the same time fostered by the system. For it removes a heavy weight of superstition, it reveals the true dignity of man, and supplies an unceasing motive for individual and collective action. The very acceptance of Positivism demands some vigour of character; it implies the braving of spiritual terrors, which were once enough to intimidate the firmest minds.

Progress, then, may be regarded under four successive aspects: Material, Physical, Intellectual, and Moral. Each of these might again be divided on the same principle, and we should then discover several intermediate phases. These cannot be investigated here; and I have only to note that the philosophical principle of this analysis is precisely the same as that on which I have based the Classification of the Sciences. In both cases the order followed is that of increasing generality and complexity in the phenomena. The only difference is in the mode in which the two arrangements are developed. For scientific purposes the lower portion of the scale has to be expanded into greater detail; while from the social point of view attention is concentrated on the higher parts. But whether it be the scale of the True or that of the Good, the conclusion is the same in both. Both alike indicate the supremacy of social considerations; both point to universal Love as the highest ideal.

I have now explained the principal purpose of Positive Philosophy, namely, spiritual reorganization; and I have shown how that purpose is involved in the Positivist motto, Order and Progress. Positivism, then, realizes the highest aspirations of mediæval Catholicism, and at the same time fulfils the conditions, the absence of which caused the failure of the Convention. It combines the opposite merits of the Catholic and the Revolutionary spirit, and by so doing supersedes them both. Theology and Metaphysics may now disappear without danger, because the service which each of them rendered is now harmonized with that of the other, and will be performed more perfectly. The principle on which this result depends is the separation of spiritual from temporal power. This, it will be remembered, had always been the chief subject of contention between the two antagonistic parties.

Application of our principles to actual politics. All government must for the present be provisional. I have spoken of the moral and mental reorganization of Western Europe as characterizing the second phase of the Revolution. Let us now see what are its relations with the present state of politics. Of course the development of Positivism will not be much affected by the retrograde tendencies of the day, whether theological or metaphysical. Still the general course of events will exercise an influence upon it, of which it is important to take account. So too, although the new doctrine cannot at present do much to modify its surroundings, there are yet certain points in which action may be taken at once. In the fourth volume of this treatise the question of a transitional policy will be carefully considered, with the view of facilitating the advent of the normal state which social science indicates in a more distant future. I cannot complete this chapter without some notice of this provisional policy, which must be carried on until Positivism has made its way to general acceptance.

The principal feature of this policy is that it is temporary. To set up any permanent institution in a society which has no fixed opinions or principles of life, would be hopeless. Until the most important questions are thoroughly settled, both in principle and practice, the only measures of the least utility are those which facilitate the process of reconstruction. Measures adopted with a view to permanence must end, as we have seen them end so often, in disappointment and failure, however enthusiastically they may have been received at first.

Inevitable as this consequence of our revolutionary position is, it has never been understood, except by the great leaders of the republican movement in 1793. Of the various governments that we have had during the last two generations, all, except the Convention, have fallen into the vain delusion of attempting to found permanent institutions, without waiting for any intellectual or moral basis. And therefore it is that none but the Convention has left any deep traces in men's thoughts or feelings. All its principal measures, even those which concerned the future more than the present, were avowedly provisional; and the consequence was that they harmonized well with the peculiar circumstances of the time. The true philosopher will always look with respectful admiration on these men, who not only had no rational theory to guide them, but were encumbered with false metaphysical notions; and who yet notwithstanding proved themselves the only real statesmen that Western Europe can boast of since the time of Frederick the Great. Indeed the wisdom of their policy would be almost unaccountable, only that the very circumstances which called for it so urgently, were to some extent calculated to suggest it. The state of things was

such as to make it impossible to settle the government on
any permanent basis. Again, amidst all the wild extravagance of the principles in vogue, the necessity of a
strong government to resist foreign invasion counteracted
many of their worst effects. On the removal of this salutary pressure, the Convention fell into the common error,
though to a less extent than the Constituent Assembly.
It set up a constitution framed according to some abstract
model, which was supposed to be final, but which did not
last so long as the period originally proposed for its own
provisional labours. It is on this first period of its government that its fame rests.

The plan originally proposed was that the government
of the Convention should last till the end of the war. If
this plan could have been carried out, it would probably
have been extended still further, as the impossibility of
establishing any permanent system would have been generally recognised. The only avowed motive for making
the government provisional was of course the urgent necessity of national defence. But beneath this temporary
motive, which for the time superseded every other consideration, there was another and a deeper motive for it,
which could not have been understood without sounder
historical principles than were at that time possible. That
motive was the utterly negative character of the metaphysical doctrines then accepted, and the consequent absence
of any intellectual or moral basis for political reconstruction. This of course was not recognised, but it was really
the principal reason why the establishment of any definite
system of government was delayed. Had the war been
brought to an end, clearer views of the subject would no
doubt have been formed; indeed they had been formed
already in the opposite camp, by men of the Neo-catholic
school, who were not absorbed by the urgent question of

defending the Republic. What blinded men to the truth was the fundamental yet inevitable error of supposing the critical doctrines of the preceding generation applicable to purposes of construction. They were undeceived at last by the utter anarchy which the triumph of these principles occasioned; and the next generation occupied itself with the counter revolutionary movement, in which similar attempts at finality were made by the various reactionist parties. For these parties were quite as destitute as their opponents of any principles suited to the task of reconstruction; and they had to fall back upon the old system as the only recognized basis on which public Order could be maintained.

And in this respect the situation is still unchanged. It still retains its revolutionary character; and any immediate attempt to reorganize political administration would only be the signal for fresh attempts at reaction, attempts which now can have no other result than anarchy. It is true that Positivism has just supplied us with a philosophical basis for political reconstruction. But its principles are still so new and undeveloped, and besides are understood by so few, that they cannot exercise much influence at present on political life. Ultimately, and by slow degrees, they will mould the institutions of the future, but meanwhile they must work their way freely into men's minds and hearts, and for this at least one generation will be necessary. Spiritual organization is the only point where an immediate beginning can be made; difficult as it is, its possibility is at last as certain as its urgency. When sufficient progress has been made with it, it will cause a gradual regeneration of political institutions. But any attempt to modify these too rapidly would only result in fresh disturbances. Such disturbances, it is true, will

Danger of attempting political reconstruction before spiritual.

never be as dangerous as they were formerly, because the anarchy of opinion is so profound that it is far more difficult for men to agree in any fixed principles of action. The absolute doctrines of the last century which inspired such intense conviction, can never regain their strength, because, when brought to the crucial test of experience as well as of discussion, their uselessness for constructive purposes and their subversive tendency became evident to every one. They have been weakened, too, by theological concessions which their supporters, in order to carry on the government at all, were obliged to make. Consequently the policy with which they are at present connected is one which oscillates between reaction and anarchy, or rather which is at once despotic and destructive, from the necessity of controlling a society which has become almost as adverse to metaphysical as to theological rule. In the utter absence, then, of any general convictions, the worst forms of political commotion are not to be feared, because it would be impossible to rouse men's passions sufficiently. But unwise efforts to set up a permanent system of government would even now lead, in certain cases, to lamentable disorder, and would at all events be utterly useless. Quiet at home depends now, like peace abroad, simply on the absence of disturbing forces; a most insecure basis, since it is itself a symptom of the extent to which the disorganizing movement has proceeded. This singular condition must necessarily continue until the *interregnum* which at present exists in the moral and intellectual region comes to an end. As long as there is such an utter want of harmony in feeling as well as in opinion, there can be no real security against war or internal disorder. The existing equilibrium has arisen so spontaneously that it is no doubt less unstable than is generally supposed. Still it is sufficiently precarious to excite continual panics, both at home and abroad, which are not only very irritating, but often exercise a most injurious influence over our policy. Now attempts at immediate reconstruction of political institutions, instead of improving this state of things, make it very much worse, by giving factitious life to the old doctrines, which, being thoroughly worn out, ought to be left to the natural process of decay. The inevitable result of restoring them to official authority will be to deter the public, and even the thinking portion of it, from that free exercise of the mental powers by which, and by which only, we may hope to arrive without disturbance at fixed principles of action.

The cessation of war therefore justifies no change in republican policy. As long as the spiritual interregnum lasts, it must retain its provisional character. Indeed this character ought to be more strongly impressed upon it than ever. For no one now has any real belief in the organic value of the received metaphysical doctrines. They would never have been revived but for the need of having some sort of political formula to work with, in default of any real social convictions. But the revival is only apparent, and it contrasts most strikingly with the utter absence of systematic principles in most active minds. There is no real danger of repeating the error of the first revolutionists and of attempting to construct with negative doctrines. We have only to consider the vast development of industry, of esthetic culture, and of scientific study, to free ourselves from all anxiety on this head. Such things are incompatible with any regard for the metaphysical teaching of ideologists or psychologists. Nor is there much to fear in the natural enthusiasm which is carrying us back to the first days of the Revolution. It will only revive the old republican spirit, and make us forget the long period of retrogression and stagnation which have elapsed since the first great outbreak; for this is the point on which the attention of posterity will be finally concentrated. But while satisfying these very legitimate feelings, the people will soon find that the only aspect of this great crisis which we have to imitate is the wise insight of the Convention during the first part of its administration, in perceiving that their policy could only be provisional, and that definite reconstruction must be reserved for better times. We may fairly hope that the next formal attempt to set up a constitution according to some abstract ideal, will convince the French nation, and ultimately the whole West, of the utter futility of such schemes. Besides, the free discussion which has now become habitual to us, and the temper of the people, which is as sceptical of political entities as of Christian mysteries, would make any such attempts extremely difficult. Never was there a time so unfavourable to doctrines admitting of no real demonstration : demonstration being now the only possible basis of permanent belief. Supposing then a new constitution to be set on foot, and the usual time to be spent in the process of elaborating it, public opinion will very possibly discard it before it is completed ; not allowing it even the short average duration of former constitutions. Any attempt to check free discussion on the subject would defeat its own object ; since free discussion is the natural consequence of our intellectual and social position.

Politically what is wanted is Dictatorship, with liberty of speech and discussion. The same conditions which require our policy to be provisional while the spiritual interregnum lasts, point also to the mode in which this provisional policy should be carried out. Had the revolutionary government of the Convention continued till the end of the war, it would probably have been prolonged up to the present time. But in one most

important respect a modification would have been necessary. During the struggle for independence what was
wanted was a vigorous dictatorship, combining spiritual
with temporal powers : a dictatorship even stronger than
the old monarchy, and only distinguished from despotism
by its ardour in the course of progress. Without complete concentration of political power, the republic could
never have been saved. But with peace the necessity for
such concentration was at an end. The only motive for
still continuing the provisional system was the absence of
social convictions. But this would also be a motive for
giving perfect liberty of speech and discussion, which till
then had been impossible or dangerous. For liberty was
a necessary condition for elaborating and diffusing a new
system of universal principles, as the only sure basis for
the future regeneration of society.

This hypothetical view of changes which might have
taken place in the Conventional government, may be applied to the existing condition of affairs. It is the policy
best adapted for the republican government which is now
arising in all the security of a settled peace, and yet amidst
the most entire anarchy of opinion. The successors of
the Convention, men unworthy of their task, degraded the
progressive dictatorship entrusted to them by the circumstances of the time into a retrograde tyranny. During
the reign of Charles X., which was the last phase of the
reaction, the central power was thoroughly undermined
by the legal opposition of the parliamentary or local
power. The central government still refused to recognize
any limits to its authority ; but the growth of free thought
made its claims to spiritual jurisdiction more and more
untenable, leaving it merely the temporal authority requisite for public order. During the neutral period which
followed the counter-revolution, the dictatorship was not

merely restricted to its proper functions, but was legally destroyed; that is, the local power as represented by parliament took the place of the central power. All pretentions to spiritual influence were abandoned by both; their thoughts being sufficiently occupied with the maintenance of material order. The intellectual anarchy of the time made this task difficult enough; but they aggravated the difficulty by unprincipled attempts to establish their government on the basis of pure self-interest, irrespectively of all moral considerations. The restoration of the republic and the progressive spirit aroused by it has no doubt given to both legislative and executive a large increase of power : to an extent indeed which a few years back would have caused violent antipathy. But it would be a grievous error for either of them to attempt to imitate the dictatorial style of the Conventional government. Unsuccessful in any true sense as the attempt would be, it might occasion very serious disturbances, which like the obsolete metaphysical principles in which they originate, would be equally dangerous to Order and to Progress.

We see, then, that in the total absence of any fixed principles on which men can unite, the policy required is one which shall be purely provisional, and limited almost entirely to the maintenance of material order. If order be preserved, the situation is in all other respects most favourable to the work of mental and moral regeneration which will prepare the way for the society of the future. The establishment of a republic in France disproves the false claims set up by official writers in behalf of constitutional government, as if it was the final issue of the Revolution. Meantime there is nothing irrevocable in the republic itself, except the moral principle involved in it, the absolute and permanent preponderance of Social Feeling; in other words, the concentration of all the powers of

Man upon the common welfare. This is the only maxim of the day which we can accept as final. It needs no formal sanction, because it is merely the expression of feelings generally avowed, all prejudices against it having been entirely swept away. But with the doctrines and the institutions resulting from them, through which this dominion of social feeling is to become an organized reality, the republic has no direct connection; it would be compatible with many different solutions of the problem. Politically, the only irrevocable point is the abolition of monarchy, which for a long time has been in France and to a less extent throughout the West, the symbol of retrogression.

That spirit of devotion to the public welfare, which is the noblest feature of republicanism, is strongly opposed to any immediate attempts at political finality, as being incompatible with conscientious endeavours to find a real solution of social problems. For before the practical solution can be hoped for, a systematic basis for it must exist; and this we can hardly expect to find in the remnants left to us of the old creeds. All that, the true philosopher desires is simply that the question of moral and intellectual reorganization shall be left to the unrestricted efforts of thinkers of whatever school. And in advocating this cause, he will plead the interests of the republic, for the safety of which it is of the utmost importance that no special set of principles should be placed under official patronage. Republicanism, then, will do far more to protect free thought, and resist political encroachment, than was done during the Orleanist government by the retrograde instincts of Catholicism. Catholic resistance to political reconstructions was strong, but blind : its place will now be more than supplied by wise indifference on the part of the public, which has learnt by experience the inevitable failure of these incoherent attempts to realise metaphysical Utopias. The only danger of the position is lest it divert the public, even the more reflective portion of it, from deep and continuous thought, to practical experiments based on superficial and hasty considerations. It must be owned that the temper of mind which now prevails would have been most unfavourable for the original elaboration of Positivism. That work, however, had already been accomplished under the Constitutional system; which, while not so restrictive as the preceding government, was yet sufficiently so to concentrate our intellectual powers, which of themselves would have been too feeble, upon the task. The original conception had indeed been formed during the preceding reign; but its development and diffusion took place under the parliamentary system. Positivism now offers itself for practical application to the question of social progress, which has become again the prominent question, and will ever remain so. Unfavourable as the present political temper would have been to the rise of Positivism, it is not at all so to its diffusion; always supposing its teachers to be men of sufficient dignity to avoid the snare of political ambition into which thinkers are now so apt to fall. By explaining, as it alone can explain, the futility and danger of the various Utopian schemes which are now competing with each other for the reorganization of society, Positivism will soon be able to divert public attention from these political chimeras, to the question of a total reformation of principles and of life.

Republicanism, then, will offer no obstacle to the diffusion of Positivist principles. Indeed, there is one point of view from which we may regard it as the commencement of the normal state. It will gradually lead to the recognition of the fundamental principle that spiritual power must be wholly

Such a dictatorship would be a step towards the separation of spiritual and temporal power.

independent of every kind of temporal power, whether central or local. It is not merely that statesmen will soon have to confess their inability to decide on the merits of a doctrine which supposes an amount of deep scientific knowledge from which they must necessarily be precluded. Besides this, the disturbance caused by the ambition of metaphysical schemers, who are incapable of understanding the times in which they live, will induce the public to withdraw their confidence from such men, and give it only to those who are content to abandon all political prospects, and to devote themselves to their proper function as philosophers. Thus Republicanism is, on the whole, favourable to this great principle of Positivism, the separation of temporal from spiritual power, notwithstanding the temptations offered to men who wish to carry their theories into immediate application. The principle seems, no doubt, in opposition to all our revolutionary prejudices. But the public, as well as the government, will be brought to it by experience. They will find it the only means of saving society from the consequences of metaphysical Utopias, by which Order and Progress are alike threatened. Thinkers too, those of them at least who are sincere, will cease to regard it with such blind antipathy, when they see that while it condemns their aspirations to political influence, it opens out to them a noble and most extensive sphere of moral influence. Independently of social considerations, it is the only way in which the philosopher can maintain the dignity to which his position entitles him, and which is at present so often compromised by the very success of his political ambition.

The political attitude which ought for the present to be assumed is so clearly indicated by all the circumstances of the time, that practical instinct has in this respect anticipated theory. The right

The motto of 1830, Liberty and Public Order.

view is well expressed in the motto, *Liberty and Public Order*, which was adopted spontaneously by the middle class at the commencement of the neutral period in 1830. It is not known who was the author of it; but it is certainly far too progressive to be considered as representing the feelings of the monarchy. It is not of course the expression of any systematic convictions; but no metaphysical school could have pointed out so clearly the two principal conditions required by the situation. Positivism while accepting it as an inspiration of popular wisdom, makes it more complete by adding two points which should have been contained in it at · first, only that they were too much opposed to existing prejudices to have been sanctioned by public opinion. Both parts of the motto require some expansion. Liberty ought to include perfect freedom of teaching; Public Order should involve the preponderance of the central power over the local. I subjoin a few brief 'remarks on these two points, which will be considered more fully in the fourth volume of this treatise.

Liberty should be extended to Education.   Positivism is now the only consistent advocate of free speech and free enquiry. Schools of opinion which do not rest on demonstration, and would consequently be shaken by any argumentative attacks, can never be sincere in their wish for Liberty, in the extended sense here given to it. Liberty of writing we have now had for a long time. But besides this we want liberty of speech; and also liberty of teaching; that is to say, the abandonment by the State of all its educational monopolies. Freedom of teaching, of which Positivists are the only genuine supporters, has become a condition of the first importance : and this not merely as a provisional measure, but as an indication of the normal state of things. In the first place, it is the only means by which any doctrine that has the power of fixing and harmonising men's convictions can become generally known. To legalise any system of education would imply that such a doctrine had been already found; it most assuredly is not the way to find it. But again, freedom of teaching is a step towards the normal state; it amounts to an admission that the problem of education is one which temporal authorities are incompetent to solve. Positivists would be the last to deny that education ought to be regularly organized. Only they assert, first, that as long as the spiritual interregnum lasts, no organization is possible; and secondly, that whenever the acceptance of a new synthesis makes it possible, it will be effected by the spiritual power to which that synthesis gives rise. In the meantime no general system of State education should be attempted. It will be well, however, to continue State assistance to those branches of instruction which are the most liable to be neglected by private enterprise, especially reading and writing. Moreover, there are certain institutions either established or revived by the Convention for higher training in special subjects; these ought to be carefully preserved, and brought up to the present state of our knowledge, for they contain the germs of principles which will be most valuable when the problem of reorganizing general education comes before us. But all the institutions abolished by the Convention ought now to be finally suppressed. Even the Academies should form no exception to this rule, for the harm which they have done, both intellectually and morally, since their reinstalment, has fully justified the wisdom of the men who decided on their abolition. Government should no doubt exercise constant vigilance over all private educational institutions; but this should have nothing to do with their doctrines, but with their morality, a point scandalously neglected in

the present state of the law.   These should be the limits
of state interference in education.   With these exceptions
it should be left to the unrestricted efforts of private associations, so as to give every opportunity for a definitive
educational system to establish itself.   For to pretend that
any satisfactory system exists at present would only be a
hypocritical subterfuge on the part of the authorities.
The most important step towards freedom of education
would be the suppression of all grants to theological or
metaphysical societies, leaving each man free to support
the religion and the system of instruction which he pre-
fers.   This, however, should be carried out in a just and
liberal spirit worthy of the cause, and without the least
taint of personal dislike or party feeling.   Full indemnity
should be given to members of Churches or Universities,
upon whom these changes would come unexpectedly.   By
acting in this spirit it will be far less difficult to carry out
measures which are obviously indicated by the position in
which we stand.   As there is now no doctrine which commands general assent, it would be an act of retrogression
to give legal sanction to any one of the old creeds, whatever their former claim to spiritual ascendancy.   It is
quite in accordance with the republican spirit to refuse
such sanction, notwithstanding the tendency that there is
to allow ideologists to succeed to the Academic offices held
under the constitutional system by psychologists.

Order de-   But Positivism will have as beneficial an in-
mands central-
ization.   fluence on public Order as on Liberty.   It
holds, in exact opposition to revolutionary prejudices, that
the central power should preponderate over the local.
The constitutionalist principle of separating the legislative
from the executive is only an empirical imitation of the
larger principle of separating temporal and spiritual power,
which was adopted in the Middle Ages.   There will always

be a contest for political supremacy between the central and local authorities; and it is an error into which, from various causes, we have fallen recently, to attempt to balance them against each other.   The whole tendency of French history has been to let the central power preponderate, until it degenerated and became retrograde towards the end of the seventeenth century.   Our present preference for the local power is therefore an historical anomaly, which is sure to cease as soon as the fear of reaction has passed away.   And as Republicanism secures us against any dangers of this kind, our political sympathies will soon resume their old course.   The advantages of the central power are, first, that it is more directly responsible than the other; and, secondly, that it is more practical and less likely to set up any claims to spiritual influence. This last feature is of the highest importance, and is likely to become every day more marked.   Whereas the local or legislative power, not having its functions clearly defined, is very apt to interfere in theoretical questions without being in any sense qualified for doing so.   Its preponderance would, then, in most cases be injurious to intellectual freedom, which, as it feels instinctively, will ultimately result in the rise of a spiritual authority destined to supersede its own.   On the strength of these tendencies, which have never before been explained, Positivists have little hesitation in siding in almost all cases with the central as against the local power.   Philosophers, whom no one can accuse of reactionist or servile views, who have given up all political prospects, and who are devoting themselves wholly to the work of spiritual reorganization, need not be afraid to take this course; and they ought to exert themselves **vigorously** in making the central power preponderant, limiting the functions of the local power to what is strictly indispensable.   And, notwithstanding all appearances to the contrary, republicanism will help to modify the revolutionary feeling on this point. It removes the distrust of authority caused naturally by the retrograde spirit of the old monarchy; and it makes it easier to repress any further tendencies of the same kind, without necessitating an entire change in the character of our policy for the sake of providing against a contingency, of which there is now so little fear. As soon as the central power has given sufficient proof of its progressive intentions, there will be no unwillingness on the part of the French public to restrict the powers of the legislative body, whether by reducing it to one-third of its present numbers, which are so far too large, or even by limiting its functions to the annual vote of the supplies. During the last phase of the counter-revolution, and the long period of parliamentary government which followed, a state of feeling has arisen on this subject, which is quite exceptional, and which sound philosophical teaching, and wise action on the part of government, will easily modify. It is inconsistent with the whole course of French history; and only leads us into the mistake of imitating the English constitution, which is adapted to no other country. The very extension which has just been given to the representative system will bring it into discredit, by showing it to be as futile and subversive in practice as philosophy had represented it to be in theory.

Intimate connection of Liberty with Order.   Such, then, is the way in which Positivism would interpret these two primary conditions of our present policy, Liberty and Public Order. But besides this, it explains and confirms the connection which exists between them. It teaches, in the first place, that true liberty is impossible at present without the vigorous control of a central power, progressive in the true sense of the word, wise enough to abdicate all spiritual influence, and keep to its own practical functions. Such a power is needed in order to check the despotic spirit of the various doctrines now in vogue. As all of them are more or less inconsistent with the principle of separation of powers, they would all be willing to employ forcible means of securing uniformity of opinion. Besides, the anarchy which is caused by our spiritual interregnum, might, but for a strong government, very probably interfere with the philosophical freedom which we now enjoy. Conversely, unless Liberty in the sense here spoken of be granted, it will be impossible for the central power to maintain itself in the position which public order requires. The obstacle to that position at present is the fear of reaction; and a scrupulous regard for freedom is the only means of removing these feelings which, though perhaps unfounded, are but too natural. All fears will be allayed at once when liberty of instruction and association becomes part of the law of the land. There will then be no hope, and indeed no wish, on the part of government to regulate our social institutions in conformity with any particular doctrine.

The object of this chapter has been to show the social value of Positivism. We have found that not merely does it throw light upon our Future policy, but that it also teaches us how to act upon the Present; and these indications have in both cases been based upon careful examination of the Past, in accordance with the fundamental laws of human development. It is the only system capable of handling the problem now proposed by the more advanced portion of our race to all who would claim to guide them. That problem is this: to reorganize human life, irrespectively of god or king; recognizing the obligation of no motive, whether public or private, other than Social Feeling, aided in due measure by the positive science and practical energy of Man.

CHAPTER III.

THE ACTION OF POSITIVISM UPON THE WORKING CLASSES.

Positivism will not for the present recommend itself to the governing classes, so much as to the People.

POSITIVISM whether looked at as a philosophical system or as an instrument of social renovation, cannot count upon much support from any of the classes, whether in Church or State, by whom the government of mankind has hitherto been conducted. There will be isolated exceptions of great value, and these will soon become more numerous: but the prejudices and passions of these classes will present serious obstacles to the work of moral and mental reorganization which constitutes the second phase of the great Western revolution. Their faulty education and their repugnance to system prejudice them against a philosophy which subordinates specialities to general principles. Their aristocratic instincts make it very difficult for them to recognise the supremacy of Social Feeling; that doctrine which lies at the root of social regeneration, as conceived by Positivism. That no support can be expected from the classes who were in the ascendant before the Revolution, is of course obvious; and we shall probably meet with opposition, quite as real though more carefully concealed, from the middle classes, to whom that revolution transferred the authority and social influence which they had long been coveting. Their thoughts are entirely engrossed with the acquisition of power; and they concern themselves but little with the mode in which it is used, or the objects to which it is directed. They were quite con-

vinced that the Revolution had found a satisfactory issue
in the parliamentary system instituted during the recent
period of political oscillation.   They will long continue to
regret that stationary period, because it was peculiarly
favourable to their restless ambition.   A movement tending
to the complete regeneration of society is almost as much
dreaded now by the middle classes as it was formerly by
the higher.   And both would at all events agree in prolonging the system of theological hypocrisy, as far as republican institutions admitted of it.   That policy is now
the only means by which retrogression is still possible.
Ignoble as it is, there are two motives for adopting it; it
secures respect and submission on the part of the masses,
and it imposes no unpleasant duties on their governors.
All their critical and metaphysical prejudices indispose
them to terminate the state of spiritual anarchy which is
the greatest obstacle to social regeneration; while at the
same time their ambition dreads the establishment of a
new moral authority, the restrictive influence of which
would of course press most heavily upon themselves.   In
the eighteenth century, men of rank, and even kings,
accepted the purely negative philosophy that was then in
vogue: it removed many obstacles, it was an easy path to
reputation, and it imposed no great sacrifice.   But we can
hardly hope from this precedent that the wealthy and
literary classes of our own time will be equally willing to
accept Positive philosophy; the avowed purpose of which
is to discipline our intellectual powers, in order to reorganize our modes of life.

The avowal of such a purpose is quite sufficient to prevent
Positivism from gaining the sympathies of any one of the
governing classes.   The classes to which it must appeal
are those who have been left untrained in the present
worthless methods of instruction by words and entities,

who are animated with strong social instincts, and who consequently have the largest stock of good sense and good feeling. In a word it is among the Working Classes that the new philosophers will find their most energetic allies. They are the two extreme terms in the social series as finally constituted; and it is only through their combined action that social regeneration can become a practical possibility. Notwithstanding their difference of position, a difference which indeed is more apparent than real, there are strong affinities between them, both morally and intellectually. Both have the same sense of the real, the same preference for the useful, and the same tendency to subordinate special points to general principles. Morally they resemble each other in generosity of feeling, in wise unconcern for material prospects, and in indifference to worldly grandeur. This at least will be the case as soon as philosophers in the true sense of that word have mixed sufficiently with the nobler members of the working classes to raise their own character to its proper level. When the sympathies which unite them upon these essential points have had time to show themselves, it will be felt that the philosopher is, under certain aspects, a member of the working class fully trained; while the working man is in many respects a philosopher without the training. Both too will look with similar feelings upon the intermediate or capitalist class. As that class is necessarily the possessor of material power, the pecuniary existence of both will as a rule be dependent upon it.

The working man who accepts his position is favourably situated for the reception of comprehensive principles and generous sympathies.
These affinities follow as a natural result from their respective position and functions. The reason of their not having been recognised more distinctly is, that at present we have nothing that can be called a philosophic class, or at least it is only represented by a few iso-

lated types.   Workmen worthy of their position are happily far less rare; but hitherto it is only in France, or rather in Paris, that they have shown themselves in their true light, as men emancipated from chimerical beliefs, and careless of the empty prestige of social position.   It is, then, only in Paris that the truth of the preceding remarks can be fully verified.

The occupations of working men are evidently far more conducive to philosophical views than those of the middle classes; since they are not so absorbing as to prevent continuous thought, even during the hours of labour.   And besides having more time for thinking, they have a moral advantage in the absence of any responsibility when their work is over.   The workman is preserved by his position from the schemes of aggrandisement, which are constantly harassing the capitalist.   Their difference in this respect causes a corresponding difference in their modes of thought; the one cares more for general principles, the other more for details.   To a sensible workman, the system of dispersive speciality now so much in vogue shows itself in its true light.   He sees it, that is, to be brutalizing, because it would condemn his intellect to the most paltry mode of culture, so much so that it will never be accepted in France, in spite of the irrational endeavours of our Anglomaniac economists.   To the capitalist, on the contrary, and even to the man of science, that system, however rigidly and consistently carried out, will seem far less degrading; or rather it will be looked upon as most desirable, unless his education has been such as to counteract these tendencies, and give him the desire and the ability for abstract and general thought.

Morally, the contrast between the position of the workman and the capitalist is even more striking.   Proud as most men are of worldly success, the degree of moral or

mental excellence implied in the acquisition of wealth or
power, even when the means used have been strictly legitimate, is hardly such as to justify that pride. Looking
at intrinsic qualities rather than at visible results, it is
obvious that practical success, whether in industry or in
war, depends far more on character than on intellect or
affection. The principal condition for it is the combination of a certain amount of energy with great caution, and
a fair share of perseverance. When a man has these
qualities, mediocrity of intellect and moral deficiency will
not prevent his taking advantage of favourable chances;
chance being usually a very important element in worldly
success. Indeed it would hardly be an exaggeration to
say that poverty of thought and feeling has often something to do with forming and maintaining the disposition
requisite for the purpose. Vigorous exertion of the active
powers is more frequently induced by the personal propensities of avarice, ambition, or vanity, than by the
higher instincts. Superiority of position, when legitimately obtained, deserves respect ; but the philosopher,
like the religionist, and with still better grounds, refuses
to regard it as a proof of moral superiority, a conclusion
which would be wholly at variance with the true theory of
human nature.

The life of the workman, on the other hand, is far more
favourable to the development of the nobler instincts. In
practical qualities he is usually not wanting, except in
caution, a deficiency which makes his energy and perseverance less useful to himself, though fully available for
society. But it is in the exercise of the higher feelings
that the moral superiority of the working class is most
observable. When our habits and opinions have been
brought under the influence of systematic principles, the
true character of this class, which forms the basis of

modern society, will become more distinct; and we shall
see that home affections are naturally stronger with them
than with the middle classes, who are too much engrossed
with personal interests for the full enjoyment of domestic
ties. Still more evident is their superiority in social feelings strictly so called, for these with them are called into
daily exercise from earliest childhood. Here it is that we
find the highest and most genuine types of friendship, and
this even amongst those who are placed in a dependent
position, aggravated often by the aristocratic prejudices of
those above them, and whom we might imagine on that
account condemned to a lower moral standard. We find
sincere and simple respect for superiors, untainted by servility, not vitiated by the pride of learning, not disturbed
by the jealousies of competition. Their personal experience of the miseries of life is a constant stimulus to the
nobler sympathies. In no class is there so strong an
incentive to social feeling, at least to the feeling of Solidarity between contemporaries; for all are conscious of the
support that they derive from union, support which is not
at all incompatible with strong individuality of character.
The sense of Continuity with the past has not, it is true,
been sufficiently developed; but this is a want which can
only be supplied by systematic culture. It will hardly be
disputed that there are more remarkable instances of
prompt and unostentatious self-sacrifice at the call of a
great public necessity in this class than in any other.
Note, too, that in the utter absence of any systematic education, all these moral excellences must be looked upon as
inherent in the class. It is impossible to attribute them
to theological influence, now that they have so entirely
shaken off the old faith. The type I have described would
be generally considered imaginary; and at present it is
only in Paris that it can be fully realized. But the fact

of its existence in the centre of Western Europe is enough
for all rational observers. A type so fully in accordance
with what we know of human nature cannot fail ultimately to spread everywhere, especially when these spontaneous tendencies are placed under the systematic guidance of Positivism.

This the Convention felt; but they encouraged the People to seek political supremacy, for which they are not fit. These remarks will prepare us to appreciate
the wise and generous instincts of the Conven-
tion in looking to the Proletariate as the main-
spring of its policy; and this not merely on
account of the incidental danger of foreign invasion, but in dealing with the larger question of social
regeneration, which it pursued so ardently, though in such
ignorance of its true principles. Owing, however, to the
want of a satisfactory system, and the disorder produced
by the metaphysical theories of the time, the spirit in
which this alliance with the people was framed, was incompatible with the real object in view. It was considered
that government ought as a rule to be in the hands of the
people. Now under the special circumstances of the time
popular government was undoubtedly very useful. The
existence of the republic depended almost entirely upon
the proletariate, the only class that stood unshaken and
true to its principles. But in the absolute spirit of the
received political theories, this state of things was regarded
as normal, a view which is incompatible with the most
important conditions of modern society. It is of course
always right for the people to assist government in carrying out the law, even to the extent of physical force,
should the case require it. Interference of this subordinate kind, whether in foreign or internal questions, so
far from leading to anarchy, is obviously a guarantee for
order which ought to exist in every properly constituted
society. Indeed in this respect our habits in France are

still very defective; men are too often content to remain mere lookers on, while the police to whom they owe their daily protection is doing its duty. But for the people to take a direct part in government, and to have the final decision of political measures, is a state of things which in modern society is only adapted to times of revolution. To recognise it as final would lead at once to anarchy, were it not so utterly impossible to realise.

Positivism rejects the metaphysical doctrine of the Sovereignty of the people. But it appropriates all that is really sound in the doctrine, and this with reference not merely to *It is only in exceptional cases that the People can be really 'sovereign.'* exceptional cases but to the normal state; while at the same time it guards against the danger involved in its application as an absolute truth. In the hands of the revolutionary party the doctrine is generally used to justify the right of insurrection. Now in Positive Polity, this right is looked upon as an ultimate resource, with which no society should allow itself to dispense. Absolute submission, which is too strongly inculcated by modern Catholicism, would expose us to the danger of tyranny. Insurrection may be regarded, scientifically, as a sort of reparative crisis, of which societies stand in more need than individuals, in accordance with the well-known biological law, that the higher and the more complicated the organism, the more frequent and also the more dangerous is the pathological state. Therefore, the fear that Positivism, when generally accepted, will encourage passive obedience, is perfectly groundless; although it is certainly not favourable to the pure revolutionary spirit, which would fain take the disease for the normal type of health. Its whole character is so essentially relative, that it finds no difficulty in accepting subordination as the rule, and yet allowing for exceptional cases of revolt; a course by which good taste and human dignity are alike satisfied. Positivism looks upon insurrection as a dangerous remedy that should be reserved for extreme cases ; but it would never scruple to sanction and even to encourage it when it is really indispensable. This is quite compatible with refusing, as a rule, to submit the decision of political questions and the choice of rulers to judges who are obviously incompetent ; and who, under the influence of Positivism, will of their own free will abdicate rights which are subversive of order.

The truth involved in the expression is that the well-being of the people should be the one great object of government. The metaphysical doctrine of the Sovereignty of the people, contains, however, a truth of permanent value, though in a very confused form. This truth Positivism separates very distinctly from its dangerous alloy, yet without weakening, on the contrary, with the effect of enforcing, its social import. There are two distinct conceptions in this doctrine, which have hitherto been confounded ; a political conception applicable to certain special cases ; a moral conception applicable to all.

In the first place the name of the whole body politic ought to be invoked in the announcement of any special measure, of which the motives are sufficiently intelligible, and which directly concern the practical interests of the whole community. Under this head would be included decisions of law courts, declarations of war, etc. When society has reached the Positive state, and the sense of universal solidarity is more generally diffused, there will be even more significance and dignity in such expressions than there is now, because the name invoked will no longer be that of a special nation, but that of Humanity as a whole. It would be absurd, however, to extend this practice to those still more numerous cases where the people is incompetent to express any opinion, and has merely to adopt the opinion of superior officers who have obtained its confidence. This may be owing either to the difficulty of the question or to the fact of its application being indirect or limited. Such, for instance, would be enactments, very often of great importance, which deal with scientific principles; or again most questions relating to special professions or branches of industry. In all these cases popular good sense would, under Positivist influence, easily be kept clear from political illusions. It is only under the stimulus of metaphysical pride that such illusions become dangerous; and the untaught masses have but little experience of this feeling.

There is, however, another truth implied in the expression, Sovereignty of the people. It implies that it is the first of duties to concentrate all the efforts of society upon the common good. And in this there is a more direct reference to the working class than to any other; first, on account of their immense numerical superiority, and, secondly, because the difficulties by which their life is surrounded require special interference to a degree which for other classes would be unnecessary. From this point of view it is a principle which all true republicans may accept. It is, in fact, identical with what we have laid down as the universal basis of morality, the direct and permanent preponderance of social feeling over all personal interests. Not merely, then, is it incorporated by Positivism, but, as was shown in the first chapter, it forms the primary principle of the system, even under the intellectual aspect. Since the decline of Catholicism the metaphysical spirit has been provisionally the guardian of this great social precept. Positivism now finally appropriates it, and purifies it for the future from all taint of anarchy. Revolutionists, as we should expect from their characteristic dislike to the separation of the two powers, had treated the question politically. Positivism avoids all danger by shifting it to the region of morality. I shall show presently that this very salutary change, so far from weakening the force of the principle, increases its permanent value, and at the same time removes the deceptive and subversive tendencies which are always involved in the metaphysical mode of regarding it.

The People's function is to assist the spiritual power in modifying the action of government. What then, it will be asked, is the part assigned to the Proletariate in the final constitution of society? The similarity of position, which I pointed out, between themselves and the philosophic class, suggests the answer. They will be of the most essential service to the spiritual power in each of its three social functions, judgment, counsel, and even education. All the intellectual and moral qualities that we have just indicated in this class concur in fitting them for this service. If we except the philosophic body, which is the recognized organ of general principles, there is no class which is so habitually inclined to take comprehensive views of any subject. Their superiority in Social Feeling is still more obvious. In this even the best philosophers are rarely their equals; and it would be a most beneficial corrective of their tendency to over-abstraction to come into daily contact with the noble and spontaneous instincts of the people. The working class, then, is better qualified than any other for understanding, and still more for sympathising with the highest truths of morality, though it may not be able to give them a systematic form. And, as we have seen, it is in social morality, the most important and the highest of the three branches of Ethics, that their superiority is most observable. Besides, independently of their intrinsic merits, whether intellectual or moral, the necessities of their daily life serve to impress them with respect for the great rules of morality, which in most cases were framed for their own protection. To secure the application of these rules in daily life, is a function of the spiritual power in the performance of which they will meet with but slight assistance from the middle classes. It is with them that temporal power naturally resides, and it is their misuse of power that has to be controlled and set right. The working classes are the chief sufferers from the selfishness and domineering of men of wealth and power. For this reason they are the likeliest to come forward in defence of public morality. And they will be all the more disposed to give it their hearty support, if they have nothing to do directly with political administration. Habitual participation in temporal power, to say nothing of its unsettling influence, would lead them away from the best remedy for their sufferings of which the constitution of society admits. Popular sagacity will soon detect the utter hollowness of the off-hand solutions that are now being obtruded upon us. The people will rapidly become convinced that the surest method of satisfying all legitimate claims lies in the moral agencies which Positivism offers, though it appeals to them at the same time to abdicate political power which either yields them nothing or results in anarchy.

So natural is this tendency of the people to rally round the spiritual power in defence of morality, that we find it to have been the case even in mediæval times. Indeed this it is which explains the sympathies which Catholicism still retains, notwithstanding its general decline, in the countries where Protestantism has failed to establish itself. Superficial observers often mistake these sympathies for evidence of sincere attachment to the old creeds, though in point of fact they are more thoroughly undermined in those countries than anywhere else. It is an historical error which will, however, soon be corrected by the reception which these nations, so wrongly imagined to be in a backward stage of political development, will give to Positivism. For they will soon see its superiority to Catholicism in satisfying the primary necessity with which their social instincts are so justly preoccupied.

In the Middle Ages, however, the relations between the working classes and the priesthood were hampered by the institution of serfage, which was not wholly abolished until Catholicism had begun to decline. In fact a careful study of history will show that one of the principal causes of its decline was the want of popular support. The mediæval church was a noble, but premature attempt. Disbelief in its doctrines, and also retrograde tendencies in its directors, had virtually destroyed it, before the Proletariate had attained sufficient social importance to support it successfully, supposing it could have deserved their support. But we are now sufficiently advanced for the perfect realization of the Catholic ideal in Positivism. And the principal means of realizing it will be the formation of an alliance between philosophers and the working classes, for which both are alike prepared by the negative and positive progress of the last five centuries.

Their combined efforts result in the formation of PublicOpinion. The direct object of their combined action will be to set in motion the force of Public Opinion. All views of the future condition of society, the views of practical men as well as of philosophic thinkers, agree in the belief that the principal feature of the state to which we are tending, will be the increased influence which Public Opinion is destined to exercise.

It is in this beneficial influence that we shall find the surest guarantee for morality ; for domestic and even for personal morality, as well as for social. For as the whole tendency of Positivism is to induce every one to live as far as possible without concealment, the public will be intrusted with a strong check upon the life of the individual. Now that all theological illusions have become so entirely obsolete, the need of such a check is greater than it was before. It compensates for the insufficiency of natural goodness which we find in most men, however wisely their education has been conducted. Except the noblest of joys, that which springs from social sympathy when called into constant exercise, there is no reward for doing right so satisfactory as the approval of our fellow-beings. Even under theological systems it has been one of our strongest aspirations to live esteemed in the memory of others. And still more prominence will be given to this noble form of ambition under Positivism, because it is the only way left us of satisfying the desire which all men feel of prolonging their life into the Future. And the increased force of Public Opinion will correspond to the increased necessity for it. The peculiar reality of Positive doctrine and its constant conformity with facts facilitate the recognition of its principles, and remove all obscurity in their application. They are not to be evaded by subterfuges like those to which metaphysical and theological principles, from their vague and absolute character, have been always liable. Again, the primary principle of Positivism, which is to judge every question by the standard of social interests, is in itself a direct appeal to Public Opinion ; since the public is naturally the judge of the good or bad effect of action upon the common welfare. Under theological and metaphysical systems no appeal of this sort was recognised ; because the objects upheld as the highest aims of life were purely personal.

In political questions the application of our principle is still more obvious. For political morality Public Opinion is almost our only guarantee. We feel its force even now in spite of the intellectual anarchy in which we live. Neutralized as it is in most cases by the wide divergences of men's convictions, yet it shows itself on the occasion of any great public excitement. Indeed, we feel it to our cost sometimes when the popular mind has taken a wrong direction; government in such cases being very seldom able to offer adequate resistance. These cases may convince us how irresistible this power will prove when used legitimately, and when it is formed by systematic accordance in general principles, instead of by a precarious and momentary coincidence of feeling. And here we see more clearly than ever how impossible it is to effect any permanent reconstruction of the institutions of society, without a previous reorganization of opinion and of life. The spiritual basis is necessary, not merely to determine the character of the temporal reconstruction, but to supply the principal motive force by which the work is to be carried out. Intellectual and moral harmony will gradually be restored, and under its influence the new political system will by degrees arise. Social improvements of the highest importance may therefore be realised long before the work of spiritual reorganization is completed. We find in mediæval history that Catholicism exercised a powerful influence on society during its emergence from barbarism, before its own internal constitution had advanced far. And this will be the case to a still greater degree with the regeneration which is now in progress.

Public opinion involves, (1) principles of social conduct, (2) their acceptance by society at large, (3) an organ through which to enunciate them. Having defined the sphere within which Public Opinion should operate, we shall find little difficulty in determining the conditions requisite for its proper organization. These are, first, the establishment of fixed principles of social action; secondly, their adoption by the public, and its consent to their application in special cases;

and, lastly, a recognised organ to lay down the principles, and to apply them to the conduct of daily life. Obvious as these three conditions appear, they are still so little understood, that it will be well to explain each of them somewhat more fully.

The first condition, that of laying down fixed principles, is, in fact, the extension to social questions of that separation between theory and practice, which in subjects of less importance is universally recognised. This is the aspect in which the superiority of the new spiritual system to the old is most perceptible. The principles of moral and political conduct that were accepted in the Middle Ages were little better than empirical, and owed their stability entirely to the sanction of religion. In this respect, indeed, the superiority of Catholicism to the systems which preceded it, consisted merely in the fact of separating its precepts from the special application of them. By making its precepts the distinct object of preliminary study, it secured them against the bias of human passions. Yet important as this separation was, the system was so defective intellectually, that the successful application of its principles depended simply on the good sense of the teachers; for the principles in themselves were as vague and as absolute as the creeds from which they were derived. The influence exercised by Catholicism was due to its indirect action upon social feeling in the only mode then possible. But the claims with which Positivism presents itself are far more satisfactory. It is based on a complete synthesis; one which embraces, not the outer world only, but the inner world of human nature. This, while in no way detracting from the practical value of social principles, gives them the imposing weight of theoretical truth; and ensures their stability and coherence, by connecting them with the whole series of laws on which the

life of man and of society depend. For these laws will
corroborate even those which are not immediately deduced
from them. By connecting all our rules of action with
the fundamental conception of social duty, we render their
interpretation in each special case clear and consistent,
and we secure it against the sophisms of passion. Principles such as these, based on reason, and rendering our conduct independent of the impulses of the moment, are the
only means of sustaining the vigour of Social Feeling, and
at the same time of saving us from the errors to which its
unguided suggestions so often lead. Direct and constant
culture of Social Feeling in public as well as in private life
is no doubt the first condition of morality. But the
natural strength of Self-love is such that something besides
this is required to control it. The course of conduct must
be traced beforehand in all important cases by the aid of
demonstrable principles, adopted at first upon trust, and
afterwards from conviction.

There is no art whatever in which, however ardent and
sincere our desire to succeed, we can dispense with knowledge of the nature and conditions of the object aimed at.
Moral and political conduct is assuredly not exempt from
such an obligation, although we are more influenced in
this case by the direct promptings of feeling than in any
other of the arts of life. It has been shown only too
clearly by many striking instances how far Social Feeling
may lead us astray when it is not directed by right principles. It was for want of fixed convictions that the noble
sympathies entertained by the French nation for the rest
of Europe at the outset of the Revolution so soon degenerated into forcible oppression, when her retrograde leader
began his seductive appeal to selfish passions. Inverse
cases are still more common; and they illustrate the connection of feeling and opinion as clearly as the others. A

false social doctrine has often favoured the natural ascendency of Self-love, by giving a perverted conception of public well-being. This has been too plainly exemplified in our own time by the deplorable influence which Malthus's sophistical theory of population obtained in England. This mischievous error met with very little acceptance in the rest of Europe, and it has been already refuted by the nobler thinkers of his own country; but it still gives the show of scientific sanction to the criminal antipathy of the governing classes in Great Britain to all effectual measures of reform.

Next to a system of principles, the most important condition for the exercise of Public Opinion is the existence of a strong body of supporters sufficient to make the weight of these principles felt. Now it was here that Catholicism proved so weak; and therefore, even had its doctrine been less perishable, its decline was unavoidable. But the defect is amply supplied in the new spiritual order, which, as I have before shown, will receive the influential support of the working classes. And the need of such assistance is as certain as the readiness with which it will be yielded. For though the intrinsic efficacy of Positive teaching is far greater than that of any doctrine which is not susceptible of demonstration, yet the convictions it inspires cannot be expected to dispense with the aid of vigorous popular support. Human nature is imperfectly organized; and the influence which Reason exercises over it is not by any means so great as this supposition would imply. Even Social Feeling, though its influence is far greater than that of Reason, would not in general be sufficient for the right guidance of practical life, if Public Opinion were not constantly at hand to support the good inclinations of individuals. The arduous struggle of Social Feeling against Self-love requires the constant assertion of true principles to remove uncertainty as to the proper course of action in each case. But it requires also something more. The strong reaction of All upon Each is needed, whether to control selfishness or to stimulate sympathy. The tendency of our poor and weak nature to give way to the lower propensities is so great that, but for this universal co-operation, Feeling and Reason would be almost inadequate to their task. In the working class we find the requisite conditions. They will, as we have seen, form the principal source of opinion, not merely from their numerical superiority, but also from their intellectual and moral qualities, as well as from the influence directly due to their social position. Thus it is that Positivism views the great problem of human life, and shows us for the first time that the bases of a solution already exist in the very structure of the social organism.

Working men's clubs. Working men, whether as individuals or, what is still more important, collectively, are now at liberty to criticise all the details, and even the general principles, of the social system under which they live ; affecting, as it necessarily does, themselves more nearly than any other class. The remarkable eagerness lately shown by our people to form clubs, though there was no special motive for it, and no very marked enthusiasm, was a proof that the checks which had previously prevented this tendency from showing itself were quite unsuited to our times. Nor is this tendency likely to pass away; on the contrary, it will take deeper root and extend more widely, because it is thoroughly in keeping with the habits, feelings, and wants of working men, who form the majority in these meetings. A consistent system of social truth will largely increase their influence, by giving them a more settled character and a more important aim. So far from being in any way destructive, they form a natural though imperfect model of the mode of life which will ultimately be adopted in the regenerate condition of Humanity. In these unions social sympathies are kept in constant action by a stimulus of a most beneficial kind. They offer the speediest and most effectual means of elaborating Public Opinion : this at least is the case when there has been a fair measure of individual training. No one at present has any idea of the extent of the advantages which will one day spring from these spontaneous meetings, when there is an adequate system of general principles to direct them. Spiritual reorganization will find them its principal basis of support, for they secure its acceptance by the people ; and this will have the greater weight, because it will be always given without compulsion or violence. The objection that meetings of this kind may lead to dangerous political agitation, rests upon a misinterpretation of the events of the Revolution. So far from their stimulating a desire for what are called political rights, or encouraging their exercise in those who possess them, their tendency is quite in the opposite direction. They will soon divert working men entirely from all useless attempts to interfere with existing political institutions, and bring them to their true social function, that of assisting and carrying out the operations of the new spiritual power. It is a noble prospect which is thus held out to them by Positivism, a prospect far more inviting than any of the metaphysical illusions of the day. The real intention of the Club is to form a provisional substitute for the Church of old times, or rather to prepare the way for the religious building of the new form of worship, the worship of Humanity ; which, as I shall explain in a subsequent chapter, will be gradually introduced under the regenerating influence of Positive doctrine. Under our present republican government all progressive tendencies are allowed free scope, and therefore it will not be long before our people accept this new vent for social sympathies, which in former times could find expression only in Catholicism.

In this theory of Public Opinion one condition yet remains to be described. A philosophic organ is necessary to interpret the doctrine; the influence of which would otherwise in most cases be very inadequate. This third condition has been much disputed; but it is certainly even more indispensable than the second. And in fact it has never been really wanting, for every doctrine must have had some founder, and usually has a permanent body of teachers. It would be difficult to conceive that a system of moral and political principles should be possessed of great social influence, and yet at the same time that the men who originate or inculcate the system should exercise no spiritual authority. It is true that this inconsistency did for a time exist under the negative and destructive influence of Protestantism and Deism, because men's thoughts were for the time entirely taken up with the struggle to escape from the retrograde tendencies of Catholicism. During this long period of insurrection, each individual became a sort of priest; each, that is, followed his own interpretation of a doctrine which needed no special teachers, because its function was not to construct but to criticise. All the constitutions that have been recently established on metaphysical principles give a direct sanction to this state of things, in the preambles with which they commence. They apparently regard each citizen as competent to form a sound opinion on all social questions, thus exempting him from the necessity of applying to any special interpreters. This extension to the normal state of things of a phase of mind only suited to the period of revolutionary transition, is an error which I have already sufficiently refuted.

In the minor arts of life, it is obvious that general principles cannot be laid down without some theoretical study ; and that the application of these rules to special cases is not to be entirely left to the untaught instinct of the artisan. And can it be otherwise with the art of Social Life, so far harder and more important than any other, and in which, from its principles being less simple and less precise, a special explanation of them in each case is even more necessary ?   However perfect the demonstration of social principles may become, it must not be supposed that knowledge of Positive doctrine, even when it has been taught in the most efficient way, will dispense with the necessity of frequently appealing to the philosopher for advice in questions of practical life, whether private or public.   And this necessity of an interpreter to intervene occasionally between the principle and its application, is even more evident from the moral than it is from the intellectual aspect.   Certain as it is that no one will be so well acquainted with the true character of the doctrine as the philosopher who teaches it, it is even more certain that none is so likely as himself to possess the moral qualifications of purity, of exalted aims, and of freedom from party spirit, without which his counsels could have but little weight in reforming individual or social conduct. It is principally through his agency that we may hope in most cases to bring about that reaction of All upon Each, which, as we have seen, is of such indispensable importance to practical morality.   Philosophers are not indeed the principal source of Public Opinion, as intellectual pride so often leads them to believe.   Public Opinion proceeds essentially from the free voice and spontaneous cooperation of the people.   But in order that the full weight of their unanimous judgment may be felt, it must be announced by some recognised organ.   There are, no doubt, rare cases where the direct expression of popular feeling is enough, but these are quite exceptional. Thus working men and philosophers are mutually necessary, not merely in the creation of Public Opinion, but also in most cases in the manifestation of it. Without the first, the doctrine, however well established, would not have sufficient force. Without the second, it would usually be too incoherent to overcome those obstacles in the constitution of man and of society, which make it so difficult to bring practical life under the influence of fixed principles.

In fact, this necessity for some systematic organ to direct and give effect to Public Opinion, has always been felt, even amidst the spiritual anarchy which at present surrounds us, on every occasion in which such opinion has played any important part. For its effect on these occasions would have been null and void but for some individual to take the initiative and personal responsibility. This is frequently verified in private life by cases in which we see the opposite state of things; we see principles which no one would think of contesting, practically inadequate, for want of some recognized authority to apply them. It is a serious deficiency, which is, however, compensated, though imperfectly, by the greater facility of arriving at the truth in such cases, and by the greater strength of the sympathies which they call forth. But in public life, with its more difficult conditions and more important claims, such entire absence of systematic intervention could never be tolerated. In all public transactions even now we may perceive the participation of a spiritual authority of one kind or other; the organs of which, though constantly varying, are in most cases metaphysicians or literary men writing for the press. Thus even in the present anarchy of feelings and convictions, Public Opinion cannot dispense with guides and interpreters.   Only it has to be content with men who at the best can only offer the guarantee of personal responsibility, without any reliable security either for the stability of their convictions or the purity of their feelings.   But now that the problem of organizing Public Opinion has once been proposed by Positivism, it cannot remain long without a solution.   It plainly reduces itself to the principle of separating the two social powers ; just as we have seen that the necessity of an established doctrine rested on the analogous principle of separating theory from practice. It is clear, on the one hand, that sound interpretation of moral and political rules, as in the case of any other art, can only be furnished by philosophers engaged in the study of the natural laws on which they rest.   On the other hand these philosophers, in order to preserve that breadth and generality of view which is their principal intellectual characteristic, must abstain scrupulously from all regular participation in practical affairs, and especially from political life : on the ground that its specialising influence would soon impair their speculative capacity. And such a course is equally necessary on moral grounds. It helps to preserve purity of feeling and impartiality of character ; qualities essential to their influence upon public as well as upon private life.

Such, in outline, is the Positive theory of Public Opinion. In each of its three constituent elements, the Doctrine, the Power, and the Organ, it is intimately connected with the whole question of spiritual reorganization ; or rather, it forms the simplest mode of viewing that great subject. All the essential parts of it are closely related to each other.   Positive principles, on the one hand, cannot count on much material support, except from the working classes ; these in their turn will for the future regard Positivism as the only doctrine with which they can sympathise.   So,

again, with the philosophic organs of opinion; without the
People, their necessary independence cannot be established
or sustained. To our literary classes the separation of the
two powers is instinctively repugnant, because it would
lay down systematic limits to the unwise ambition which
we now see in them. And it will be disliked as strongly
by the rich classes, who will look with fear upon a new
moral authority destined to impose an irresistible check
upon their selfishness. At present it will be generally
understood and welcomed only by the proletary class, who
have more aptitude for general views and for social sympathy. In France especially they are less under the delusion of metaphysical sophisms and of aristocratic prestige
than any other class; and the Positivist view of this primary condition of social regeneration will find a ready
entrance into their minds and hearts.

All three conditions of Public Opinion exist, but have not yet been combined. Our theory of Public Opinion shows us at
once how far we have already gone in organiz-
ing this great regulator of modern society; how
far we still fall short of what is wanted. The
Doctrine has at last arisen : there is no doubt of the existence of the Power; and even the Organ is not wanting.
But they do not as yet stand in their right relation to each
other. The effective impulse towards social regeneration
depends, then, on one ultimate condition; the formation of
a firm alliance between philosophers and proletaries.

Of this powerful coalition I have already spoken. I
have now to explain the advantages which it offers to the
people in the way of obtaining sufficient recognition of all
legitimate claims.

Of these advantages, the principal, and that by which
the rest will speedily be developed and secured, is the
important social function which is hereby conferred upon
them. They become auxiliaries of the new spiritual power;

auxiliaries indispensable to its action.   This vast proletary
class, which ever since its rise in the Middle Ages has
been shut out from the political system, will now assume
the position for which by nature it is best adapted, and
which is most conducive to the general well-being of
society.   Its members, independently of their special vocation, will at last take a regular and most important part in
public life, a part which will compensate for the hardships
inseparable from their social position.   Their combined
action, far from disturbing the established order of things,
will be its most solid guarantee, from the fact of being
moral, not political.   And here we see definitely the alteration which Positivism introduces in the revolutionary
conception of the action of the working classes upon society.
For stormy discussions about rights, it substitutes peaceable definition of duties.   It supersedes useless disputes
for the possession of power, by inquiring into the rules
that should regulate its wise employment.

A superficial observer of the present state of *Spontaneous*
things might imagine our working classes to be *tendencies of
the people in
a right direc-*
as yet very far from this frame of mind.   But *tion.   Their
Communism.*
he who looks deeper into the question will see
that the very experiment which they are now trying, of
extending their political rights, will soon have the effect
of showing them the hollowness of a remedy which has so
slight a bearing upon the objects really important to them.
Without making any formal abdication of rights, which
might seem inconsistent with their social dignity, there is
little doubt that their instinctive sagacity will lead them
to the still more efficacious plan of indifference.   Positivism will readily convince them that whereas spiritual
power, in order to do its work, must ramify in every direction, it is essential to public order that political power
should be as a rule concentrated.   And this conviction

will grow upon them, as they see more clearly that the primary social problems which are very properly absorbing their attention are essentially moral rather than political.

One step in this direction they have already taken of their own accord, though its importance has not been duly appreciated. The well-known scheme of Communism, which has found such rapid acceptance with them, serves, in the absence of sounder doctrine, to express the way in which they are now looking at the great social problem. The experience of the first part of the Revolution has not yet wholly disabused them of political illusions, but it has at least brought them to feel that Property is of more importance than Power in the ordinary sense of the word. So far Communism has given a wider meaning to the great social problem, and has thereby rendered an essential service, which is not neutralised by the temporary dangers involved in the metaphysical forms in which it comes before us. Communism should therefore be carefully distinguished from the numerous extravagant schemes brought forward in this time of spiritual anarchy; a time which stimulates incompetent and ill-trained minds to the most difficult subjects of thought. The foolish schemes referred to have so few definite features, that we have to distinguish them by the names of their authors. But Communism bears the name of no single author, and is something more than an accidental product of anomalous circumstances. We should look upon it as the natural progress in the right direction of the revolutionary spirit; progress of a moral rather than intellectual kind. It is a proof that revolutionary tendencies are now concentrating themselves upon moral questions, leaving all purely political questions in the back-ground. It is quite true that the solution of the problem which Communists are now putting forward, is still as essentially political as that of their predecessors ; since the only mode by which they propose to regulate the employment of property, is by a change in the mode of its tenure. Still it is owing to them that the question of property is at last brought forward for discussion : and it is a question which so evidently needs a moral solution, the solution of it by political means is at once so inadequate and so destructive, that it cannot long continue to be debated, without leading to the more satisfactory result offered by Positivism. Men will see that it forms a part of the final regeneration of opinion and of life, which Positivism is now inaugurating.

To do justice to Communism, we must look at the generous sympathies by which it is inspired, not at the shallow theories in which those sympathies find expression provisionally, until circumstances enable them to take some other shape. Our working classes, caring but very little for metaphysical principles, do not attach nearly the same importance to these theories, as is done by men of literary education. As soon as they see a better way of bringing forward the points on which they have such legitimate claims, they will very soon adopt the clear and practical conceptions of Positivism, which can be carried out peaceably and permanently, in preference to these vague and confused chimeras, which, as they will instinctively feel, lead only to anarchy. Till then they will naturally abide by Communism, as the only method of bringing forward the most fundamental of social problems in a way which there shall be no evading. The very alarm which their present solution of the problem arouses helps to stir public attention, and fix it on this great subject. But for this constant appeal to their fears, the metaphysical delusions and aristocratic self-seeking of the govern-

ing classes would shelve the question altogether, or pass it
by with indifference.   The errors of Communism must be
rectified; but there is no necessity for giving up the name,
which is a simple assertion of the paramount importance
of Social Feeling.   However, now that we have happily
passed from monarchy to republicanism, the name of
Communist is no longer indispensable; the word *Republican* expresses the meaning as well, and without the same
danger.   Positivism, then, has nothing to fear from Communism; on the contrary, it will probably be accepted by
most Communists among the working classes, especially in
France, where abstractions have but little influence on
minds thoroughly emancipated from theology.   The people
will gradually find that the solution of the great social
problem which Positivism offers is better than the Communistic solution.

Its new title of Socialism.   A tendency in this direction has already
shown itself since the first edition of this work
was published.   The working classes have now adopted a
new expression, *Socialism*, thus indicating that they accept
the problem of the Communists while rejecting their solution.   Indeed that solution would seem to be finally disposed of by the voluntary exile of their leader.   Yet, if
the Socialists at present keep clear of Communism, it is
only because their position is one of criticism or inaction.
If they were to succeed to power, with principles so far
below the level of their sympathies, they would inevitably
fall into the same errors and extravagances which they
now instinctively feel to be wrong.   Consequently the
rapid spread of Socialism very naturally alarms the upper
classes; and their resistance, blind though it be, is at present the only legal guarantee for material order.   In fact,
the problem brought forward by the Communists admits
of no solution but their own, so long as the revolution-

ary confusion of temporal and spiritual power continues. Therefore the universal blame that is lavished on these utopian schemes cannot fail to inspire respect for Positivism, as the only doctrine which can preserve Western Europe from some serious attempt to bring Communism into practical operation. Positivists stand forward now as the party of construction, with a definite basis for political action; namely, systematic prosecution of the wise attempt of mediæval statesmen to separate the two social powers. On this basis they are enabled to satisfy the Poor, and at the same time to restore the confidence of the Rich. It is a final solution of our difficulties which will make the titles of which we have been speaking unnecessary. Stripping the old word *Republican* of any false meaning at present attached to it, we may retain it as the best expression of the social sympathies on which the regeneration of society depends. For the opinions, manners, and even institutions of future society, *Positivist* is the only word suitable.

The peculiar reality of Positivism, and its invariable tendency to concentrate our intellectual powers upon social questions, are attributes, *Property is in its nature social, and needs control.* both of which involve its adoption of the essential principle of Communism; that principle being, that Property is in its nature social, and that it needs control.

Property has been erroneously represented by most modern jurists as conferring an absolute right upon the possessor, irrespectively of the good or bad use made of it. This view is instinctively felt by the working classes to be unsound, and all true philosophers will agree with them. It is an anti-social theory, due historically to exaggerated reaction against previous legislation of a peculiarly oppressive kind, but it has no real foundation either in justice or in fact. Property can neither be created, nor even trans-

mitted by the sole agency of its possessor. The co-operation of the public is always necessary, whether in the
assertion of the general principle or in the application of
it to each special case. Therefore the tenure of property
is not to be regarded as a purely individual right. In
every age and in every country the state has intervened,
to a greater or less degree, making property subservient to
social requirements. Taxation evidently gives the public
an interest in the private fortune of each individual; an
interest which, instead of diminishing with the progress
of civilization, has been always on the increase, especially
in modern times, now that the connection of each member
of society with the whole is becoming more apparent.
The practice of confiscation, which also is in universal use,
shows that in certain extreme cases the community considers itself authorised to assume entire possession of private property. Confiscation has, it is true, been abolished
for a time in France. But this isolated exception is
due only to the abuses which recently accompanied the
exercise of what was in itself an undoubted right; and it
will hardly survive when the causes which led to it are
forgotten, and the power which introduced it has passed
away. In their abstract views of property, then, Communists are perfectly able to maintain their ground against
the jurists.

They are right, again, in dissenting as deeply as they
do from the Economists, who lay it down as an absolute
principle that the application of wealth should be entirely
unrestricted by society. This error, like the one just
spoken of, is attributable to instances of unjustifiable interference. But it is utterly opposed to all sound philosophical teaching, although it has a certain appearance of
truth, in so far as it recognises the subordination of social
phenomena to natural laws. But the Economists seem to

have adopted this important principle only to show how incapable they are of comprehending it. Before they applied the conception of Law to the higher phenomena of nature, they ought to have made themselves well acquainted with its meaning, as applied to the lower and more simple phenomena. Not having done so, they have been utterly blind to the fact that the Order of nature becomes more and more modifiable as it grows more complicated. This conception lies at the very root of our whole practical life; therefore nothing can excuse the metaphysical school of Economists for systematically resisting the intervention of human wisdom in the various departments of social action. That the movement of society is subject to natural laws is certain; but this truth, instead of inducing us to abandon all efforts to modify society, should rather lead to a wiser application of such efforts, since they are at once more efficacious, and more necessary in social phenomena than in any other.

So far, therefore, the fundamental principle of Communism is one which the Positivist school must obviously adopt. Positivism not only confirms this principle, but widens its scope, by showing its application to other departments of human life; by insisting that, not wealth only, but that all our powers shall be devoted in the true republican spirit to the continuous service of the community. The long period of revolution which has elapsed since the Middle Ages has encouraged individualism in the moral world, as in the intellectual it has fostered the specialising tendency. But both are equally inconsistent with the final order of modern society. In all healthy conditions of Humanity, the citizen, whatever his position, has been regarded as a public functionary, whose duties and claims were determined more or less distinctly by his faculties. The case of property is certainly no exception to this general principle. Proprietorship is regarded by the Positivist as an important social function; the function, namely, of creating and administering that capital by means of which each generation lays the foundation for the operations of its successor. This is the only tenable view of property; and wisely interpreted, it is one which, while ennobling to its possessor, does not exclude a due measure of freedom. It will in fact place his position on a firmer basis than ever.

But Positiv-
ism rejects the
Communist so-
lution of the
problem. Pro-
perty is to be
controlled by
moral not legal
agencies.

But the agreement here pointed out between sociological science and the spontaneous inspirations of popular judgment, goes no farther. Positivists accept, and indeed enlarge, the programme of Communism; but we reject its practical solution on the ground that it is at once inadequate and subversive. The chief difference between our own solution and theirs is that we substitute moral agencies for political. Thus we come again to our leading principle of separating spiritual from temporal power; a principle which, disregarded as it has hitherto been in the system of modern renovators, will be found in every one of the important problems of our time to be the sole possible issue. In the present case, while throwing such light on the fallacy of Communism, it should lead us to excuse the fallacy, by reminding us that politicians of every accredited school are equally guilty of it. At a time when there are so very few, even of cultivated minds, who have a clear conception of this the primary principle of modern politics, it would be harsh to blame the people for still accepting a result of revolutionary empiricism, which is so universally adopted by other classes.

I need not enter here into any detailed criticism of the utopian scheme of Plato. It was conclusively refuted

twenty-two centuries ago, by the great Aristotle, who
thus exemplified the organic character, by which, even in
its earliest manifestations, the Positive spirit is distinguished.   In modern Communism, moreover, there is one
fatal inconsistency, which while it proves the utter weakness of the system, testifies at the same time to the honorable character of the motives from which it arose.   Modern
Communism differs from the ancient, as expounded by
Plato, in not making women and children common as well
as property ; a result to which the principle itself obviously
leads.   Yet this, the only consistent view of Communism,
is adopted by none but a very few literary men, whose
affections, in themselves too feeble, have been perverted
by vicious intellectual training.   Our untaught proletaries,
who are the only Communists worthy our consideration,
are nobly inconsistent in this respect.   Indivisible as their
erroneous system is, they only adopt that side of it which
touches on their social requirements.   The other side is
repugnant to all their highest instincts, and they utterly
repudiate it.

Without discussing these chimerical schemes in detail,
it will be well to expose the errors inherent in the method
of reasoning which leads to them, because they are common to all the other progressive schools, the Positivist
school excepted.   The mistake consists in the first place,
in disregarding or even denying the natural laws which
regulate social phenomena ; and secondly, in resorting to
political agencies where moral agency is the real thing
needed.   The inadequacy and the danger of the various
utopian systems which are now setting up their rival
claims to bring about the regeneration of society, are all
attributable in reality to these two closely-connected errors.
For the sake of clearness, I shall continue to refer specially
to Communism as the most prominent of these systems.

But it will be easy to extend the bearing of my remarks to all the rest.

Individuali-   The ignorance of the true laws of social life
zation of func-
tions as neces-   under which Communists labour is evident in
sary as co-
operation.   their dangerous tendency to suppress individuality.   Not only do they ignore the inherent preponderance in our nature of the personal instincts; but they
forget that, in the collective Organism, the separation of
functions is a feature no less essential than the co-operation
of functions.   Suppose for a moment that the connection
between men could be made such that they were physically
inseparable, as has been actually the case with twins in
certain cases of monstrosity; society would obviously be
impossible.   Extravagant as this supposition is, it may
illustrate the fact that in social life individuality cannot
be dispensed with.   It is necessary in order to admit of
that variety of simultaneous efforts which constitutes the
immense superiority of the Social Organism over every
individual life.   The great problem for man is to harmonize, as far as possible, the freedom resulting from
isolation, with the equally urgent necessity for convergence.   To dwell exclusively upon the necessity of convergence would tend to undermine not merely our practical energy, but our true dignity; since it would do away
with the sense of personal responsibility.   In exceptional
cases where life is spent in forced subjection to domestic
authority, the comforts of home are often not enough to
prevent existence from becoming an intolerable burden,
simply from the want of sufficient independence.   What
would it be, then, if everybody stood in a similar position
of dependence towards a community that was indifferent
to his happiness?   Yet no less a danger than this would
be the result of adopting any of those utopian schemes
which sacrifice true liberty to uncontrolled equality, or

even to an exaggerated sense of fraternity. Wide as the divergence between Positivism and the Economic schools is, Positivists adopt substantially the strictures which they have passed upon Communism; especially those of Dunoyer, their most advanced writer.

There is another point in which Communism is equally inconsistent with the laws of Sociology. Acting under false views of the constitution of our modern industrial system, it proposes to remove its directors, who form so essential a part of it. An army can no more exist without officers than without soldiers; and this elementary truth holds good of Industry as well as of War. The organization of modern industry has not been found practicable as yet; but the germ of such organization lies unquestionably in the division which has arisen spontaneously between Capitalist and Workman. No great works could be undertaken if each worker were also to be a director, or if the management, instead of being fixed, were entrusted to a passive and irresponsible body. It is evident that under the present system of industry there is a tendency to a constant enlargement of undertakings: each fresh step leads at once to still further extension. Now this tendency, so far from being opposed to the interests of the working classes, is a condition which will most seriously facilitate the real organization of our material existence, as soon as we have a moral authority competent to control it. For it is only the larger employers that the spiritual power can hope to penetrate with a strong and habitual sense of duty to their subordinates. Without a sufficient concentration of material power, the means of satisfying the claims of morality would be found wanting, except at such exorbitant sacrifices as would be incompatible with all industrial progress. This is the

Industry requires its captains as well as War.

weak point of every plan of reform which limits itself
to the mode of acquiring power, whether public power
or private, instead of aiming at controlling its use in
whosoever hands it may be placed. It leads to a waste
of those forces which, when rightly used, form our
principal resource in dealing with grave social difficulties.

Communism is deficient in the historical spirit. The motives, therefore, from which modern
Communism has arisen, however estimable, lead
at present, in the want of proper scientific teaching, to a very wrong view both of the nature of the
disease and of its remedy. A heavier reproach against it
is, that in one point it shows a manifest insufficiency of
social instinct. Communists boast of their spirit of social
union; but they limit it to the union of the present generation, stopping short of historical continuity, which yet
is the principal characteristic of Humanity. When they
have matured their moral growth, and have followed out
in Time that connection which at present they only recognise in Space, they will at once see the necessity of these
general conditions which at present they would reject.
They will understand the importance of inheritance, as the
natural means by which each generation transmits to its
successor the result of its own labours and the means of
improving them. The necessity of inheritance, as far as
the community is concerned, is evident, and its extension to the individual is an obvious consequence. But
whatever reproaches Communists may deserve in this
respect are equally applicable to all the other progressive
sects. They are all pervaded by an anti-historic spirit,
which leads them to conceive of Society as though it
had no ancestors; and this, although their own ideas for
the most part can have no bearing except upon posterity.

Serious as these errors are, a philosophic
mind will treat the Communism of our day,
so far as it is adopted in good faith, with indulgence, whether he look at the motives from
which it arose, or at the practical results which will follow
from it. It is hardly fair to criticise the intrinsic merits
of a doctrine, the whole meaning and value of which are
relative to the peculiar phase of society in which it is proposed. Communism has in its own way discharged an important function. It has brought prominently forward the
greatest of social problems ; and, if we except the recent
Positivist explanation, its mode of stating it has never
been surpassed. And let no one suppose that it would
have been enough simply to state the problem, without
hazarding any solution of it. Those who think so do not
understand the exigencies of man's feeble intellect. In far
easier subjects than this, it is impossible to give prolonged
attention to questions which are simply asked, without
any attempt to answer them. Suppose, for instance, that
Gall and Broussais had limited themselves to a simple
statement of their great problems without venturing on
any solution ; their principles, however incontestable,
would have been barren of result, for want of that motive
power of renovation which nothing can give but a systematic solution of some kind or other, hazardous as the attempt
must be at first. Now it is hardly likely that we should
be able to evade this condition of our mental faculties in
subjects which are not only of the highest difficulty, but
also more exposed than any others to the influence of passion. Besides, when we compare the errors of Communism
with those of other social doctrines which have recently
received official sanction, we shall feel more disposed to
palliate them. Are they, for instance, more shallow and
more really dangerous than the absurd and chimerical

In fact, as a system, it is worthless, though prompted by noble feelings.

notion which was accepted in France for a whole generation, and is still upheld by so many political teachers ; the
notion that the great Revolution has found its final issue
in the constitutional system of government, a system peculiar to England during her stage of transition ? Moreover,
our so-called conservatives only escape the errors of Communism by evading or ignoring its problems, though they
are becoming every day more urgent.   Whenever they
are induced to deal with them, they render themselves
liable to exactly the same dangers, dangers common to all
schools which reject the division of the two powers, and
which consequently are for ever trying to make legislation do the work of morality.   Accordingly we see the
governing classes now-a-days upholding institutions of a
thoroughly Communist character, such as alms-houses,
foundling hospitals, etc. ; while popular feeling strongly
and rightly condemns such institutions, as being incompatible with that healthy growth of home affection which
should be common to all ranks.

Were it not that Communism is provisionally useful in
antagonising other doctrines equally erroneous, it would
have, then, no real importance, except that due to the
motives which originated it ; since its practical solution is
far too chimerical and subversive ever to obtain acceptance.   Yet, from the high morality of these motives, it
will probably maintain and increase its influence until our
working men find that their wants can be more effectually
satisfied by gentler and surer means.   Our republican system seems at first sight favourable to the scheme ; but it
cannot fail soon to have the reverse effect, because, while
adopting the social principle which constitutes the real
merit of Communism, it repudiates its mischievous illusions.   In France, at all events, where property is so easy
to acquire and is consequently so generally enjoyed, the

doctrine cannot lead to much practical harm ; rather its reaction will be beneficial, because it will fix men's minds more seriously on the just claims of the People. The danger is far greater in other parts of Western Europe ; especially in England, where aristocratic influence is less undermined, and where consequently the working classes are less advanced and more oppressed. And even in Catholic countries, where individualism and anarchy have been met by a truer sense of fraternity, Communistic disturbances can only be avoided finally by a more rapid dissemination of Positivism, which will ultimately dispel all social delusions, by offering the true solution of the questions that gave rise to them.

The nature of the evil shows us at once that the remedy we seek must be almost entirely of a moral kind. This truth, based as it is on real knowledge of human nature, the people will soon come to feel instinctively. And here Communists are, without knowing it, preparing the way for the ascendancy of Positivism. They are forcing upon men's notice in the strongest possible way a problem to which no peaceable and satisfactory solution can be given, except by the new philosophy.

That philosophy, abandoning all useless and irritating discussion as to the origin of wealth and the extent of its possession, proceeds at *Property is a public trust, not to be interfered with legally.* once to the moral rules which should regulate it as a social function. The distribution of power among men, of material power especially, lies so far beyond our means of intervention, that to set it before us as our main object to rectify the defects of the natural order in this respect, would be to waste our short life in barren and interminable disputes. The chief concern of the public is that power, in whosever hands it may be placed, should be exercised for their benefit ; and this is a point to which we may direct our efforts with far greater effect. Besides, by regulating the employment of wealth, we do, indirectly, modify its tenure; for the mode in which wealth is held has some secondary influence over the right use of it.

The regulations required should be moral, not political in their source; general, not special, in their application. Those who accept them will do so of their own free will, under the influence of their education. Thus their obedience, while steadily maintained, will have, as Aristotle long ago observed, the merit of voluntary action. By converting private property into a public function, we would subject it to no tyrannical interference; for this, by the destruction of free impulse and responsibility, would prove most deeply degrading to man's character. Indeed, the comparison of proprietors with public functionaries will frequently be applied in the inverse sense; with the view, that is, of strengthening the latter rather than of weakening the former. The true principle of republicanism is, that all forces shall work together for the common good. With this view we have on the one hand, to determine precisely what it is that the common good requires; and on the other, to develop the temper of mind most likely to satisfy the requirement. The conditions requisite for these two objects, are a recognised Code of principles, an adequate Education, and a healthy direction of Public Opinion. For such conditions we must look principally to the philosophic body which Positivism proposes to establish at the apex of modern society. Doubtless this purely moral influence wonld not be sufficient of itself. Human frailty is such that Government in the ordinary sense of the word, will have, as before, to repress by force the more palpable and more dangerous class of delinquencies. But this additional control, though necessary, will not fill so important a place as it did in the Middle Ages under the sway of Catholicism. Spiritual rewards and punishments will preponderate over temporal, in proportion as human development evokes a stronger sense of the ties which unite each with all, by the threefold bond of Feeling, Thought, and Action.

Positivism, being more pacific and more effi- *Inheritance favourable to its right employment.* cacious than Communism, because more true, is also broader and more complete in its solution of great social problems. The superficial view of property, springing too often from envious motives, which condemns Inheritance because it admits of possession without labour, is not subversive merely, but narrow. From the moral point of view we see at once the radical weakness of these empirical reproaches. They show blindness to the fact that this mode of transmitting wealth is really that which is most likely to call out the temper requisite for its right employment. It saves the mind and the heart from the mean and sordid habits which are so often engendered by slow accumulation of capital. The man who is born to wealth is more likely to feel the wish to be respected. And thus those whom we are inclined to condemn as idlers may very easily become the most useful of the rich classes, under a wise reorganization of opinions and habits. Of course too, since with the advance of Civilization the difficulty of living without industry increases, the class that we are speaking of becomes more and more exceptional. In every way, then, it is a most serious mistake to wish to upset society on account of abuses which are already in course of removal, and which admit of conversion to a most beneficial purpose.

Again, another feature in which the Posi- *Intellect needs moral control as much as wealth.* tivist solution surpasses the Communist, is the remarkable completeness of its application. Communism takes no account of anything but wealth ;

as if wealth were the only power in modern society badly distributed and administered. In reality there are greater abuses connected with almost every other power that man possesses; and especially with the powers of intellect; yet these our visionaries make not the smallest attempt to rectify. Positivism being the only doctrine that embraces the whole sphere of human existence, is therefore the only doctrine that can elevate Social Feeling to its proper place, by extending it to all departments of human activity without exception. Identification, in a moral sense, of private functions with public duties is even more necessary in the case of the scientific man or the artist, than in that of the proprietor; whether we look at the source from which his powers proceed, or at the object to which they should be directed. Yet the men who wish to make material wealth common, the only kind of wealth that can be held exclusively by an individual, never extend their utopian scheme to intellectual wealth, in which it would be far more admissible. In fact the apostles of Communism often come forward as zealous supporters of what they call literary property. Such inconsistencies show the shallowness of the system; it proclaims its own failure in the very cases that are most favourable for its application. The extension of the principle here suggested would expose at once the inexpediency of political regulations on the subject, and the necessity of moral rules; for these and these only can ensure the right use of all our faculties without distinction. Intellectual effort, to be of any value, must be spontaneous; and it is doubtless an instinctive sense of this truth which prevents Communists from subjecting intellectual faculties to their utopian regulations. But Positivism can deal with these faculties, which stand in the most urgent need of wise direction, without inconsistency and without disturbance. It leaves to them their fair measure of free action ; and in the case of other faculties which, though less eminent, are hardly less dangerous to repress, it strengthens their freedom.   When a pure morality arises capable of impressing a social tendency upon every phase of human activity, the freer our action becomes the more useful will it be to the public. The tendency of modern civilization, far from impeding private industry, is to entrust it more and more with functions, especially with those of a material kind, which were originally left to government.   Unfortunately this tendency, which is very evident, leads economists into the mistake of supposing that industry may be left altogether without organization.   All that it really proves is that the influence of moral principles is gradually preponderating over that of governmental regulations.

Action of organized public opinion upon Capitalists. Strikes.   The method which is peculiar to Positivism of solving our great social problems by moral agencies, will be found applicable also to the settlement of industrial disputes, so far as the popular claims involved are well founded.   These claims will thus become clear from all tendency to disorder, and will consequently gain immensely in force ; especially when they are seen to be consistent with principles which are freely accepted by all, and when they are supported by a philosophic body of known impartiality and enlightenment. This spiritual power, while impressing on the people the duty of respecting their temporal leaders, will impose duties upon these latter, which they will find impossible to evade.   As all classes will have received a common education, they will all alike be penetrated with the general principles on which these special obligations will rest.   And these weapons, derived from no source but that of Feeling and Reason, and aided solely by Public Opinion, will wield an influence over practical life, of which nothing

12

in the present day can give any conception. We might compare it with the influence of Catholicism in the Middle Ages, only that men are too apt to attribute the results of Catholicism to the chimerical hopes and fears which it inspired, rather than to the energy with which praise and blame were distributed. With the new spiritual power praise and blame will form the only resource; but it will be developed and consolidated to a degree which, as I have before shown, was impossible for Catholicism.

This is the only real solution of the disputes that are so constantly arising between workmen and their employers. Both parties will look to this philosophic authority as a supreme court of arbitration. In estimating its importance, we must not forget that the antagonism of employer and employed has not yet been pushed to its full consequences. The struggle between wealth and numbers would have been far more serious, but for the fact that combination, without which there can be no struggle worth speaking of, has hitherto only been permitted to the capitalist. It is true that in England combinations of workmen are not legally prohibited. But in that country they are not yet sufficiently emancipated, either intellectually or morally, to make such use of the right as would be the case in France. When French workmen are allowed to concert their plans as freely as their employers, the antagonism of interests that will then arise will make both sides feel the need of a moral power to arbitrate between them. Not that the conciliating influence of such a power will ever be such as to do away entirely with extreme measures; but it will greatly restrict their application, and in cases where they are unavoidable, will mitigate their excesses. Such measures should be limited on both sides to refusal of co-operation; a power which every free agent ought to be allowed to exercise, on his own personal responsibility, with the object of impressing on those who are treating him unjustly the importance of the services which he has been rendering. The workman is not to be compelled to work any more than the capitalist to direct. Any abuse of this extreme protest on either side will of course be disapproved by the moral power; but the option of making the protest is always to be reserved to each element in the collective organism, by virtue of his natural independence. In the most settled times functionaries have always been allowed to suspend their services on special occasions. It was done frequently in the Middle Ages by priests, professors, judges, etc. All we have to do is to regulate this right, and embody it into the industrial system. This will be one of the secondary duties of the philosophic body, who will naturally be consulted on most of these occasions, as on all others of public or private moment. The formal sanction or positive order which it may give for a suspension of work, will render that measure far more effective than it is at present. The operation of the measure is but partial at present, but it might in this way extend, first to all who belong to the same trade, then to other branches of industry, and even ultimately to every Western nation that accepts the same spiritual guides. Of course persons who think themselves aggrieved may always resort to this extreme course on their own responsibility, against the advice of the philosophic body. True spiritual power confines itself to giving counsel: it never commands. But in such cases, unless the advice given by the philosophers has been wrong, the suspension of work is not likely to be sufficiently general to bring about any important result.

This theory of trade-unions is, in fact, in the industrial world, what the power of insurrection is with regard to the higher social functions; it is an ultimate resource which every collective organism must reserve. The principle is the same in the simpler and more ordinary cases as in the more unusual and important. In both the intervention of the philosophic body, whether solicited or not, whether its purpose be to organize popular effort or to repress it, will largely influence the result.

We are now in a position to state with more precision the main practical difference between the policy of Positivism, and that of Communism or of Socialism. All progressive political schools agree in concentrating their attention upon the problem, How to give the people their proper place as a component element of modern Society, which ever since the Middle Ages has been tending more and more distinctly to its normal mode of existence. They also agree that the two great requirements of the working classes are, the organization of Education, and the organization of Labour. But here their agreement ends. When the means of effecting these two objects have to be considered, Positivists find themselves at issue with all other progressive schools. They maintain that the organization of Industry must be based upon the organization of Education. It is commonly supposed that both may be begun simultaneously: or indeed that Labour may be organized irrespectively of Education. It may seem as if we are making too much of a mere question of arrangement; yet the difference is one which affects the whole character and method of social reconstruction. The plan usually followed is simply a repetition of the old attempt to reconstruct politically, without waiting for spiritual reconstruction; in other words, to raise the social edifice before its intellectual and moral foundations have been laid. Hence the attempts made to satisfy popular requirements by measures of a purely political kind, because they appear to meet the evil directly; a course which is as useless as it is destructive. Positivism, on the contrary, substitutes for such agencies, an influence which is sure and peaceful, although it be gradual and indirect; the influence of a more enlightened morality, supported by a purer state of Public Opinion; such opinion being organized by competent minds, and diffused freely amongst the people. In fact, the whole question, whether the solution of the twofold problem before us is to be empirical, revolutionary, and therefore confined simply to France; or whether it is to be consistent, pacific, and applicable to the whole of Western Europe, depends upon the preference or the postponement of the organization of Labour to the organization of Education.

This conclusion involves a brief explanation of the general system of education which Positivism will introduce. This the new spiritual power regards as its principal function, and as its most efficient means of satisfying the working classes in all reasonable demands.

Public Opinion must be based upon a sound system of Education.

It was the great social virtue of Catholicism, that it introduced for the first time, as far as circumstances permitted, a system of education common to all classes without distinction, not excepting even those who were still slaves. It was a vast undertaking, yet essential to its purpose of founding a spiritual power which was to be independent of the temporal power. Apart from its temporary value, it has left us one imperishable principle, namely that in all education worthy of the name, moral training should be regarded as of greater importance than scientific teaching. Catholic education, however, was of course extremely defective; owing partly to the circumstances of the time, and partly to the weakness of the doctrine on which it rested. Having reference almost exclusively to the oppressed masses, the principal lesson which it

taught was the duty of almost passive resignation, with
the exception of certain obligations imposed upon rulers.
Intellectual culture in any true sense there was none. All
this was natural in a faith which directed men's highest
efforts to an object unconnected with social life, and which
taught that all the phenomena of nature were regulated
by an impenetrable Will. Catholic Education was consequently quite unsuited to any period but the Middle
Ages; a period during which the advanced portion of
Humanity was gradually ridding itself of the ancient institution of slavery, by commuting it first into serfdom, as
a preliminary step to entire personal freedom. In the
ancient world Catholic education would have been too
revolutionary; at the present time it would be servile and
inadequate. Its function was that of directing the long
and difficult transition from the social life of Antiquity to
that of Modern times. Personal emancipation once obtained, the working classes began to develop their powers
and rise to their true position as a class; and they soon
became conscious of intellectual and social wants which
Catholicism was wholly incapable of satisfying.

And yet this is the only real system of universal education which the world has hitherto seen. For we cannot
give that name to the so-called University system which
metaphysicians began to introduce into Europe at the
close of the Middle Ages; and which offered little more
than the special instruction previously given to the priesthood; that is, the study of the Latin language, with
the dialectical training required for the defence of their
doctrines. Morals were untaught except as a part of the
training of the professed theologian. All this metaphysical and literary instruction was of no great service to
social evolution, except so far as it developed the critical
power; it had, however, a certain indirect influence on the

constructive movement, especially on the development of Art. But its defects, both practical and theoretical, have been made more evident by its application to new classes of society, whose occupations, whether practical or speculative, required a very different kind of training. And thus, while claiming the title of Universal, it never reached the working classes, even in Protestant countries, where each believer became to a certain extent his own priest.

The theological method being obsolete, and the metaphysical method inadequate, the task of founding an efficient system of popular education belongs to Positivism; the only doctrine capable of reconciling those two orders of conditions, the intellectual and the moral, which are equally necessary, but which since the Middle Ages have always proved incompatible. Positivist education, while securing the supremacy of the heart over the understanding more efficiently than Catholicism, will yet put no obstacle in the way of intellectual growth. The function of Intellect, in education as in practical life, will be to regulate Feeling; the culture of which, beginning at birth, will be maintained by constant exercise of the three classes of duties relative to Self, to the Family, and to Society.

I have already explained the mode in which the principles of universal morality will be finally co-ordinated; a task which, as I have shown, is connected with the principal function of the new spiritual power. I have now only to point out the paramount influence of morality in every part of Positive Education. It will be seen to be connected at first spontaneously, and afterwards in a more systematic form, with the entire system of human knowledge.

Positive Education, adapting itself to the requirements of the Organism with which it has to deal, subordinates intellectual conditions to social. Social conditions are considered as the main object, intellectual as but the means of attaining it. Its principal aim is to induce the working classes to accept their high social function of supporting the spiritual power, while at the same time it will render them more efficient in their own special duties.

Education has two stages; from birth to puberty, from puberty to adolescence. The first, consisting of physical and esthetic training, to be given at home. Presuming that Education extends from birth to manhood, we may divide it into two periods, the first ending with puberty, that is, at the beginning of industrial apprenticeship. Education here should be essentially spontaneous, and should be carried on as far as possible in the bosom of the family. The only studies required should be of an esthetic kind. In the second period, Education takes a systematic form, consisting chiefly of a public course of scientific lectures, explaining the essential laws of the various orders of phenomena. These lectures will be the groundwork of Moral Science, which will co-ordinate the whole, and point out the relation of each part to the social purpose common to all. Thus, at about the time which long experience has fixed as that of legal majority, and when in most cases the term of apprenticeship closes, the workman will be prepared intellectually and morally for his public and private service.

The first years of life, from infancy to the end of the period of second dentition, should be devoted to education of the physical powers, carried on under the superintendence of the parents, especially of the mother. Physical education, as usually practised, is nothing but mere muscular exercise ; but a more important object is that of training the senses, and giving manual skill, so as to develope from the very first our powers of observation and action. Study, in the ordinary acceptation, there should be none during this period, not even reading or writing. An acquaintance with facts of various kinds, such as may spontane-

ously attract the growing powers of attention, will be the
only instruction received.   The philosophic system of the
infant individual, like that of the infant species, consists
in pure Fetichism, and its natural development should not
be disturbed by unwise interference.   The only care of the
parents will be to impress those feelings and habits for
which a rational basis will be given at a later period.   By
taking every opportunity of calling the higher instincts
into play, they will be laying down the best foundation
for true morality.

During the period of about seven years comprised between the second dentition and puberty, Education will
become somewhat more systematic ; but it will be limited
to the culture of the fine arts ; and it will be still most
important, especially on moral grounds, to avoid separation from the family.   The study of Art should simply
consist in practising it more or less systematically.   No
formal lectures are necessary, at least for the purposes of
general education, though of course for professional purposes they may still be required.   There is no reason why
these studies should not be carried on at home by the
second generation of Positivists, when the culture of the
parents will be sufficiently advanced to allow them to
superintend it.   They will include Poetry, the art on
which all the rest are based ; and the two most important
of the special arts, music and drawing.   Meantime the
pupil will become familiar with the principal Western
languages, which are included in the study of Poetry,
since modern poetry cannot be properly appreciated without them.   Moreover, independently of esthetic considerations, a knowledge of them is most important morally, as
a means of destroying national prejudices, and of forming
the true Positivist standard of Occidental feeling.   Each
nation will be taught to consider it a duty to learn the

language of contiguous countries; an obvious principle,
which, in the case of Frenchmen, will involve their learning all the other four languages, as a consequence of that
central position which gives them so many advantages.
When this rule becomes general, and the natural affinities
of the five advanced nations are brought fully into play, a
common Occidental language will not be long in forming
itself spontaneously, without the aid of any metaphysical
scheme for producing a language that shall be absolutely
universal.

During the latter portion of primary Education, which
is devoted to the culture of the imaginative powers, the
philosophic development of the individual, corresponding
to that of the race, will carry him from the simple Fetichism with which he began to the stage of Polytheism.
This resemblance between the growth of the individual
and that of society has always shown itself more or
less, in spite of the irrational precautions of Christian
teachers. They have never been able to give children a
distaste for those simple tales of fairies and genii, which
are natural to this phase. The Positivist teacher will let
this tendency take its own course. It should not, however, involve any hypocrisy on the part of the parents,
nor need it lead to any subsequent contradiction. The
simple truth is enough. The child may be told that these
spontaneous beliefs are but natural to his age, but that
they will gradually lead him on to others, by the fundamental law of all human development. Language of
this kind will not only have the advantage of fami-
liarising him with a great principle of Positivism, but
will stimulate the nascent sense of sociability, by leading him to sympathize with the various nations who
still remain at his own primitive stage of intellectual
development.

The second part of Positivist Education can- *The second part consists of public lectures on the Sciences, from Mathematics to Sociology.* not be conducted altogether at home, since it involves public lectures, in which of course the part taken by the parent can be only accessory. But this is no reason for depriving the pupil of the advantages of family life ; it remains as indispensable as ever to his moral development, which is always to be the first consideration, It will be easy for him to follow the best masters without weakening his sense of personal and domestic morality, which is the almost inevitable result of monastic seclusion of modern schools. The public-school system is commonly thought to compensate for these disadvantages, by the knowledge of the world which it gives ; but this is better obtained by free intercourse with society, where sympathies are far more likely to be satisfied. Recognition of this truth would do much to facilitate and improve popular education ; and it applies to all cases, except perhaps to some special professions, where seclusion of the pupils may still be necessary, though even in these cases probably it may be ultimately dispensed with.

The plan to be followed in this period of education, will obviously be that indicated by the encyclopædic law of Classification, which forms part of my Theory of Development. Scientific study, whether for the working man or the philosopher, should begin with the inorganic world around us, and then pass to the subject of Man and Society ; since our ideas on these two subjects form the basis of our practical action. The first class of studies, as I have stated before, includes four sciences which we may arrange in pairs : Mathematics and Astronomy forming the first pair ; Physics and Chemistry the second. To each of these pairs, two years may be given. But as the first ranges over a wide field, and is of greater logical importance, it will require two lectures weekly ; whereas, for all the subsequent studies one lecture will be sufficient. Besides, during these two years, the necessities of practical life will not press heavily, and more time may fairly be spent in mental occupation. From the study of inorganic science, the pupil will proceed to Biology: this subject may easily be condensed in the fifth year into a series of forty lectures, without really losing either its philosophic or its popular character. This concludes the introductory part of Education. The student will now co-ordinate all his previous knowledge by the direct study of Sociology, statically and dynamically viewed. On this subject also forty lectures will be given, in which the structure and growth of human societies, especially those of modern times, will be clearly explained. With this foundation we come to the last of the seven years of pupillage, in which the great social purpose of the scheme is at last reached. It will be devoted to a systematic exposition of Moral Science, the principles of which may be now fully understood by the light of the knowledge previously obtained of the World, of Life, and of Humanity.

During this course of study, part of the three unoccupied months of each year will be spent in public examinations, to test the degree to which the instruction has been assimilated. The pupils will of their own accord continue their esthetic pursuits, even supposing their natural tastes in this direction not to be encouraged as they ought to be. During the last two years the Latin and Greek languages might be acquired, as an accessory study, which would improve the poetic culture of the student, and be useful to him in the historical and moral questions with which he will then be occupied. For the purposes of Art, Greek is the more useful of the two; but in the second object, that of enabling us to realize our social Filiation, Latin is of even greater importance.

In the course of these seven years the philosophic development of the individual, preserving its correspondence with that of the race, will pass through its last phase. As the pupil passed before from Fetichism to Polytheism, so he will now pass, as spontaneously, into Monotheism, induced by the influence on his imaginative powers which hitherto have been supreme, of the spirit of discussion. No interference should be offered to this metaphysical transition, which is the homage that he pays to the necessary conditions under which mankind arrives at truth. There is something in this provisional phase which evidently harmonizes well with the abstract and independent character of Mathematics, with which the two first years of the seven are occupied. As long as more attention is given to deduction than to induction, the mind cannot but retain a leaning to metaphysical theories. Under their influence the student will soon reduce his primitive theology to Deism of a more or less distinct kind; and this during his physico-chemical studies will most likely degenerate into a species of Atheism; which last phase, under the enlightening influence of biological and still more of sociological knowledge, will be finally replaced by Positivism. Thus at the time fixed for the ultimate study of moral science, each new member of Humanity will have been strongly impressed by personal experience, with a sense of historical Filiation, and will be enabled to sympathise with his ancestors and contemporaries, while devoting his practical energies to the good of his successors.

There is an excellent custom prevalent among the working men of France and creditable to their good sense, with which our educational scheme seems at first sight incompatible. I refer to the custom of travelling from place to place during the last years of apprenticeship; which is as beneficial to their mind and

Travels of Apprentices.

character, as the purposeless excursions of our wealthy and idle classes are in most cases injurious. But there is no necessity for its interfering with study, since it always involves long residence in the chief centres of production, where the workman is sure to find annual courses of lectures similar to those which he would otherwise have been attending at home. As the structure and distribution of the philosophic body will be everywhere the same, there need be no great inconvenience in these changes. For every centre not more than seven teachers will be required; each of whom will take the whole Encyclopædic scale successively. Thus the total number of lectures will be so small as to admit of a high standard of merit being everywhere attained, and of finding everywhere a fair measure of material support. So far from discouraging the travelling system, Positivism will give it a new character, intellectually and socially, by extending the range of travel to the whole of Western Europe, since there is no part of it in which the workman will not be able to prosecute his education. The difference of language will then be no obstacle. Not only would the sense of fraternity among Western nations be strengthened by such a plan, but great improvement would result esthetically. The languages of Europe would be learnt more thoroughly, and there would be a keener appreciation of works of art, whether musical, pictorial, or architectural; for these can never be properly appreciated but in the country which gave them birth.

Concentration of study. Judging by our present practice, it would seem impossible to include such a mass of important scientific studies, as are here proposed, in three hundred and sixty lectures. But the length to which courses of lectures on any subject extend at present, is owing partly to the special or professional object with which the

course is given, and still more to the discursive and unphi-
losophical spirit of most of the teachers, consequent on the
miserable manner in which our scientific system is organized. Such a regeneration of scientific studies as Positivism proposes, will animate them with a social spirit,
and thus give them a larger and more comprehensive tendency. Teachers will become more practised in the art of
condensing, and their lectures will be far more substantial.
They will not indeed be a substitute for voluntary effort,
on which all the real value of teaching depends. Their
aim will be rather to direct such effort. A striking example, which is not so well remembered as it should be,
will help to explain my meaning. At the first opening of
the Polytechnic School, courses of lectures were given,
very appropriately named *Revolutionary Courses*, which
concentrated the teaching of three years into three months.
What was in that case an extraordinary anomaly, due
to republican enthusiasm, .may become the normal state
when a moral power arises not inferior in energy, and
yet based upon a consistent intellectual synthesis, of
which our great predecessors of the Revolution could have
no conception.

Little attention has hitherto been given to the didactic
value of Feeling. Since the close of the Middle Ages, the
heart has been neglected in proportion as the mind has
been cultivated. But it is the characteristic principle of
Positivism, a principle as fertile in intellectual as in moral
results, that the Intellect, whether we look at its natural
or at its normal position, is subordinate to Social Feeling.
Throughout this course of popular education, parents and
masters will seize every suitable occasion for calling Social
Feeling into play ; and the most abstruse subjects will
often be vivified by its influence. The office of the mind
is to strengthen and to cultivate the heart ; the heart

again should animate and direct the mental powers. This mutual influence of general views and generous feelings will have greater effect upon scientific study, from the esthetic culture previously given, in which such habits of mind will have been formed, as will give grace and beauty to the whole life.

Governmental assistance not required, except for certain special institutions, and this only as a provisional measure.

When I speak of this education as specially destined for the people, I am not merely using words to denote its comprehensiveness and philosophic character. It is, in my opinion, the only education, with the exception of certain special branches, for which public organization is needed. It should be, looked on as a sacred debt which the republic owes to the working classes. But the claim does not extend to other classes, who can easily pay for any special instruction that they may require. Besides such instruction will be only a partial development of the more general teaching, or an application of it to some particular purpose. Therefore if the general training be sound, most people will be able to prosecute accessory studies by themselves. Apprenticeship to any business involves very little, except the practice of it. Even in the highest arts, no course of systematic instruction is necessary. The false views now prevalent on the subject are due to the unfortunate absence of all general education, since the decay of Catholicism. The special institutions founded in Europe during the last three centuries, and carefully remodelled in France by the Convention, are only valuable as containing certain germs of truth, which will be found indispensable when general education is finally reorganized. But important as they may be from a scientific aspect, their practical utility, which seems to have been the motive for establishing them, is exceedingly doubtful. The arts which they were intended to promote could have done perfectly well without them. I include in these remarks such institutions as the Polytechnic School, the Museum of Natural History, etc. Their value, like that of all good institutions of modern times, is purely provisional. Viewed in this light, it may be worth our while to reorganize them. Positivist principles, discarding all attempts to make them permanent, will be all the better able to adapt them to their important temporary purpose. Indeed there are some new institutions which it might be advisable to form; such, for instance, as a School of Comparative Philology, the object of which would be to range all human languages according to their true affinities. This would compensate the suppression of Greek and Latin professorships, which is certainly an indispensable measure. But the whole of this provisional framework would no doubt disappear before the end of the nineteenth century, when a system of general education will have been thoroughly organized. The present necessity for a provisional system should lead to no misconception of its character and purpose. Working men are the only class who have a real claim upon the State for instruction; and this, if wisely organized, dispenses with the necessity of special institutions. The adoption of these views would at once facilitate and ennoble popular education. Nations, provinces, and towns will vie with one another in inviting the best teachers that the spiritual authorities of Western Europe can supply. And every true philosopher will take pride in such teaching, when it becomes generally understood that the popular character of his lectures implies that they shall be at the same time systematic. Members of the new spiritual power will in most cases regard teaching as their principal occupation, for at least a considerable portion of their public life.

We are not ripe for this system at present; and Government must not attempt to hasten its introduction.

What has been said makes it clear that any organization of such education as this at the present time would be impossible. However sincere the intentions of governments to effect this great result might be, any premature attempt to do it would but injure the work, especially if they put in a claim to superintend it. The truth is that a system of education, if it deserve the name, presupposes the acceptance of a definite philosophical and social creed to determine its character and purpose. Children cannot be brought up in convictions contrary to those of their parents; indeed, the influence of the parent is essential to the instructor. Opinions and habits that have been already formed may subsequently be strengthened by an educational system; but the carrying out of any such system is impossible, until the principles of combined action and belief have been well established. Till then the organization that we propose can only be effected in the case of individuals who are ripe for it. Each of these will endeavour to repair the faults and deficiencies of his own education in the best way he can, by the aid of the general doctrine which he accepts. Assuming that the doctrine is destined to triumph, the number of such minds gradually increases, and they superintend the social progress of the next generation. This is the natural process, and no artificial interference can dispense with it. So far, then, from inviting government to organize education, we ought rather to exhort it to abdicate the educational powers which it already holds, and which, I refer more especially to France, are either useless or a source of discord. There are only two exceptions to this remark, namely, primary education, and special instruction in certain higher branches. Of these I have already spoken. But with these exceptions, it is most desirable that government, whether municipal or central, should surrender its unreasonable monopoly, and establish real liberty of teaching; the condition of such liberty being, as I said before, the suppression of all annual grants whatsoever for theological or metaphysical purposes. Until some universal faith has been accepted on its own merits, all attempts made by Government to reform education must necessarily be reactionary; since they will always be based on some one of the retrogressive creeds which it is our object to supersede altogether.

It is with adults, then, that we must deal. We must endeavour to disseminate systematic convictions among them, and thus open the door to a real reform of education for the next generation. The press and the power of free speech offer many ways of bringing about this result. The most important of these would be a more or less connected series of popular lectures on the various positive sciences, including history, which may now be ranked among them. Now for these lectures to produce their full effect, they must, even when treating of the most elementary point in mathematics, be thoroughly philosophic and consequently animated by a social spirit. They must be entirely independent of government, so as not to be hampered by any of the authorized views. Lastly, there is a condition in which all the rest are summed up. These lectures should be Occidental, not simply National. What we require is a free association of philosophers throughout Western Europe, formed by the voluntary co-operation of all who can contribute efficiently to this great preliminary work; their services being essentially gratuitous. It is a result which no system but Positivism is capable of effecting. By its agency that coalition between philosophers and the working classes, on which so much depends, will speedily be established.

While the work of propagating Positivist convictions is going on in the free and unrestricted manner here described, the spiritual authority will at the same time be forming itself, and will be prepared to make use of these convictions as the basis for social regeneration. Thus the transitional state will be brought as nearly as possible into harmony with the normal state; and this the more in proportion as the natural affinity between philosophers and workmen is brought out more distinctly. The connection between Positivist lectures and Positivist clubs will illustrate my meaning. While the lectures prepare the way for the Future, the clubs work in the same direction by judging the Past, and advising for the Present; so that we have at once a beginning of the three essential functions of the new spiritual power.

We have now a clear conception of popular education in its provisional, and in its normal state. Long before the normal state can be realised, the mutual action of philosophers and workmen will have done great service to both. Meeting with such powerful support from the people, the rising spiritual power will win the respect if not the affection of their rulers, even of those among them who are now the most contemptuous of every influence but that of material power. Their excess of pride will often be so far humbled that they will invite its mediation in cases where their people have been roused to just indignation. The force of numbers seems at first so violent as to carry all before it; but in the end it usually proves far inferior to that of wealth. It cannot exist for any length of time without complete convergence of opinion and feeling. Hence, a spiritual power has very great weight in controlling or directing its action. Philosophers will never, indeed, be able to manage the working classes as they please, as some unprincipled agitators have imagined; but

when they exercise their authority rightly, whether it be in
the cause of Order or that of Progress, they will have great
power over their passions and conduct.   Such influence
can only spring from long cherished feelings of gratitude
and trust, due not merely to presumed capacity, but to
services actually rendered.   No one is a fit representative
of his own claims ; but the philosopher may honourably
represent the cause of working men before the governing
classes ; and the people will in their turn compel their
rulers to respect the new spiritual power.   By this habitual
exchange of services the aspirations of the people will be
kept clear of all subversive tendencies, and philosophers
will be led to abandon the folly of seeking political power.
Neither class will degrade itself by making its own interest the chief consideration : each will find its own reward in keeping to the nobler course of its own social
duty.

To complete this view of the political attitude which Positivism recommends to the
working class, I have now to speak of the
intellectual and moral conditions which that
attitude requires, and on which the character of their
spiritual leaders depends.   What is wanted is only a
more perfect development of tendencies which already
exist in the people, and which have already shown
themselves strong in Paris, the centre of the great
Western movement.

Intellectual attitude of the people. Emancipation from theological belief.

Intellectually the principal conditions are two ; Emancipation from obsolete beliefs, and a sufficient amount of
mental culture.

The emancipation of the working classes from theology
is complete, at least in Paris.   In no other class has it so
entirely lost its power.   The shallow Deism, which satisfies
so many of our literary men, finds little favour with the.

people. They are happily unversed in studies of words
and abstractions, without which this last stage in the process of emancipation speedily comes to an end. We only
require a stronger expression of popular feeling on this
point, so as to avoid all deception and false statement as
to the intellectual character of the reorganization that is
going on. And the freedom that we are now enjoying
will admit of these feelings being unmistakeably manifested, especially now that they have the new philosophy
for their exponent. A distinct declaration of opinion on
this subject is urgently needed on social grounds. That
hypocritical affectation of theological belief against which
we have to fight, is designed to prevent, or at least has the
effect of preventing, the just enforcement of popular claims.
These unscrupulous attempts to mystify the people involve
their mental subjection. The result is, that their legitimate aspirations for real progress are evaded, by diverting
their thoughts towards an imaginary future state. It is
for the working classes themselves to break through this
concerted scheme, which is even more contemptible than
it is odious. They have only to declare without disguise
what their intellectual position really is ; and to do this so
emphatically as to make any mistake on the part of the
governing classes impossible. They will consequently
reject all teachers who are insufficiently emancipated, or
who in any way support the system of theological hypocrisy, which, from Robespierre downwards, has been the
refuge of all reactionists, whether democrat or royalist.
But there are teachers of another kind, who sincerely
maintain that our life here on earth is a temporary banish-
ment, and that we ought to take as little interest in it as
possible. A prompt answer may be given to such instructors as these. They should be requested to follow out
their principle consistently, and to cease to interfere in the

management of a world which is so alien to what, in their ideas, is the sole aim of life.

Metaphysical principles have more hold on our working classes than theological; yet their *From metaphysical doctrines.* abandonment is equally necessary. The subtle extravagances by which the German mind has been so confused, find, it is true, little favour in Catholic countries. But even in Paris the people retains a prejudice in favour of metaphysical instruction, though happily it has not been able to obtain it. It is most desirable that this last illusion of our working classes should be dissipated, as it forms the one great obstacle to their social action. One reason for it is that they fall into the common error of confounding knowledge with intelligence, and imagine in their modesty that none but instructed men are capable of governing. Now this error, natural as it is, often leads them to choose incompetent leaders. A truer estimate of modern society would teach them that it is not among our literary, or even our scientific men, proud as they may be of their attainments, that the largest number of really powerful intellects are to be found. There are more of them among the despised practical class, and even amongst the most uninstructed working men. In the Middle Ages this truth was better known than it is now. Education was thought more of than instruction. A knight would be appreciated for his sagacity and penetration, and appointed to important posts, though he might be extremely ignorant. Clear-sightedness, wisdom, and even consistency of thought, are qualities which are very independent of learning; and, as matters now stand, they are far better cultivated in practical life than in scholastic study. In breadth of view, which lies at the root of all political capacity, our literary classes have certainly shown themselves far below the average.

Their mistaken preference of literary and rhetorical talent to real intellectual power. And now we come to another and a deeper reason for the prejudice 'of which I am speaking. It is that they make no distinction between one kind of instruction and another. The unfortunate confidence which they still bestow on literary men and lawyers shows that the prestige of pedantry lingers among them longer than the prestige of theology or monarchy. But all this will soon be altered under the influence of republican government, and the strong discipline of a sound philosophical system. Popular instinct will soon discover that constant practice of the faculty of expression, whether in speech or in writing, is no guarantee for real power of thought; indeed that it has a tendency to incapacitate men from forming a clear and decided judgment on any question. The instruction which such men receive is utterly deficient in solid principles, and it almost always either presupposes or causes a total absence of fixed convictions. Most minds thus trained, while skilled in putting other men's thoughts into shape, become incapable of distinguishing true from false in the commonest subjects, even when their own interest requires it. The people must give up the feeling of blind respect which leads them to intrust such men with their highest interests. Reverence for superiors is doubtless indispensable to a well-ordered state; only it needs to be better guided than it is now.

What then, working men may ask, is the proper training for themselves, and consequently for those who claim to guide them? The answer is, systematic cultivation of the Positive spirit. It is already called into exercise by their daily occupations; and all that is wanted is to strengthen it by a course of scientific study. Their daily work involves a rudimentary application of the Positive method: it turns their attention to many most important natural laws. In fact, the workmen of Paris, whom I take as the best type of their class, have a clearer sense of that union of reality with utility by which the Positive spirit is characterised, than most of our scientific men. The speciality of their employment is no doubt disadvantageous with respect to breadth and coherence of ideas. But it leaves the mind free from responsibility, and this is the most favourable condition for developing these qualities to which all vigorous intellects are naturally disposed. But nothing will so strongly impress on the people the importance of extending and organizing their scientific knowledge, as their interest in social questions. Their determination to rectify a faulty condition of society will suggest to them that they must first know what the laws of Social life really are ; knowledge which is obviously necessary in every other subject. They will then feel how impossible it is to understand the present state of society, without understanding its relation on the one hand with the Past, and on the other with the Future. Their desire to modify the natural course of social phenomena will make them anxious to know the antecedents and consequences of these phenomena, so as to avoid all mischievous or useless interference. They will thus discover that Political Art is even more dependent than other arts, upon its corresponding Science. And then they will soon see that this science is no isolated department of knowledge, but that it involves preliminary study of Man and of the World. In this way they will pass downwards through the hierarchic scale of Positive conceptions, until they come back to the inorganic world, the sphere more immediately connected with their own special avocations. And thus they will reach the conclusion that Positivism is the only system which can satisfy either the intellectual or material wants of the people, since its subject-matter and its objects are

identical with their own, and since, like themselves, it
subordinates everything to social considerations. All that
it claims is to present in a systematic form principles
which they already hold instinctively. By co-ordinating
these principles of morality and good sense, their value,
whether in public or in private questions, is largely increased; and the union of the two forms of wisdom,
theoretiçal and practical wisdom, is permanently secured.
When all this is understood, the people will feel some
shame at having entrusted questions of the greatest complexity to minds that have never quite comprehended
the difference between a cubic inch and a cubic foot. As
to men of science, in the common acceptation of the word,
who are so respected by the middle classes, we need not
be afraid of their gaining much influence with the people.
They are alienated from them by their utter indifference
to social questions ; and before these their learned puerilities fade into insignificance. Absorbed in the details of
their own special science, they are quite incapable of
satisfying unsophisticated minds. What the people want
is to have clear conceptions on all subjects, *des clartés de
tout*, as Molière has it. Whenever the savants of our
time are drawn by their foolish ambition into politics,
ordinary men find to their surprise that, except in a few
questions of limited extent and importance, their minds
have become thoroughly narrow under the influence of
the specialising system of which they are so proud. Positivism explains the mystery, by showing that, since the
necessity for the specialising system now no longer exists,
it naturally results, if prolonged, in a sort of academic
idiocy. During the last three centuries it did real service
to society, by laying down the scientific groundwork for
the renovation of Philosophy projected by Bacon and
Descartes. But as soon as the groundwork was suffici-

ently finished to admit of the formation of true Science, that is, of Science viewed relatively to Humanity, the specialising method became retrograde. It ceased to be of any assistance to the modern spirit; and indeed it is now, especially in France, a serious obstacle to its diffusion and systematic working. The wise revolutionists of the Convention were well aware of this when they took the bold step of suppressing the Academy of Sciences. The beneficial results of this statesman-like policy will soon be appreciated by our workmen. The danger lest, in withdrawing their confidence from metaphysicians or literary men, they should fall into the bad scientific spirit, is not therefore very great. With the social aims which they have in view, they cannot but see that generality in their conceptions is as necessary as positivity. The Capitalist class by which industry is directed, being more concentrated on special objects, will always look on men of pure science with more respect. But the people will be drawn by their political leanings towards philosophers in the true sense of that word. The number of such men is but very small at present; but it will soon increase at the call of the working classes, and will indeed be recruited from their ranks.

This, then, should be the attitude of the working class, intellectually. Morally, what is required is, that they should have a sufficient sense of the dignity of labour, and that they should be prepared for the mission that now lies before them.

Moral attitude of the people. The workman should regard himself as a public functionary.

The workman must learn to look upon himself, morally, as a public servant, with functions of a special and also of a general kind. Not that he is to receive his wages for the future from the State instead of from a private hand. The present plan is perfectly well adapted to all services which are so direct and definite, that a common standard of value can be at once applied to them. Only let it be understood that the service is not sufficiently recompensed, without the social feeling of gratitude towards the agent that performs it. In what are called liberal professions, this feeling already obtains. The client or patient is not dispensed from gratitude by payment of his fee. In this respect the republican instincts of the Convention have anticipated the teaching of philosophy. They valued the workman's labour at its true worth. Workmen have only to imagine labour suppressed or even suspended in the trade to which they may belong, to see its importance to the whole fabric of modern society. Their general functions as a class, the function of forming public opinion, and of supporting the action of the spiritual power, it is of course less easy for them to understand at present. But, as I have already shown, it follows so naturally from their character and position, and corresponds so perfectly with their requirements as a class, that they cannot fail to appreciate its importance, when the course of events allows, or rather compels them to bring it into play. The only danger lies in their insisting on the possession of what metaphysicians call political rights, and in engaging in useless discussions about the distribution of power, instead of fixing their attention on the manner in which it is used. Of this, however, there is no great fear, at all events in France, where the metaphysical theory of Right has never reached so fanatical a pitch with the working classes as elsewhere. Ideologists may blame them, and may use their official influence as they will; but the people have too much good sense to be permanently misled as to their true function in society. Deluged as they have been with electoral votes, they will soon voluntarily abandon this useless qualification, which now has not even the charm of a privilege.   Questions of pure politics have ceased to interest the people; their attention is fixed, and will remain fixed, on social questions, which are to be solved for the most part through moral agencies.   That substitutions of one person or party for another, or that mere modifications of any kind in the administration should be looked on as the final issue of the great Revolution, is a result in which they will never acquiesce.

And if this is to be the attitude of the people, it must be the attitude no less of those who seek to gain their confidence.   With them, as with the people, political questions should be subordinate to social questions; and with them the conviction should be even more distinct, that the solution of social problems depends essentially on moral agencies.   They must, in fact, accept the great principle of separation of spiritual from temporal power, as the basis on which modern society is to be permanently organized.   So entirely does this principle meet the wants of the people, that they will soon insist on its adoption by their teachers.   They will accept none who do not formally abandon any prospects they may have of temporal power, parliamentary as well as administrative.   And by thus dedicating their lives without reservation to the priesthood of Humanity, they will gain confidence, not merely from the people, but from the governing classes.   Governments will offer no impediment to social speculations which do not profess to be susceptible of immediate application; and thus the normal state may be prepared for in the future without disturbance, and yet without neglecting the present.   Practical statesmen meanwhile, no longer interfered with by pretentious sophists, will give up their retrograde tendencies, and will gradually adapt their policy to the new ideas current in the public mind, while discharging the indispensable function of maintaining material order.

For the people to rise to the true level of their position, they have only to develope and cultivate certain dispositions which already exist in them spontaneously. And the most important of these is, absence of ambition for wealth or rank. Political metaphysicians would say that the sole object of the Great Revolution was to give the working classes easier access to political and civil power. But this, though it should always be open to them, is very far from meeting their true wants. Individuals among them may be benefited by it, but the mass is left unaffected, or rather is placed often in a worse position, by the desertion of the more energetic members. The Convention is the only government by which this result has been properly appreciated. It is the only government which has shown due consideration for working men as such ; which has recognised the value of their services, and encouraged what is the chief compensation for their condition of poverty, their participation in public life. All subsequent governments, whether retrograde or constitutional, have, on the contrary, done all they could to divert the people from their true social function, by affording opportunity for individuals among them to rise to higher positions. The monied classes, under the influence of blind routine, have lent their aid to this degrading policy, by continually preaching to the people the necessity of saving; a precept which is indeed incumbent on their own class, but not on others. Without saving, capital could not be accumulated and administered ; it is therefore of the highest importance that the monied classes should be as economical as possible. But in other classes and especially in those dependent on fixed wages, parsimonious habits are uncalled for and injurious ; they lower the character of the labourer, while they do little or nothing to improve his physical condition ; and neither the working classes nor their teachers should encourage them. Both the one and the other will find their truest happiness in keeping clear of all serious practical responsibility, and in allowing free play to their mental and moral faculties in public as well as private life. In spite of the Economists, savings-banks are regarded by the working classes with unmistakable repugnance. And the repugnance is justifiable; they do harm morally, by checking the exercise of generous feelings. Again, it is the fashion to declaim against wine-shops; and yet after all they are at present the only places where the people can enjoy society. Social instincts are cultivated there which deserve our approval far more than the self-helping spirit which carries men to the savings-bank. No doubt this unconcern for money, wise as it is, involves real personal risk; but it is a danger which civilization is constantly tending to diminish, without effacing qualities which do the workman honour, and which are the source of his most cherished pleasures. The danger ceases when the mental and moral faculties are called into stronger exercise. The interest which Positivism will arouse among the people in public questions, will lead to the substitution of the club for the wine-shop. In these questions, the generous inspirations of popular instinct hold out a model which philosophers will do well to follow themselves. Fondness for money is as much a disqualification for the spiritual government of Humanity, as political ambition. It is a clear proof of moral incompetence, which is generally connected in one way or other with intellectual feebleness.

One of the principal results of the spiritual power exercised by philosophers and the working classes under the Positivist system, will be to compensate by a just distribution of blame and praise for the imperfect arrangements of social rank, in which wealth must always preponderate.

Leaving the present subordination of offices untouched, each functionary will be judged by the intrinsic worth of his mind and heart, without servility and yet without any encouragement to anarchy. It must always be obvious that the political importance which high position gives, is out of all proportion to the real merit implied in gaining that position. The people will come to see more and more clearly that real happiness, so far from depending on rank, is far more compatible with their own humble station. Exceptional men no doubt there are, whose character impels them to seek power; a character more dangerous than useful, unless there be sufficient wisdom in the social body to turn it to good account. The best workmen, like the best philosophers, will soon cease to feel envy for greatness, laden, as it always must be, with heavy responsibilities. At present, the compensation which I hold out to them has not been realized; but when it exists, the people will feel that their spiritual and temporal leaders are combining all the energies of society for the satisfaction of their wants. Recognizing this, they will care but little for fame that must be bought by long and tedious meditation, or for power burdened with constant care. There are men whose talents call them to these important duties, and they will be left free to perform them; but the great mass of society will be well satisfied that their own lot is one far more in keeping with the constitution of our nature; more compatible with that harmonious exercise of the faculties of Thought, Feeling, and Action, which is most conducive to happiness. The immediate pressure of poverty once removed, the highest reward of honorable conduct will be found in the permanent esteem, posthumous as it may be sometimes, of that portion of Humanity which has witnessed it. In a word the title, *servus servorum*, which is still retained by the Papacy from false humility, but which originated in anticipation of a social truth, is applicable to all functionaries in high position.   They may be described as the involuntary servants of voluntary subordinates.   It is not chimerical to conceive Positivist society so organised that its theoretical and practical directors, with all their personal advantages, will often regret that they were not born, or that they did not remain, in the condition of workmen.   The only solid satisfaction which great minds have hitherto found in political or spiritual power has been that, being more occupied with public interests, they had a wider scope for the exercise of social feeling.   But the excellence of the future condition of society will be, that the possibility of combining public and private life will be open to all.   The humblest citizen will be able to influence society, not by command but by counsel, in proportion to his energy and worth.

All the views brought forward in this chapter bear out the statement with which it began, that the Proletariate forms the principal basis of the social system, not merely as finally constituted, but in its present state of transition; and admitting this, the present state will be seen to have no essential difference from the normal future to which it tends.   The principal conditions of our transitional policy were described at the conclusion of the last chapter.   The security for these conditions is to be found in the natural tendencies of the people of Western Europe, and especially of France.   Our governors will do well to follow these tendencies instead of attempting to lead them ; for they are in perfect keeping with the two great requirements of the present time, Liberty and Public Order.

Liberty of thought and speech is enjoyed in France, and especially in Paris, to an extent impossible in any other country ; and it is due

The working classes are the best guarantee for Liberty and for Order.

14

principally to the intellectual emancipation of our workmen. They have rid themselves of theology in all its forms, and yet have not accepted any metaphysical system. At the same time, though totally devoid at present of systematic convictions, there is in them a submissiveness of mind which predisposes them to receive convictions combining reality with utility. In all other classes there is a tendency to use forcible measures in spreading their doctrines when discussion fails. It is only to the people that philosophers can look for the support and extension of Liberty, which is so essential to their objects; and from this they derive moral confidence far more reassuring than any legal security. However reactionary or stationary the views of particular leaders or sects may be, with such a population as that of Paris, no real oppression is possible. Of all the claims which France has to the leadership of Europe, this is the strongest. The resistance which is still offered to freedom of association and freedom of education will soon be overcome by the force of its liberal sympathies. A population of such strong social feeling as ours will certainly not allow itself to be permanently deprived of the power of meeting together freely in clubs; institutions most conducive both to its culture and to the protection of its interests. It will insist with equal force upon perfect liberty of teaching, feeling deeply the need of solid instruction, and the incapacity of metaphysicians and theologians to give it. Without popular pressure, the essential conditions of educational liberty will always be evaded.

And if Liberty depends upon popular support, Public Order, whether at home or abroad, depends upon it no less. The inclinations of the working classes are altogether on the side of peace. Their strong dislike of war is the principal reason of the present remarkable tranquillity of

Europe. The foolish regret expressed by all the retrograde parties for the decline of the military spirit is a sufficient indication of what the popular feeling is ; but even more significant is the necessity for compulsory enlistment, which began in France and has extended to other parts of Europe. There has been much factitious indignation on the subject, but at least it must be allowed, that in our armies, the officers are the only volunteers. Again, the working class is more free than any other from international prejudices, which still disunite the great family of Western nations, although they are very much weaker than formerly. They are strongest in the middle classes, a fact principally due to industrial competition. But working men feel how similar their wants and their conditions are in all countries, and this feeling checks their animosity. And the consciousness of union will become far stronger, now that the great social problem of their incorporation into modern society is being raised everywhere. No errors that statesmen can commit, whether in matters of war or peace, can prevent this from becoming the preponderating question in every European country ; and thus it tends to preserve their mutual concord.

Popular sympathies of this sort are, it may be said, less conducive to internal tranquillity than to pacific foreign relations. But the alarm which is naturally aroused by the spiritual anarchy around us must not blind us to the real guarantees for Order which popular tendencies, rightly interpreted, hold out. It is to the people that we must look for the ascendency of central over local power, which, as we have seen, is so indispensable to public order. The executive authority, provided only that it gives no cause to fear reaction, will always have their support when opposed by an assembly the prevalent tendencies of

which will usually be adverse to their interests. They
will always turn instinctively to the dictatorial rather
than to the parliamentary branch of the administration;
feeling that from its practical character and the directness
of its action, it is more likely to meet their wants. Useless discussions on constitutional questions may suit ambitious members of the middle classes, by facilitating their
arrival to power. But the people take very little interest
in all this unmeaning agitation, and often treat it with
merited contempt. They know that it can be of no use to
them, and that its only result is to evade their real wants
by undermining the only authority that can do them justice.
Consequently the people are certain to give their support
to every government that deserves it; especially in France,
where political passions have already yielded to the
superior and more permanent interest of social questions.
And while strengthening the government, they may do
much to elevate its character; by confining it strictly to
its practical function, and resisting any attempts that it
may make to interfere with opinion. In all these respects
the spontaneous influence of the working classes will be
of material assistance in carrying out the systematic conceptions of social philosophy.

It is from
them that we
shall obtain
the dictatorial
power which
is provision-
ally required.
But a more striking proof of the political
influence to be exercised by the people is this.
The dictatorship which our transitional policy
requires, as long as the spiritual interregnum
lasts, must arise in the first instance from their ranks.

In the word *People*, especially in the French language,
there is a fortunate ambiguity, which may serve to remind
us that the proletariate class is not, properly speaking, a
class at all, but constitutes the body of society. From it
proceed the various special classes, which we may regard
as organs necessary to that body. Since the abolition of

royalty, the last remnant of caste, our political leaders
have been recruited, and will continue to be so, from the
working class. In the normal state, however, it will be
required as a preliminary condition, that the holder of
dictatorial power shall have first received the political
training which is given by the exercise of authority in
his own business. In a settled state of society, Government, strictly so called, is a mere extension of civil influence. Ultimately, therefore, political power will fall into
the hands of the great leaders of industry. As spiritual
reorganization proceeds, they will gradually become more
worthy of it than they are at present. Besides, the tenure
of power will become less burdensome, because it will be
confined to duties of a purely practical kind.

As yet, however, the case is very different; and therefore the wealthy, though ultimately they will be the
administrators of power, are not those to whom it should
as a rule be entrusted in our present condition. Special
departments may be given to them with advantage, as we
have seen proved recently, and that in cases where the
functions to be performed had no relation whatever to
industrial skill. But they are not competent as yet for
dictatorial power, the power which has to supply the place
of royalty. Individual exceptions, of course, there may be,
though none have appeared hitherto, and at least they are
not enough for our provisional system to rely on. As yet
the wealthy classes have shown themselves too debased in
thought and feeling for an office of such importance. Nor
do we find greater aptitude for it outside the industrial
class. Scientific men are most assuredly unfit for it,
especially in France, where the system of Academies has
narrowed the mind, withered the feelings, and enervated
the character to such an extent, that most of them fail
in the conduct of common life, and are utterly unworthy

of the smallest post of authority, even in their own department.

All other classes failing us, we have to look to the working class, which has been left more free to form broad views, and in which the sense of duty has been better cultivated. On historical grounds I feel convinced that the workmen of France are more likely than any other class to supply men competent for supreme power, as long as the spiritual interregnum lasts; that is, for at least one generation.

On looking at this question calmly and without scholastic or aristocratic prejudice, it will be seen, as I pointed out at the beginning of this chapter, that the working class is better situated than any other with respect to generality of views and generosity of feeling. In knowledge and experience of administration they would ordinarily be deficient; they would therefore not be fit for the work of any special department. But this is no disqualification for the supreme power, or indeed for any of the higher offices for which breadth of view rather than special knowledge is required. These may be filled by working men, whose good sense and modesty will at once lead them to choose their agents for special departments from the classes who have usually furnished them before. The practical character and progressive spirit of such a government being beyond suspicion, special talent of whatever kind may be made available, even in the case of men who, if they had been placed in a higher position, would have proved thoroughly hostile to republican institutions. Of all the diversified elements of modern society, there is not one which may not be of real service in assisting the transition. Among soldiers and magistrates, for instance, there are many who will join the popular movement, and become sincere supporters of republicanism. A government of this kind would tranquillize the people, would obviate the necessity for violent compressive measures, and would at the same time have a most beneficial influence on the capitalist class. It would show them the necessity of attaining to greater purity of feeling and greater breadth of view, if they are to become worthy of the position for which they are ultimately destined.

Thus, whether we look at the interests of Public Order, or at those of Liberty, it appears necessary as a provisional measure, during the continuance of our spiritual interregnum, that the holders of dictatorial power shall be chosen from the working class. The success of a few working men in the pursuit of wealth has exercised an unsettling influence on the rest; but in the present instance we need not fear this result. It will be obvious that the career of a proletary governor is a rare exception, and one which requires peculiar endowments.

In examining the mode in which this anomalous policy should be carried out, we must bear in mind the object with which it was instituted. It is most important to get rid of the custom, based on motives of self-interest, which has grown up during the last generation, of insisting on parliamentary experience as an apprenticeship for executive power; executive power being always the real object of ambition. We have found from experience what we might have anticipated on theoretical grounds, that this plan excludes all except mere talkers of the Girondin type, men totally devoid of statesman-like qualities. To working men it offers almost insurmountable obstacles; and even supposing these obstacles to be overcome, we may be sure that they would lose the straightforwardness and native vigour which constitute their best claim to the exceptional position proposed for them.

It is best, then, that they should reach the position

assigned to them at once, without the circuitous process of a parliamentary career. Our transition towards the normal state will then exhibit its true character. It will be tranquil and yet decisive; for it will rest on the combined action of philosophers without political ambition, and dictators adverse to spiritual encroachment. The teacher who attempts to govern, the governor who attempts to educate, will both incur severe public censure, as enemies alike of peace and progress. The whole result will be a change in our revolutionary condition identical with that which the Convention would have realised, if, as its founders contemplated, it had lasted till the Peace.

Such, then, is the nature of the compact into which all true philosophers should enter with the leading members of the proletary class. Their object is to direct the organic and final phase through which the Great Revolution is now passing. What they have to do is carefully to prolong the provisional system adopted by the Convention, and to ignore, as far as possible, the traditions of all succeeding governments, whether stationary or retrograde. Comprehensiveness of view and social sympathy predominate alike in both members of this great alliance; and it is thus a guarantee for our present state of transition, and a sure earnest of the normal future. The people are the spontaneous representatives of this alliance; the philosophers its systematic organ. The intellectual deficiencies of the former will easily be remedied by philosophers, who will show them how essential it is on social grounds that they should understand the true meaning of history; since otherwise their conception of the union of mankind must be limited to the present generation, ignoring the more important truth of the continuity of the Present with the Past and the Future. A far greater obstacle is the moral deficiency of most philosophers of our time.

But the wholesome influence of the people upon them, combined with a deep philosophic conviction of the preponderance of Feeling in every subject of thought, will do much to overcome the ambitious instincts which weaken and distract their energies in the common cause of social renovation.

CHAPTER IV.

THE INFLUENCE OF POSITIVISM UPON WOMEN.

Women represent the affective element in our nature, as philosophers and people represent the intellectual and practical elements. In their action, then, upon society, philosophers may hope for the energetic support of the working classes. But the regenerating movement requires still the co-operation of a third element, an element indicated by our analysis of human nature, and suggested also by historical study of the great crisis of modern times.

The moral constitution of man consists of something more than Intellect and Activity. These are represented in the constitution of society by the philosophic body and the proletariate. But besides these there is Feeling, which, in the theory put forward in the first chapter of this work, was shown to be .the predominating principle, the motive power of our being, the only basis on which the various parts of our nature can be brought into unity. Now the alliance between philosophers and working men, which has been just described, however perfectly it may be realised, does not represent the element of Feeling with sufficient distinctness and prominence.

Certainly without Social Feeling, neither philosophers nor proletaries can exercise any real influence. But in their case its source is not sufficiently pure nor deep to sustain them in the performance of their duty. A more spontaneous and more perennial spring of inspiration must be found.

With the philosopher social sympathies will never be

wanting in coherence, since they will be connected with his whole system of thought; but this very scientific character will deaden their vigour, unless they are revived by impulses in which reflection has no share. Roused as he will be by the consciousness of public duty to a degree of activity of which abstract thinkers can form no conception, the emotions of private life will yet be not less necessary for him than for others. Intercourse with the working classes will be of the greatest benefit to him; but even this is not enough to compensate the defects of a life devoted to speculation.

The sympathies of the people again, though stronger and more spontaneous than those of the philosopher, are, in most cases, less pure and not so lasting. From the pressure of daily necessities it is difficult for them to maintain the same consistent and disinterested character. Great as are the moral advantages which will result from the incorporation of the people in modern society, they are not enough by themselves to outweigh the force of self-interest aroused by the precarious nature of their position. Emotions of a gentler and less transient kind must be called into play. Philosophers may relieve the working classes from the necessity of pressing their own claims and grievances; but the fact still remains, that the instincts by which those claims are prompted are personal rather than social.

Thus, in the alliance which has been here proposed as necessary for social reorganization, Feeling, the most influential part of human nature, has not been adequately represented. An element is wanting which shall have the same relation to the moral side of our constitution, as the philosophic body has with Intellect, and the people with Activity. On this, as well as on other grounds, it is indispensable that Women be associated in the work of regeneration as soon as its tendencies and conditions can be explained to them. With the addition of this third element, the constructive movement at last assumes its true character. We may then feel confident that our intellectual and practical faculties will be kept in due subordination to universal Love. The digressions of intellect, and the subversive tendencies of our active powers will be as far as possible prevented.

Women have stood aloof from the modern movement, because of its antihistoric and destructive character. Indispensable to Positivism as the co-operation of women is, it involves one essential condition. Modern progress must rise above its present imperfect character, before women can thoroughly sympathise with it.

At present the general feeling amongst them is antipathy to the Revolution. They dislike the destructive character which the Revolution necessarily exhibited in its first phase. All their social sympathies are given to the Middle Ages. And this is not merely due, as is supposed, to the regret which they very naturally feel for the decline of chivalry, although they cannot but feel that the Middle Ages are the only period in which the feeling of reverence for women has been properly cultivated. But the real ground of their predilection is deeper and less interested. It is that, being morally the purest portion of Humanity, they venerate Catholicism, as the only system which has upheld the principle of subordinating Politics to Morals. This, I cannot doubt, is the secret cause of most of the regret with which women still regard the irrevocable decay of mediæval society.

They do not disregard the progress which modern times have made in various special directions. But our erroneous tendencies towards bringing back the old supremacy of Politics over Morality, are, in their eyes, a retrograde movement so comprehensive in its character that no partial improvements can compensate for it. True, we are able to justify this deviation provisionally, since the decay of Catholicism renders political dictatorship necessary. But women, having comparatively little to do with the practical business of life, can hardly appreciate this necessity without a more satisfactory theory of history than they at present possess. It is a complete mistake to charge women with being retrograde on account of these feelings of regret which are most honourable to them. They might retort the charge with far better reason on the revolutionists, for their blind admiration of Greek and Roman society, which they still persist in asserting to be superior to Catholic Feudalism ; a delusion, the continuance of which is principally due to our absurd system of classical education, from which women are fortunately preserved.

However this may be, the feelings of women upon these subjects are a very plain and simple demonstration of the first condition of social regeneration, which is, that Politics must again be subordinated to Morality ; and this upon a more intelligible, more comprehensive, and more permanent basis than Catholicism could supply. A system which supplied such a basis would natually involve reverence for women as one of its characteristic results. Such, then, are the terms on which women will cordially co-operate in the progressive movement. Nothing but incapacity to satisfy these terms could induce any thinkers to condemn the conception as retrograde.

It is not, then, to the Revolution itself that women feel antipathy, but to the anti-historic spirit which prevailed in its first phase. The blind abuse lavished on the Middle Ages wounds their strongest sympathies. They care little for metaphysical theories of society in which human happiness is made to consist in a continual exercise of political rights ; for political rights, however attractively presented,

will always fail to interest them. But they give their cordial sympathy to all reasonable claims of the people ; and
these claims form the real object of the revolutionary crisis.
They will wish all success to philosophers and workmen
when they see them endeavouring to transform political
disputes into social compacts, and proving that they have
greater regard for duties than for rights. If they regret
the decline of the gentle influence which they possessed in
former times, it is principally because they find it superseded by coarse and egotistic feelings, which are now no
longer counterbalanced by revolutionary enthusiasm. Instead of blaming their antipathies, we should learn from
them the urgent necessity of putting an end to the moral
and intellectual anarchy of our times ; for this it is which
gives a ground of real justice to their reproaches.

But they will sympathize with constructive tendencies; and will distinguish sound philosophy from scientific specialities.   Women will gladly associate themselves with
the Revolution as soon as its work of recon-
struction is fairly begun. Its negative phase
must not be prolonged too far. It is difficult
enough for them to understand how such a
phase could ever be necessary ; therefore they
cannot be expected to excuse its aberrations. The true
connection of the Revolution with the Middle Ages must
be fairly stated. History, when rightly interpreted, will
show them that its real object is, while laying down a
surer basis for Morality, to restore it to the old position of
superiority over Politics in which the mediæval system
first placed it. Women will feel enthusiasm for the
second phase of the Revolution, when they see republicanism in the light in which Positivism presents it, modified
by the spirit of ancient chivalry.

Then, and not till then, will the movement of social
regeneration be fairly begun. The movement can have
no great force until women give cordial support to it ; for

it is they who are the best representatives of the fundamental principle on which Positivism rests, the victory of social over selfish affections. On philosophers rests the duty of giving logical coherence to this principle, and saving it from sophistical attacks. Its practical working depends upon the proletary class, without whose aid it would almost always be evaded. But to maintain it in all its purity, as an inspiration that needs neither argument nor compulsion, is the work of women only. So constituted, the alliance of the three classes will be the foreshadowed image of the normal state to which Humanity is tending. It will be the living type of perfect human nature.

Unless the new philosophy can obtain the support of women, the attempt to substitute it for theology in the regulation of social life had better be abandoned. But if the theory stated in my first chapter be true, Positivism will have even greater influence with women than with the working classes. In the principle which animates it, in its manner of regarding and of handling the great problem of human life, it is but a systematic development of what women have always felt instinctively. To them, as to the people, it offers a noble career of social usefulness, and it holds out a sure prospect of improvement in their own personal position.

Nor is it surprising that the new philosophy should possess such qualities. They follow naturally from the reality which is one of its chief claims to acceptance ; in other words, from the exactness with which it takes account of the facts of every subject that it deals with. Strong as the prejudices of women are upon religious questions, it cannot be long before they find out that Positivism satisfies, not merely their intellectual, but their moral and social wants better than Catholicism. They will then have no further reason for clinging to the old system, of the decayed condition of which they are perfectly aware. At present they not unnaturally confound Positivism with the scientific specialities on which it is based. Scientific studies have, as they see, a hardening influence, which they cannot suppose that the new school of philosophers, who insist so strongly upon the necessity of studying science, can have escaped. Closer acquaintance with the subject will show them where their error lies. They will see that the moral danger of scientific studies arises almost entirely from want of purpose and from irrational speciality, which always alienate them from the social point of view. But for the Positivist this danger does not exist; since, however far he may carry these preliminary studies, he does so simply in order to gain a stronger grasp of social questions. His one object is to concentrate all the powers of Man upon the general advancement of the race. And so long as this object be kept in view, women's good sense will readily distinguish between the training necessary for it, and the puerilities of the learned societies. The general spirit of this work, however, makes further explanation unnecessary.

Women's position in society. Like philosophers and people, their part is not to govern, but to modify.
The social mission of Woman in the Positive system follows as a natural consequence from the qualities peculiar to her nature.

In the most essential attribute of the human race, the tendency to place social above personal feeling, she is undoubtedly superior to man. Morally, therefore, and apart from all material considerations, she merits always our loving veneration, as the purest and simplest impersonation of Humanity, who can never be adequately represented in any masculine form. But these qualities do not involve the possession of political power, which some visionaries have claimed for women, though

without their own consent. In that which is the great
object of human life, they are superior to men; but in the
various means of attaining that object they are undoubtedly
inferior. In all kinds of force, whether physical, intellectual, or practical, it is certain that Man surpasses Woman,
in accordance with a general law which prevails throughout the animal kingdom. Now practical life is necessarily
governed by force rather than by affection, because it
requires unremitting and laborious activity. If there
were nothing else to do but to love, as in the Christian
utopia of a future life in which there are no material
wants, Woman would be supreme. But life is surrounded
with difficulties, which it needs all our thoughts and
energies to avoid; therefore Man takes the command, notwithstanding his inferiority in goodness. Success in all
great efforts depends more upon energy and talent than
upon goodwill, although this last condition reacts strongly
upon the others.

Thus the three elements of our moral constitution do
not act in perfect harmony. Force is naturally supreme,
and all that women can do is to modify it by affection.
Justly conscious of their superiority in strength of feeling,
they endeavour to assert their influence in a way which is
often attributed by superficial observers to the mere love
of power. But experience always teaches them that in a
world where the simplest necessaries of life are scarce and
difficult to procure, power must belong to the strongest,
not to the most affectionate, even though the latter may
deserve it best. With all their efforts they can never do
more than modify the harshness with which men exercise
their authority. And men submit more readily to this
modifying influence, from feeling that in the highest attributes of Humanity women are their superiors. They see
that their own supremacy is due principally to the material

15

necessities of life, provision for which calls into play the self-regarding rather than the social instincts. Hence we find it the case in every phase of human society that women's life is essentially domestic, public life being confined to men. Civilization, so far from effacing this natural distinction, tends, as I shall afterwards show, to develop it, while remedying its abuses.

Thus the social position of women is in this respect very similar to that of philosophers and of the working classes. And we now see why these three elements should be united. It is their combined action which constitutes the moral or modifying force of society.

Philosophers are excluded from political power by the same fatality as women, although they are apt to think that their intellectual eminence gives them a claim to it. Were our material wants more easily satisfied, the influence of intellect would be less impeded than it is by the practical business of life. But, on this hypothesis, women would have a better claim to govern than philosophers. For the reasoning faculties would have remained almost inert had they not been needed to guide our energies; the constitution of the brain not being such as to favour their spontaneous development. Whereas the affective principle is dependent on no such external stimulus for its activity. A life of thought is a more evident disqualification for the government of the world even than a life of feeling, although the pride of philosophers is a greater obstacle to submission than the vanity of women. With all its pretensions, intellectual force is not in itself more moral than material force. Each is but an instrument; the merit depends entirely upon its right employment. The only element of our nature which is in itself moral is Love; for Love alone tends of itself towards the preponderance of social feeling over self-interest. And since even Love

cannot govern, what can be the claim of Intellect? In
practical life precedence must always depend upon superior energy. Reason, even more than Feeling, must be
restricted to the task of modifying. Philosophers therefore must be excluded from government, at least as rigidly
as women. It is in vain for intellect to attempt to command; it never can do more than modify. In fact, the
morality which it indirectly possesses is due to this impossibility of exercising compulsory power, and would be
ruined by the attainment of it, supposing it were possible.
Intellect may do much to amend the natural order of
things, provided that it does not attempt to subvert it.
What it can do is by its power of systematic arrangement
to effect the union of all the classes who are likely to exert
a beneficial influence on material power. It is with this
view that every spiritual power has availed itself of the
aid of women, as we see was the case in the Middle Ages.

Proceeding with our sociological analysis of moral force,
we shall find an equally striking resemblance between the
influence of Women and that exercised by the People.

In the first stage of progress, there is no modifying
power except what springs from Feeling: afterwards Intellect combines with it, finding itself unable to govern.
The only element now wanting is Activity; and this want,
which is indispensable, is supplied by the co-operation of
the people. The fact is, that although the people constitute the basis on which all political power rests, yet they
have as little to do directly with the administration of
power as philosophers or women.

. Power, in the strict sense of the word, power, that is,
which controls action without persuading the will, has
two perfectly distinct sources, numbers and wealth. The
force of numbers is usually considered the more material
of the two; but in reality it is the more moral. Being

created by co-operation, it involves some convergence of
ideas and feelings, and therefore it does not give such free
scope for the self-regarding instincts as the more concentrated power of wealth. But for this very reason, it is
too indirect and precarious for the ordinary purposes of
government. It can influence government morally, but
cannot take an active part in it. The same causes which
exclude philosophers and women apply in the case of the
people. Our material necessities are so urgent, that those
who have the means of providing for them will always be
the possessors of power. Now the wealthy have these
means; they hold in their hands the products of labour,
by which each generation facilitates the existence and prepares the operations of its successor. Consequently the
power of the capitalist is one of so concentrated a kind,
that numbers can very seldom resist it successfully. Even
in military nations we find the same thing; the influence
of numbers, though more direct, affects only the mode of
acquiring wealth, not its tenure. But in industrial states,
where wealth is acquired by other ways than violence, the
law is evident. And with the advance of civilization it
will operate not less, but more strongly. Capital is ever
on the increase, and consequently is ever creating means
of subsistence for those who possess nothing. In this sense,
but in no other, the cynical maxim of Antiquity, *Paucis
nascitur humanum genus*, will always bear a true meaning.
The few provide subsistence for the many. We come back,
then, to the conclusion of the last chapter; that the working classes are not destined for political power, but that they
tend to become a most important source of moral power.
The moral value of their influence is even more indirect
than that of philosophers, and depends even more in their
case upon subordination politically. In the few cases where
government passes for a time into the hands of the masses,

wealth in its turn assumes a sort of moral influence foreign to its nature. It moderates the violence with which government is apt to be administered in such cases. The high intellectual and moral qualities belonging to the working classes are, as we have seen, in great part due to their social position. They would be seriously impaired if the political authority that belongs to wealth were habitually transferred to numbers.

Such, in outline, is the Positive theory of Moral Force. By it the despotism of material force may be in part controlled. It rests upon the union of the three elements in society who are excluded from the sphere of politics strictly so called. *The united action of philosophers, women, and proletaries constitutes Moral Force.* In their combined action lies our principal hope of solving, so far as it can be solved, the great problem of man's nature, the successful struggle of Social Feeling against Self-love. Each of the three elements supplies a quality indispensable to the task. Without women this controlling power would be deficient in purity and spontaneous impulse; without philosophers, in wisdom and coherence; without the people, in energy and activity. The philosophic element, although neither the most direct nor the most efficient, is yet the distinctive feature of this power, because its function is to organize its constitution and direct its operations in accordance with the true laws of social life. As being the systematic organ of the spiritual power it has become identified with it in name. This, however, may lead to an erroneous conception. The moral aspect of the spiritual power is more important than the intellectual. While retaining the name as an historical tradition of real value, Positivists attach a somewhat different meaning to it. It originated in a time when theories of society were unknown, and when Intellect was considered as the central principle of human nature.

Spiritual power, as interpreted by Positivism, begins
with the influence of women in the family; it is afterwards moulded into a system by thinkers, while the people
are the guarantees for its political efficiency. Although
it is the intellectual class that institutes the union, yet its
own part in it, as it should never forget, is less direct than
that of women, less practical than that of the people.
The thinker is socially powerless except so far as he is
supported by feminine sympathy and popular energy.

Thus the necessity of associating women in the movement of social regeneration creates no obstacle whatever to
the philosophy by which that movement is to be directed.
On the contrary, it aids its progress, by showing the true
character of the moral force which is destined to control
all the other forces of man. It involves as perfect an
inauguration of the normal state as our times of transition
admit. For the chief characteristic of that state will be a
more complete and more harmonious union of the same
three classes to whom we are now looking for the first
impulse of reform. Already we can see how perfectly
adapted to the constitution of man this final condition of
Humanity will be. Feeling, Reason, Activity, whether
viewed separately or in combination, correspond exactly to
the three elements of the regenerative movement, Women,
Philosophers, and People.

Verification of this theory may be found more or less
distinctly in every period of history. Each of the three
classes referred to have always borne out the biological
law that the life of relation or animal life, is subordinated
to the life of nutrition. Still more striking is the application to this case of another general principle, namely,
that Progress is the development of Order; a principle
which, as I showed in the second chapter, connects every
dynamical question in Sociology with the corresponding

statical conception. For with the growth of society, the modifying influence of moral force is always increasing, both by larger scope being given to each of its three elements specially, and also by the more perfect consolidation of their union. Robertson has made an important remark on the gradual improvement in the condition of women, which is but a particular case of this sociological law. The general principle on which progress in all three classes depends, is the biological law, that the preponderance of vegetable life over animal life diminishes, as the organism is higher in the scale and is more perfectly developed.

During the various phases of ancient Polytheism, the controlling power consisted simply of the moral influence exerted by women in the Family. In public life the influence of thinkers had not made itself independent of the governmental authority, of which it was sometimes the source, sometimes the instrument. Mediæval Catholicism went a step further, and took the first step in systematizing moral force. It created an independent spiritual authority to which political governments were subordinated, and this authority was always supported by women. But the complete organization of moral force was reserved for modern times. It is only recently that the working classes have begun to interfere actively in social questions; and, as I have shown in the preceding chapter, it is from their co-operation that the new spiritual power will derive its practical efficiency. Limited originally to the sphere of Feeling, and subsequently extended to the intellectual sphere, it henceforward embraces the sphere of Activity; and this without losing its spiritual character, since the influences of which it consists are entirely distinct from the domain of practical politics. Each of its three elements persuades, advises, judges; but except in isolated cases, never commands, The social mission of Positivism is to regulate and combine their spontaneous action, by directing each to the objects for which it is best adapted.

And this mission, in spite of strong prejudices to the contrary, it will be found well calculated to fulfil. I have already shown its adaptation to the case of the people and of the philosophic body, whether regarded separately or in combination : I have now to show that it is equally adapted to the case of women.

In proof of this I have but to refer to the principle on which, as stated in the first chapter, the whole system of Positivism is based ; the preponderance of affection in our nature. Such a principle is of itself an appeal to women to associate themselves with the system, as one of its essential elements. In Catholicism their co-operation, though valuable, was not of primary importance, because Catholicism claimed a divine origin independent of their assistance. But to Positivism they are indispensable, as being the purest and simplest embodiment of its fundamental principle. It is not merely in the Family that their influence will be required. Their duty will often be to call philosophers and people back to that unity of purpose which originated in the first place with themselves, and which each of the other elements is often disposed to violate.

All true philosophers will no doubt accept and be profoundly influenced by the conviction, that in all subjects of thought the social point of view should be logically and scientifically preponderant. They will consequently admit the truth that the Heart takes precedence of the Understanding. Still they require some more direct incentive to universal Love than these convictions can supply. Knowing, as they do, how slight is the practical result of purely intellectual considerations, they will welcome so precious an incentive, were it only in the interest of their own mission. I recognised its necessity myself, when I wrote on the 11th of March, 1846, to her who, in spite of death, will always remain my constant companion : " I was incomplete as a philosopher, until the experience of deep and pure passion had given me fuller insight into the emotional side of human nature." Strong affection exercises a marvellous influence upon mental effort. It elevates the intellect at once to the only point of view which is really universal. Doubtless, the method of pure science leads up to it also ; but only by a long and toilsome process, which exhausts the powers of thought, and leaves little energy for following out the new results to which this great principle gives rise. The stimulation of affection under feminine influence is necessary, therefore, for the acceptance of Positivism, not merely in those classes for whom a long preliminary course of scientific study could be impossible. It is equally necessary for the systematic teachers of Positivism, in whom it checks the tendency, which is encouraged by habits of abstract speculation, to deviate into useless digressions ; these being always easier to prosecute than researches of real value.

Under this aspect the new spiritual system is obviously superior to the old. By the institution of celibacy, which was indispensable to Catholicism, its priests were entirely removed from the beneficial influence exercised by women. Only those could profit from it who did not belong to the ecclesiastical body ; the members of that body, as Ariosto has remarked in his vigorous satire, were excluded. Nor could the evil be remedied, except in very rare cases, by irregular attachment, which inevitably corrupted the priest's character by involving the necessity of perpetual hypocrisy.

Superiority of the new spiritual power to the old. Self-regarding tendencies of Catholic doctrine.

And when we look at the difference of the spirit by
which the two systems are pervaded, we shall find still
more striking evidence that the new system offers a far
larger sphere of moral influence to women than the old.

Both are based upon the principle of affection; but in
Positivism the affection inculcated is social, in Catholicism
it is essentially personal. The object of Catholic devotion
is one of such stupendous magnitude, that feelings which
are unconnected with it are in danger of being crushed.
The priesthood, it is true, wise interpreters in this respect
of a general instinct, brought all the more important social
obligations within the compass of religion, and held them
out as necessary for salvation. Indirectly, the nobler feelings were thus called into action; but at the same time
they were rendered far less spontaneous and pure. There
could be no perfectly disinterested affection under a system
which promised eternal rewards for all acts of self-denial.
For it was impossible, and indeed it would have been
thought sinful, to keep the future out of sight; and thus
all spontaneous generosity was unavoidably tainted by
self-interest. Catholicism gave rise to an ignoble theory
of morals which became very mischievous when it was
adopted by the metaphysicians; because, while retaining
the vicious principle, they swept away the checks by which
the priesthood had controlled it. But even when we look
at the purest form in which the love of God was exhibited,
we cannot call it a social feeling, except in so far as the
same object of worship was held out simultaneously to all.
Intrinsically, it is anti-social, since, when attained in absolute perfection, it implies the entire sacrifice of all other
love. And in the best representatives of Christian thought
and feeling, this tendency is very apparent. No one has
portrayed the Catholic ideal with such sublimity and
pathos as the author of the Imitation, a work which so

well deserved the beautiful translation of Corneille. And yet, reading it as I do daily, I cannot help remarking how grievously the natural nobleness of his heart was impaired by the Catholic system, although in spite of all obstacles he rises at times to the purest ardour. Certainly those of our feelings which are purely unselfish must be far stronger and more spontaneous than has ever yet been supposed, since even the oppressive discipline of twelve centuries could not prevent their growth.

Positivism, from the fact of its conformity with the constitution of our nature, is the only system calculated to develop, both in public and in private life, those high attributes of Humanity which, for want of adequate systematic culture, are still in their rudimentary stage. Catholicism, while appealing to the Heart, crushed Intellect, and Intellect naturally struggled to throw off the yoke. Positivism, on the contrary, brings Reason into complete harmony with Feeling, without impairing the activity of either.

The spirit of Positivism, on the contrary, is essentially social. The Heart and the Intellect mutually strengthen each other.

Scientific study of the relation which each individual bears to the whole race is a continual stimulus to social sympathy. Without a theory of society, it is impossible to keep this relation distinctly and constantly in view. It is only noticed in a few exceptional cases, and unconnected impressions are soon effaced from the memory. But the Positivist teacher, taking the social point of view invariably, will make this notion far more familiar to us than it has ever been before. He will show us the impossibility of understanding any individual or society apart from the whole life of the race. Nothing but the bewilderment caused by theological and metaphysical doctrines can account for the shallow explanations of human affairs given by our teachers, attributing as they do to Man what is really due to Humanity. But with the sounder theory that we now possess, we can see the truth as it really stands. We have but to look each of us at our own life under its physical, intellectual, or moral aspects, to recognize what it is that we owe to the combined action of our predecessors and contemporaries. The man who dares to think himself independent of others, either in feelings, thoughts, or actions, cannot even put the blasphemous conception into words without immediate self-contradiction, since the very language he uses is not his own. The profoundest thinker cannot by himself form the simplest language ; it requires the co-operation of a community for several generations. Without further illustration, the tendency of Positive doctrine is evident. It appeals systematically to our social instincts, by constantly impressing upon us that only the Whole is real ; that the Parts exist only in abstraction.

But independently of the beneficial influence which, in this final state of Humanity, the mind will exercise upon the heart, the direct culture of the heart itself will be more pure and more vigorous than under any former system. It offers us the only means of disengaging our benevolent affections from all calculations of self-interest. As far as the imperfection of man's nature admits, these affections will gradually become supreme, since they give deeper satisfaction than all others, and are capable of fuller development. Setting the rewards and punishments of theology aside, we shall attain at last to that which is the real happiness of man, pure and disinterested love. This is truly the Sovereign Good, sought for so long by former systems of philosophy in vain. That it surpasses all other good one fact will show, known to the tender-hearted from personal experience ; that it is even better to love than to be loved. Overstrained as this may seem to many, it is

yet in harmony with a general truth, that our nature is in
a healthier state when active than when passive.   In the
happiness of being loved, there is always some tinge of
self-love ; it is impossible not to feel pride in the love of
one whom we prefer to all others.   Since, then, loving
gives purer satisfaction than being loved, the superiority
of perfectly disinterested affection is at once demonstrated.
It is the fundamental defect of our nature, that intrinsically these affections are far weaker than the selfish propensities connected with the preservation of our own
existence.   But when they have once been aroused, even
though the original stimulus may have been personal,
they have greater capacity of growth, owing to the peculiar charm inherent in them.   Besides, in the exercise of
these feelings, all of us can co-operate with and encourage
one another, whereas the reverse is the case with the selfish
instincts.   There is, therefore, nothing unreasonable in
supposing that Positivism, by regulating and combining
these natural tendencies, may rouse our sympathetic instincts to a condition of permanent activity hitherto unknown.   When the heart is no longer crushed by theological dogmas, or hardened by metaphysical theories, we
soon discover that real happiness, whether public or private, consists in the highest possible development of the
social instincts.   Self-love comes to be regarded as an
incurable infirmity, which is to be yielded to only so far
as is absolutely necessary.   Here lies the universal adapta-
bility of Positivism to every type of character and to all
circumstances.   In the humblest relations of life, as in
the highest, regenerate Humanity will apply the obvious
truth, It is better to give than to receive.

The Heart thus aroused will in its turn react beneficially upon the Intellect ; and it is especially from women
that this reaction will proceed.   I have spoken of it so

fully before, that I need not now describe it further. It is in Feeling that I find the basis on which the whole structure of Positivism, intellectually as well as morally considered, rests. The only remark I have now to add is, that by following out this principle, philosophical difficulties of the most formidable kind are at once surmounted. From moral considerations, the intellect may be readily induced to submit to scientific restrictions, the propriety of which would remain for a long time matter of debate, were philosophical discussions the only means of indicating it. Attempt, for instance, to convince a pure mathematician, however conscientious and talented, that Sociology is both logically and scientifically superior to all other studies. He would not readily admit this; and severe exertion of the inductive and deductive faculties can alone convince him of it. But by the aid of Feeling, an artisan or a woman can, without education, readily grasp this great encyclopædic principle, and apply it practically to the common affairs of life. But for this, the larger conceptions of philosophy would have but a limited range, and very few would be capable of the course of study which is yet so important on social grounds for all. Comprehensiveness of mind is no doubt favourable to sympathy, but is itself more actively stimulated by it. When the Positivist method of education is accepted, moral excellence will be very generally regarded as a guarantee of real intellectual capacity. The revolutionist leaders of the Convention showed their sense of this connection by allowing, as they did sometimes, republican ardour to outweigh scientific attainment. Of course, so long as men remain without a systematic theory of morals, such policy would be likely to fail of its object, and indeed would become positively mischievous. But the reproach is usually that it was a retrograde policy, a reproach far more applicable to the present system, in which the standard of fitness for any office is regulated exclusively by intellectual considerations, the heart being altogether disregarded. Historically we can explain this practice by the fact that the religious faith in which our moral nature has hitherto been trained has been of a most oppressive character. Ever since the Middle Ages, the intellect and the heart have been unavoidably at issue. Positivism is the only system which can put an end to their antagonism, because, as I have before explained, while subordinating Reason to Feeling, it does so in such a way as not to impair the development of either. With its present untenable claims to supremacy, intellect is in reality the principal source of social discord. Until it abdicates in favour of the Heart, it can never be of real service in reconstruction. But its abdication will be useless, unless it is entirely voluntary. Now this is precisely the result which Positivism attains, because it takes up the very ground on which the claims of intellect are defended, namely, scientific demonstration, a ground which the defenders of intellect cannot repudiate without suspicion at once attaching to their motives. But theological or metaphysical remedies can only exasperate the disease. By oppressing the intellect they provoke it to fresh insurrection against the heart.

For all these reasons, women, who are better judges of moral questions than ourselves, will admit that Positivism, incontestably superior as it is to other systems intellectually, surpasses them yet more in dealing with the affections. Their only objection arises from confounding Positive Philosophy itself with its preliminary course of scientific study.

Intellectual and moral affinities of women with Positivism.

Women's minds no doubt are less capable than ours of generalizing very widely, or of carrying on long processes of deduction. They are, that is, less capable than men of

abstract intellectual exertion.   On the other hand, they are
generally more alive to that combination of reality with
utility which is one of the characteristics of Positive speculation.   In this respect they have much in common intellectually with the working classes; and fortunately they
have also the same advantage of being untrammelled by the
present absurd system of education.   Nor is their position
far removed from what it should be normally; being less
engaged than men in the business of life, their contempla-
tive faculties are called into activity more easily.   Their
minds are neither preoccupied nor indifferent; the most
favourable condition for the reception of philosophical truth.
They have far more affinity intellectually with philosophers who truly deserve the name, than we find in the
scientific men of the present day.   Comprehensiveness of
thought they consider as important as positivity, whereas
our savants care for nothing but the latter quality, and
even that they understand imperfectly.   Molière's remarkable expression, *des clartés de tout*, which I applied
in the last chapter to popular education, was used by him
in reference to women.   Accordingly we find that women
took a vivid interest in the very first attempt made to
systematize Positive speculation ; the Cartesian philosophy.   No more striking proof could be given of their
philosophical affinities ; and the more so that in the Cartesian system moral and social speculations were necessarily
excluded.   Surely, then, we may expect them to receive
Positivism far more favourably, a system of which the
principal subject of speculation is the moral problem in
which both sexes are alike interested.

Women, therefore, may, like the people, be counted
among the future supporters of the new philosophy.
Without their combined aid it could never hope to sur-
mount the strong repugnance to it which is felt by our

cultivated classes, especially in France, where the question of its success has first to be decided.

But when women have sufficient acquaint- *Catholicism purified love, but did not directly strengthen it.* ance with Positivism, to see its superiority to Catholicism in questions of feeling, they will support it from moral sympathy even more than from intellectual adhesion. It will be the heart even more than the mind which will incline them to the only system of philosophy which has fully recognised the preponderance of Feeling. They cannot fail to be drawn towards a system which regards women as the embodiment of this principle; the unity of human nature, of which this principle is the basis, being thus entrusted to their special charge. The only reason of their regret for the past, is that the present fails to satisfy their noblest social instincts. Not that Catholicism ever really satisfied them; indeed in its general character it is even less adapted to women than to men, since the dominant quality of woman's nature is in direct contradiction with it. Christianity, notwithstanding its claims to moral perfection, has always confounded the quality of tenderness with that of purity. And it is true that love cannot be deep unless it is also pure. But Catholicism, although it purified love from the animal propensities which had been stimulated by Polytheism, did nothing otherwise to strengthen it. It has given us indeed too many instances of purity, pushed to the extent of fanaticism, without tenderness. And this result is especially common now, because the austerity of the Christian spirit is not corrected, as it used to be, by the inspiring influences of Chivalry. Polytheism, deficient as it was in purity, was really far more conducive than Christianity, to tenderness. Love of God, the supreme affection round which Catholicism endeavoured to concentrate all other feelings, was essentially

16

a self-regarding principle, and as such conflicted with woman's noblest instincts. Not only did it encourage monastic isolation, but if developed to the full extent, it became inconsistent with love for our fellow men. It was impiety for the knight to love. his Lady better than his God; and thus the best feelings of his nature were repressed by his religious faith. Women, therefore, are not really interested in perpetuating the old system; and the very instincts by which their nature is characterised, will soon incline them to abandon it. They have only been waiting until social life should assume a less material character; so that morality, for the preservation of which they justly consider themselves responsible, may not be compromised. And on this head Positivism satisfies their heart no less than their understanding with all the guarantees that they can require. Based as it is upon accurate knowledge of our nature, it can combine the simple affectionate spirit of Polytheism with the exquisite purity of Catholicism, without fear of taint from the subversive sophisms engendered by the spiritual anarchy of our times. Not however that purity is to be placed on the same level with tenderness. Tenderness is the more essential of the two qualities, because more closely connected with the grand object of all human effort, the elevation of Social Feeling over Self-love. In a woman without tenderness there is something even more monstrous, than in a man without courage. Whatever her talents and even her energy may be, they will in most cases prove mischievous both to herself and to others, unless indeed they should be nullified by the restraint of theological discipline. If she has force of character it will be wasted in a struggle against all legitimate authority; while her mental power will be employed only in destructive sophisms. Too many cases of this kind present themselves in the social anarchy of the present time.

Such is the Positivist theory on the subject of Women. It marks out for them a noble field of social usefulness. It extends the scope of their influence to public as well as private life, and yet in a way thoroughly in harmony with their nature. Without leaving the family, they will participate in the controlling power exercised by philosophers and workmen, seeking even in their own domestic sphere rather to modify than to govern. In a word, as I shall show more fully in the last chapter of this introductory work, Woman is the spontaneous priestess of Humanity. She personifies in the purest form the principle of Love upon which the unity of our nature depends; and the culture of that principle in others is her special function.

All classes, therefore, must be brought under women's influence; for all require to be reminded constantly of the great truth that Reason and Activity are subordinate to Feeling. Of their influence upon philosophers I have spoken. If they are men worthy of their mission, they will be conscious of the tendency which their life has to harden them and lead them into useless speculation ; and they will feel the need of renewing the ardour of their social sympathy at its native source. Feeling, when it is pure and deep, corrects its own errors, because they clash with the good to which it is ever tending. But erroneous use of the intellectual or practical faculties, cannot be even recognised, much less corrected, without the aid of Affection, which is the only part of our nature that suffers directly from such errors. Therefore whenever either the philosopher or the people deviate from duty, it will be the part of women to remonstrate with them gently, and recall them to the true social principles which are entrusted to their special charge.

Women's influence over the working classes and their teachers.

With the working classes, the special danger to be contended against is their tendency to abuse their strength, and to resort to force for the attainment of their objects, instead of persuasion. But this danger is after all less than that of the misuse of intellectual power to which philosophers are so liable. Thinkers who try to make reasoning do the work of feeling can very seldom be convinced of their error. Popular excitement, on the contrary, has often yielded to feminine influence, exerted though it has been hitherto without any systematic guidance. The difference is no doubt partly owing to the fact that there are now few or none who deserve the name of philosophers. For we cannot give that name to the superficial sophists and rhetoricians of our time, whether psychologists or ideologists, men wholly incapable of deep thought on any subject. Independently of this, however, the difference is explained by the character of the two classes. Women will always find it harder to deal with intellectual pride than with popular violence. Appeals to social feeling are their only weapons; and the social feelings of the workman are stronger than those of the philosopher. Sophistry is far more formidable to them than passion. In fact, were it not that the working classes are even now so amenable to female influence, society would be in extreme danger from the disorder caused by intellectual anarchy. There are many sophisms which maintain themselves in spite of scientific refutation, and which would be destructive of all order, were it not for our moral instincts. Of this the Communists offer a striking example, in avoiding, with that admirable inconsistency to which I have already called attention, the extension of their principle to the Family. Surrounded by the wildest theories, such as, if they were put in practice, would utterly destroy or paralyse society, we see large numbers of working men showing in their daily life a degree of affection and respect for women, which is un-equalled by any other class. It is well to reflect on facts like these, not only because they lead us to judge the Communist school with more justice, but because, occurring as they do in the midst of social anarchy, they show what powerful agencies for good will be at our disposal in more settled times. Certainly they cannot be attributed to theological teaching, which has rather had the effect of strengthening the errors which it attacks by the absurdity of its refutations. They are simply the result of the influence which women have spontaneously exercised on the nobler feelings of the people. In Protestant countries, where their influence is less, the mischievous effects of Communistic theories have been far greater. We owe it to women that the Family has been so little injured by the retrograde spirit of those republican reformers, whose ideal of modern society is to absorb the Family into the State, as was done by a few small tribes in ancient Greece.

The readiness shown by women in applying practical remedies to erroneous theories of morality is shown in other cases where the attractiveness of the error would seem irresistible to the coarser nature of men. The evils consequent on divorce, which has been authorized in Germany for three centuries, have been much lessened by women's instinctive repugnance to it. The same may be said of recent attacks upon marriage, which are still more serious, because the anarchy of modern life revives all the extravagances of the metaphysical spirit in ancient times. In no one case has a scheme of society hostile to marriage met with any real favour from women, plausible as many of them seemed. Unable in their ignorance of social science to see the fallacy of such schemes themselves, our revolutionary writers cannot conceive that women will not be convinced by them. But happily women, like the people, judge in these matters by the heart rather than by the head. In the absence of any guiding principle to direct the understanding and prevent the deviations to which it is always exposed, the heart is a far safer guide.

There is no need at present of pursuing these remarks farther. It is abundantly clear that women are in every respect adapted for rectifying the moral deviations to which every element in the social organism is liable. And if we already feel the value of their influence, springing as it does from the unaided inspirations of the heart, we may be sure it will become far more consolidated and will be far more widely felt, when it rests on the basis of a sound philosophical system, capable of refuting sophisms and exposing fallacies from which their unassisted instinct is insufficient to preserve us.

Their social influence in the *salon*. Thus the part to be played by women in public life is not merely passive. Not only will they give their sanction individually and collectively to the verdicts of public opinion as formed by philosophers and by the people; but they will themselves interfere actively in moral questions. It will be their part to maintain the primary principle of Positivism, which originated with themselves, and of which they will always be the most natural representatives.

But how, it may be asked, can this be reconciled with my previous remark that women's life should still be essentially domestic?

For the ancients, and for the greater part of the human race at the present time, it would be irreconcileable. But in Western Europe the solution has long ago been found. From the time when women acquired, as they did in the Middle Ages, a fair measure of domestic freedom, opportunities for social intercourse arose, which combined most

happily the advantages of private and of public life, and
in these women presided. The practice afterwards extended, especially in France, and these meetings became
the laboratories of public opinion. It seems now as if they
had died out, or had lost their character. The intellectual
and moral anarchy of our times is most unfavourable to
free interchange of thoughts and feelings. But a custom
so social, and which did such good service in the philosophical movement preceding the Revolution, is assuredly
not destined to perish. In the more perfect social state to
which we are tending, it will be developed more fully than
ever, when men's minds and hearts have accepted the
rallying-point offered by the new philosophy.

This is, then, the mode in which women can with propriety participate in public life. Here all classes will
recognize their authority as paramount. Under the new
system these meetings will entirely lose their old aristocratic character, which is now simply obstructive. The
Positivist salon will complete the series of social meetings,
in which the three elements of the spiritual power will be
able to act in concert. First, there is the religious assemblage in the Temple of Humanity. Here the philosopher
will naturally preside, the other two classes taking only a
secondary part. In the Club again it is the people who
will take the active part; women and philosophers would
support them by their presence, but without joining in the
debate. Lastly, women in their salons will promote active
and friendly intercourse between all three classes; and
here all who may be qualified to take a leading part will
find their influence cordially accepted. Gently and without effort a moral control will thus be established, by which
acts of violence or folly may be checked in their source.
Kind advice, given indirectly but earnestly, will often save
the philosopher from being blinded by ambition, or from

deviating, through intellectual pride, into useless digressions.   Working men at these meetings will learn to
repress the spirit of violence or envy that frequently arises
in them, recognizing the sacredness of the care thus manifested for their interests.   And the great and the wealthy
will be taught from the manner in which praise and blame
is given by those whose opinion is most valued, that the
only justifiable use of power or talent is to devote it to the
service of the weak.

But the Fami-   But, however important the public duties
ly is their prin-
cipal sphere of   that women will ultimately be called upon to
action.   perform, the Family is after all their highest
and most distinctive sphere of work.   It was in allusion
to their domestic influence that I spoke of them as the
originators of spiritual power.   Now the Family, although
it is the basis of all human society, has never been satis-
factorily defended by any received system of society.   All
the corrosive power of metaphysical analysis has been
employed upon it; and of many of the sophisms put forward no rational refutation has been given.   On the other
hand, the protection of the theologians is no less injurious.
For they still persist in connecting the institutions of the
Family with their obsolete dogmas, which, however useful
they may have been formerly, are now simply dangerous.
From the close of the Middle Ages the priesthood has
been powerless, as the licentious songs of the troubadours
prove, to protect the sanctity of marriage against the
shallow but mischievous attacks which even then were
made against it.   And afterwards, when these false principles became more generally prevalent, and even royal
courts disgraced themselves by giving public approval to
them, the weakness of the priests became still more manifest.   Thus nothing can be more monstrous than these
ignorant assertions that theological doctrines have been

the safeguard of the Family. They have done nothing to preserve it from the most subversive attacks, under which it must have succumbed, but for the better instincts of society, especially of the female portion of it. With the exception of a foolish fiction about the origin of Woman, theology has put forward no systematic defence of marriage; and as soon as theological authority itself fell into discredit, the feeble sanction which it gave to domestic morality became utterly powerless against sophistical attacks. But now that the Family can be shown on Positive principles to rest on scientific laws of human nature or of society, the danger of metaphysical controversy and theological feebleness is past. These principles will be discussed systematically in the second volume of the larger Treatise to which this work is the Introduction. But the few remarks to which I must at present limit myself, will, I hope, at least satisfy the reader as to the capability of Positivism to re-establish morality upon a firm basis.

According to the lower views of the subject, such as those coarsely expressed by the great hero of reaction, Napoleon, procreation and maternity are the only social functions of Woman. Indeed many theorists object even to her rearing her children, and think it preferable to leave them to the abstract benevolence of the State. But in the Positivist theory of marriage, the principal function of Woman is one quite unconnected with procreation. It is a function dependent on the highest attributes of our nature. *Woman's mission as a wife. Conjugal love an education for universal sympathy.*

Vast as is the moral importance of maternity, yet the position of wife has always been considered even more characteristic of woman's nature; as shown by the fact that the words woman and wife are in many languages synonymous. Marriage is not always followed by children; and besides this, a bad wife is very seldom indeed a good mother. The first aspect then, under which Positivism considers Woman, is simply as the companion of Man, irrespective of her maternal duties.

Viewed thus, Marriage is the most elementary and yet the most perfect mode of social life. It is the only association in which entire identity of interests is possible. In this union, to the moral completeness of which the language of all civilised nations bears testimony, the noblest aim of human life is realised, as far as it ever can be. For the object of human existence, as shown in the second chapter, is progress of every kind; progress in morality, that is to say in the subjection of Self-interest to Social Feeling, holding the first rank. Now this unquestionable principle leads us by a very sure and direct path to the true theory of marriage.

Different as the two sexes are by nature, and increased as that difference is by the diversity which happily exists in their social position, each is consequently necessary to the moral development of the other. In practical energy and in the mental capacity which usually accompanies it, Man is evidently superior to Woman. Woman's strength, on the other hand, lies in Feeling. She excels Man in love, as Man excels her in force. It is impossible to conceive of a closer union than that which binds these two beings to the mutual service and perfection of each other, saving them from all danger of rivalry. The voluntary character too of this union gives it a still further charm, when the choice has been on both sides a happy one. In the Positive theory, then, of marriage, its principal object is considered to be that of completing and confirming the education of the heart by calling out the purest and strongest of human sympathies.

It is true that sexual instinct, which, in man's case at all

events, was the origin of conjugal attachment, is a feeling
purely selfish. It is also true that its absence would in
the majority of cases, diminish the energy of affection.
But woman, with her more loving heart, has usually far
less need of this coarse stimulus than man. The influence
of her purity reacts on man, and ennobles his affection.
And affection is in itself so sweet, that when once it has
been aroused by whatever agency, its own charm is sufficient to maintain it in activity. When this is the case,
conjugal union becomes a perfect ideal of friendship; yet
still more beautiful than friendship, because each possesses
and is possessed by the other. For perfect friendship,
difference of sex is essential, as excluding the possibility
of rivalry. No other voluntary tie can admit of such full
and unrestrained confidence. It is the source of the most
unalloyed happiness that man can enjoy; for there can
be no greater happiness than to live for another.

But independently of the intrinsic value of this sacred
union, we have to consider its importance from the social
point of view. It is the first stage in our progress towards that which is the final object of moral education,
namely, universal Love. Many writers of the so-called
socialist school, look upon conjugal love and universal
benevolence, the two extreme terms in the scale of affections, as opposed to each other. In the second chapter, I
pointed out the falseness and danger of this view. The
man who is incapable of deep affection for one whom he
has chosen as his partner in the most intimate relations of
life, can hardly expect to be believed when he professes
devotion to a mass of human beings of whom he knows
nothing. The heart cannot throw off its original selfishness, without the aid of some complete and enduring
affection. And conjugal love, concentrated as it is upon
one object exclusively, is more enduring and complete

than any other. From personal experience of strong love
we rise by degrees to sincere affection for all mankind;
although, as the scope of feeling widens, its energy must
decrease. The connection of these two states of feeling is
instinctively recognised by all; and it is clearly indicated
by the Positive theory of human nature, which has now
placed it beyond the reach of metaphysical attacks. When
the moral empire of Woman has been more firmly established by the diffusion of Positivist principles, men will
see that the common practice of looking to the private life
of a statesman as the best guarantee of his public conduct
had deep wisdom in it. One of the strongest symptoms
of the general laxity of morals to which mental anarchy
has brought us, is that disgraceful law passed in France
thirty years ago, and not yet repealed; the avowed object
of which was to surround men's lives with a "wall" of
privacy; a law introduced by psychologist politicians who
no doubt needed such a wall.*

Conditions of   The purpose of marriage once clearly under-
marriage. In-   stood, it becomes easy to define its conditions.
dissoluble mo-
nogamy.   The intervention of society is necessary; but
its only object is to confirm and to develop the order of
things which exists naturally.

It is essential in the first place to the high purposes for
which marriage has been instituted, that the union shall
be both exclusive and indissoluble. So essential indeed
are both conditions, that we frequently find them even
when the connection is illegal. That any one should have
ventured to propound the doctrine that human happiness
is to be secured by levity and inconstancy in love, is a
fact which nothing but the utter deficiency of social and
moral principles can explain. Love cannot be deep unless

---

* This law was introduced by Royer-Collard. It forbids discussion of the
private affairs of public men.

it remains constant to a fixed object. The very possibility of change is a temptation to it. So differently constituted as man and woman are, is our short life too much for perfect knowledge and love of one another? Yet the versatility to which most human affection is liable makes the intervention of society necessary. Without some check upon indecision and caprice, life might degenerate into a miserable series of experiments, each ending in failure and degradation. Sexual love may become a powerful engine for good: but only on the condition of placing it under rigorous and permanent discipline. Those who doubt the necessity for this, have only to cast a glance beyond Western Europe at the countries where no such discipline has been established. It has been said that the adoption or rejection of polygamy is a simple question of climate. But for this hypothesis there is no ground whatever. It is as contrary to common observation as to philosophic theory. Marriage, like every other human institution, has always been improving. Beginning in all countries with unrestricted polygamy, it tends in all to the purest monogamy. Tracing back the history of Northern Europe, we find polygamy there as well as in the South; and Southern nations, like Northern, adopt polygamy as their social life advances. We see the tendency to it in those parts of the East which come into contact with Western civilization.

Monogamy, then, is one of the most precious gifts which the Middle Ages have bequeathed to Western Europe. The striking superiority of social life in the West is probably due to it more than to any other cause. Protestant countries have seriously impaired its value by their laws of divorce. But this aberration will hardly be permanent. It is alien to the purer feelings of women and of the people, and the mischief done by it is limited to the privi-

leged classes. France is now threatened with a revival of
the metaphysical delusions of the Revolution, and it is
feared by some that the disastrous example of Germany in
this respect will be imitated. But all such tendencies, being
utterly inconsistent with the habits of modern life, will
soon be checked by the sounder philosophical principles
which have now arisen. The mode of resistance to these
errors which Positivism adopts will render the struggle
most useful in hastening the adoption of the true theory
of marriage. The spirit of Positivism being always relative, concessions may be made to meet exceptional cases,
without weakening or contradicting the principle; whereas
the absolute character of theological doctrine was incompatible with concession. The rules of morality should be
general and comprehensive; but in their practical application exceptions have often to be made. By no philosophy but the Positive can these two conditions be reconciled.

Perpetual widowhood. To the spirit of anarchy, however, Positivism
yields nothing. The unity essential to mar-
riage, it renders more complete than ever. It develops
the principle of monogamy, by inculcating, not as a legal
institution, but as a moral duty, the perpetuity of widowhood. Affection so firmly concentrated has always been
regarded with respect, even on man's side. But hitherto
no religion has had sufficient purity or influence to secure
its adoption. Positivism, however, from the completeness of
its synthesis, and from the fact that its rules are invariably
based on the laws of nature, will gain such influence, and
will find little difficulty in inducing all natures of delicate
feeling to accept this additional obligation. It follows
from the very principle which to the Positivist is the object of all marriage, the raising and purifying of the heart.
Unity of the tie which is already recognised as necessary
in life, is not less so in death. Constancy in widowhood

was once common among women; and if its moral beauty is less appreciated now, it is because all systematic morality has been forgotten. But it is none the less, as careful study of human nature will show, a most precious source of moral good, and one which is not beyond the reach of nobler natures, even in their youth. Voluntary widowhood, while it offers all the advantages which chastity can confer on the intellectual and physical as well as on the moral nature, is yet free from the moral dangers of celibacy. Constant adoration of one whom Death has implanted more visibly and deeply on the memory, leads all high natures, and especially philosophers, to give themselves more unreservedly to the service of Humanity; and thus their public life is animated by the ennobling influence of their innermost feelings. Alike from a sense of their own truest happiness and from devotion to public duty, they will be led to this result.

Deep as is the satisfaction in this prolongation of the sacredness of marriage, it may be carried by those who recognise its value yet further. As the death of one did not destroy the bond, so neither should the death of both. Let, then, those whom death could not divide be laid in the same grave together. A promise of this solemn act of perpetuation might be given beforehand, when the organs of public opinion judged it merited. A man would find a new motive for public exertion, if it were felt to be a pledge that the memory of her whom he loved should be for ever coupled with his own. We have a few instances where this union of memories has taken place spontaneously, as in the case of Laura and Petrarch, and of Dante and Beatrice. Yet these instances are so exceptional, that they hardly help us to realise the full value of the institution proposed. There is no reason for limiting it to cases of **extraordinary** genius. In the more healthy state of society to which we are tending, where private and public life will be far more closely connected than they have been hitherto, this recompense of service may be given to all who have deserved it, by those who have come within their circle of influence.

Such, then, are the consolations which Positivist sympathy can give. They leave no cause to regret the visionary hopes held out by Christianity, hopes which now are as enfeebling to the heart as to the intellect. Here, as in all other respects, the moral superiority of Positivism is shown, for the comfort which it gives to the bereaved implies a strengthening of the tie. Christian consolation, of which so much has been said, rather encourages a second union. By so doing it seriously impairs the value of the institution; for a division of affection arises, which indeed seems hardly compatible with the vague utopia of a future life. The institutions of perpetual widowhood and of union in the tomb have found no place in any previous system, though both were wanting to make monogamy complete. Here, as elsewhere, the best reply which the new philosophy can give to ignorant prejudice or malignant calumny, is to take new steps forward in the moral advancement of Man.

Thus the theory of marriage, as set forward by the Positivist, becomes totally independent of any physical motive. It is regarded by him as the most powerful instrument of moral education; and therefore as the basis of public or individual welfare. It is no overstrained enthusiasm which leads us to elevate the moral purity of marriage. We do so from rigorous examination of the facts of human nature. All the best results, whether personal or social, of marriage may follow, when the union, though more impassioned, is as chaste as that of brother and sister. The sexual instinct has no doubt something to do in most cases with the first formation of the passion; but it is not necessary in all cases to gratify the instinct. Abstinence, in cases where there is real ground for it on both sides, will but serve to strengthen mutual affection.

We have examined the position of Woman as a wife, without supposing her to be a mother. We shall find that maternity, while it extends her sphere of moral influence, does not alter its nature. *Woman's mission as a mother.*

As a mother, no less than as a wife, her position will be improved by Positivism. She will have, almost exclusively, the direction of household education. Public education given subsequently, will be little but a systematic development of that which has been previously given at home.

For it is a fundamental principle that education, in the normal condition of society, must be entrusted to the spiritual power; and in the family the spiritual power is represented by Woman. There are strong prejudices against *Education of children belongs to mothers. They only can guide the development of character.* entrusting the education of children to mothers: prejudices springing from the revolutionary spirit of modern times. Since the close of the Middle Ages, the tendency has been to place the intellect above the heart. We have neglected the moral side of education, and have given undue importance to its intellectual side. But Positivism having superseded this revolutionary phase by demonstrating the preponderance of the heart over the intellect, moral education will resume its proper place. Certainly the present mode of instruction is not adapted for Woman's teaching. But their influence over the education of the future will be even greater than it was in the Middle Ages. For in the first place, in every part of it, moral considerations will be paramount: and moreover, until puberty, nothing will be studied continuously except Art and Poetry. The knights of old times were usually brought up in this way under feminine guidance, and on them most assuredly it had no enervating influence.   The training can hardly be supposed less adapted to a pacific than to a warlike state of society.   For instruction, theoretical and practical, as distinguished from education, masters are no doubt necessary. But moral education will be left entirely to women, until the time arrives for systematic teaching of moral science in the years immediately preceding majority.   Here the philosopher is necessary.   But the chief duties of the philosopher lie with adults; his aim being to recall them, individually or collectively, to principles impressed on them in childhood, and to enforce the right application of these principles to special cases as they may arise. That part of education which has the greatest influence on life, what may be called the spontaneous training of the feelings, belongs entirely to the mother.   Hence it is, as I have already observed, of the greatest importance to allow the pupil to remain with his family, and to do away with the monastic seclusion of our public schools.

The peculiar fitness of women for inculcating these elementary principles of morality is a truth which every true philosopher will fully recognise.   Women, having stronger sympathies than men, must be better able to call out sympathies in others.   Men of good sense have always felt it more important to train the heart than the head; and this is the view adopted by Positive Philosophy. There is a danger of exaggerating the importance of system and of forgetting the conditions on which its utility depends; but the Positivist is preserved from this danger by the peculiar reality of his philosophy.   In morals, even more than in other subjects, we can only systematize what has existed previously without system.   The feelings must first be stimulated to free and direct action, before we attempt to bring them under philosophic discipline. And this process, which begins with birth, and lasts during the whole period of physical growth, should be left for women to superintend. So specially are they adapted for it, that failing the mother, a female friend, if well chosen, and if she can make herself sufficiently a member of the family, will in most cases do better than the father himself. The importance of the subject can only be appreciated by minds dominated, as women's minds are, by feeling. Women can see, what men can seldom see, that most actions, and certainly the actions of youth and childhood, ought not to be judged in themselves so much as by the tendencies which they show or by the habits to which they lead. Viewed with reference to their influence on character, no actions are indifferent. The simplest events in a child's life may serve as an occasion for enforcing the fundamental principle by which the early as well as later stages of Positivist education should be directed; the strengthening of Social Feeling, the weakening of Self-love. In fact, actions of an unimportant kind are precisely those in which it is easiest to appreciate the feelings which prompted them; since the mind of the observer, not being occupied with the consequences of such actions, is more free to examine their source. Moreover, it is only by teaching the child to do right in small things that he can be trained for the hard inward struggle that lies before him in life; the struggle to bring the selfish instincts more and more completely under the control of his higher sympathies. In these respects the best tutor, however sympathetic his nature, will be always far inferior to a good mother. A mother may often not be able to explain the reason of the principle on which she acts, but the wisdom of her plans will generally show itself in the end. Without formal teaching, she will take every opportunity of showing her children, as no other instructor could show them, the joy that springs from generous feelings, and the misery of yielding to selfishness.

From the relation of mother we return by a natural transition to Woman's position as a wife. The mother, though her authority of course tends to decrease, continues to superintend the growth of character until the ordinary age of marriage. Up to that time feminine influence over Man has been involuntary on his part. By marriage he enters into a voluntary engagement of subordination to Woman for the rest of his life. Thus he completes his moral education. Destined himself for action, he finds his highest happiness in honourable submission to one in whom the dominant principle is affection.

Positivism holds out to woman a most important sphere of public and private duty. This sphere, as we may now see, is nothing but a larger and more systematic development of the qualities by which she is characterised. Her mission is so uniform in its nature and so clearly defined, that there seems hardly room for much uncertainty as to her proper social position. It is a striking instance of the rule which applies universally to all human effort; namely, that the order of things instituted by man ought to be simply a consolidation and improvement of the natural order.

Modern so-phisms about Women's rights. The domesticity of her life follows from the prin-ciple of Separa-tion of Powers. In all ages of transition, as in our own, there have been false and sophistical views of the social position of Woman. But we find it to be a natural law that Woman should pass the greater part of her life in the family; and this law has never been affected to any important extent. It has always been accepted instinctively, though the sophis-tical arguments against it have never yet been adequately refuted. The institution of the family has survived the subtle attacks of Greek metaphysics, which then were in all the vigour of their youth, and which were acting on minds that had no systematic principles to oppose to them. Therefore, profound as the intellectual anarchy of the present day may be, we need not be seriously alarmed when we see that nothing worse comes of it than shallow plagiarisms from ancient utopias, against which the vigorous satire of Aristophanes was quite enough to rouse general indignation.   True, there is a more complete absence of social principles now, than when the world was passing from Polytheism to Monotheism; but our intellectual powers are more developed than they were then, and in moral culture our superiority is even greater.   Women in those times were too degraded to offer even the opposition of their silence to the pedants who professed to be taking up their cause; the only resistance offered was of a purely intellectual kind.   But happily in modern times the women of the West have been free; and have consequently been able to manifest such unmistakeable aversion for these ideas, and for the want of moral discipline which gives rise to them, that, though still unrefuted philosophically, their mischievous effects have been neutralised.   Nothing but women's antipathy has prevented the practical outrages which seem logically to follow from these subversive principles.   Among our privileged classes the danger is aggravated by indolence; moreover, the possession of wealth has a bad influence on women's moral nature. Yet even here the evil is not really very deep or widely spread.   Men have never been seriously perverted, and women still less so, by flattery of their bad propensities. The really formidable temptations are those which act upon our better instincts, and give them a wrong direction.   Schemes which are utterly offensive to female delicacy will never really be adopted, even by the wealthier classes, who are less averse to them than others.   The

repugnance shown to them by the people, with whom the
mischief that they would cause would be irreparable, is far
more decided. The life which working people lead makes
it very clear to both sexes what the proper position of each
should be. Thus it will be in the very class where the
preservation of the institution of the family is of the
greatest importance, that Positivists will find the least
difficulty in establishing their theory of the social position
of women, as consequent on the sphere of public and private duty which has been here assigned to them.

Looking at the relation of this theory to other parts of
the Positive system, we shall see that it follows from the
great principle which dominates every other social problem, the principle of separating spiritual and temporal
power. That Woman's life should be concentrated in her
family, and that even there her influence should be that
of persuasion rather than that of command, is but an
extension of the principle which excludes the spiritual
power from political administration. Women, as the
purest and most spontaneous of the moral forces of society,
are bound to fulfil with rigorous exactness all the conditions which the exercise of moral force demands. Effectually to perform their mission of controlling and guiding
our affections, they must abstain altogether from the practical pursuits of the stronger sex. Such abstinence, even
when the arrangements of society may leave it optional, is
still more desirable in their case than in the case of philosophers. Active life, incompatible as it is with the clearness and breadth of philosophic speculation, is even more
injurious to delicacy of feeling, which is women's highest
claim to our respect and the true secret of their influence.
The philosophic spirit is incompatible with a position of
practical authority, because such a position occupies the
mind with questions of detail. But to purity of feeling

it is even more dangerous, because it strengthens the instincts of power and of gain. And for women it would be harder to avoid the danger of such a position than for men. Abounding as they do in sympathy, they are generally deficient in energy, and are therefore less able to withstand corrupting influences. The more we examine this important subject, the clearer it becomes that the present condition of women does not hamper them in their true work; that, on the contrary, it is well calculated to develope and even improve their highest qualities. The natural arrangements of society in this as in other respects are far less faulty than certain blind declaimers would have us believe. But for the existence of strong material forces, moral force would soon deteriorate, because its distinctive purpose would be gone. Philosophers and proletaries would soon lose their intellectual and moral superiority by the acquisition of power. On women its effect would be still more disastrous. From instances in the upper classes of society, where wealth gives them independence and sometimes unfortunately even power, we see but too clearly what the consequences would be. And this is why we have to look to the poorer classes for the highest type of womanly perfection. With the people sympathy is better cultivated, and has a greater influence upon life. Wealth has more to do with the moral degradation of women among the privileged classes than even idleness and dissipation.

Progress, in this respect as in every other, is only a more complete development of the pre-existing Order. Equality in the position of the two sexes is contrary to their nature, and no tendency to it has at any time been exhibited. All history assures us that with the growth of society the peculiar features of each sex have become not less but more

The position of the sexes tends to differentiation rather than identity.

distinct. By Catholic Feudalism the social condition of women in Western Europe was raised to a far higher level. But it took away from them the priestly functions which they had held under Polytheism; a religion in which the priesthood was more occupied with Art than with Science. So too with the gradual decline of the principle of Caste, women have been excluded more and more rigidly from royalty and from every other kind of political authority. Again, there is a visible tendency towards the removal of women from all industrial occupations, even from those which might seem best suited to them. And thus female life, instead of becoming independent of the Family, is being more and more concentrated in it; while at the same time their proper sphere of moral influence is constantly extending. The two tendencies, so far from being opposed, are inseparably connected.

Without discussing the absurd and retrograde schemes which have been recently put forward on the subject, there is one remark which may serve to illustrate the value of the order which now exists. If women were to obtain that equality in the affairs of life which their so-called champions are claiming for them without their wish, not only would they suffer morally, but their social position would be endangered. They would be subject in almost every occupation to a degree of competition which they would not be able to sustain. Moreover, by rivalry in the pursuits of life, mutual affection between the sexes would be corrupted at its source.

Woman to be maintained by Man. Leaving these subversive dreams, we find a natural principle which, by determining the practical obligations of the Active to the Sympathetic sex, averts this danger. It is a principle which no philosophy but Positivism has been sufficiently real and practical to bring forward systematically for general acceptance. It is no new invention, however, but a universal tendency, confirmed by careful study of the whole past history of Man. The principle is, that Man should provide for Woman. It is a natural law of the human race; a law connected with the essentially domestic character of female life. We find it in the rudest forms of social life; and with every step in the progress of society its adoption becomes more extensive and complete. A still larger application of this fundamental principle will meet all the material difficulties under which women are now labouring. All social relations, and especially the question of wages, will be affected by it. The tendency to it is spontaneous; but it also follows from the high position which Positivism has assigned to Woman as the sympathetic element in the spiritual power. The intellectual class, in the same way, has to be supported by the practical class, in order to have its whole time available for the special duties imposed upon it. But in the case of women, the obligation of the other sex is still more sacred, because the sphere of duty in which protection for them is required, is the home. The obligation to provide for the intellectual class, affects society as a whole; but the maintenance of women is, with few exceptions, a personal obligation. Each individual should consider himself bound to maintain the woman he has chosen to be his partner in life. There are cases, however, in which men should be considered collectively responsible for the support of the other sex. Women who are without husband or parents should have their maintenance guaranteed by society; and this not merely from compassion for their dependent position, but with the view of enabling them to render public service of the greatest moral value.

The direction, then, of progress in the social condition of woman is this: to render her life more and more domestic;

to diminish as far as possible the burden of out-door labour; and so to fit her more completely for her special office of educating our moral nature. Among the privileged classes it is already a recognised rule that women should be spared all laborious exertion. It is the one point in the relations of the sexes in which the working classes would do well to imitate the habits of their employers. In every other respect the people of Western Europe have a higher sense of their duties to women than the upper classes. Indeed there are few of them who would not be ashamed of the barbarity of subjecting women to their present burdensome occupations, if the present state of our industrial system allowed of its abolition. But it is chiefly among the higher and wealthier classes that we find those degrading and very often fraudulent bargains, connected with unscrupulous interference of parents in the question of marriage, which are so humiliating to one sex and so corrupting to the other. Among the working classes the practice of giving dowries is almost extinct; and as women's true mission becomes more recognised, and as choice in marriage becomes less restricted, this relic of barbarism, with all its debasing results, will rapidly die out. With this view the application of our theory should be carried one step further. Women should not be allowed to inherit. If inheritance be allowed, the prohibition of dowries would be evaded in a very obvious manner by discounting the reversionary interest. Since women are to be exempt from the labour of production, capital, that is to say, the instruments of labour produced by each generation for the benefit of the next, should revert to men. This view of inheritance, so far from making men a privileged class, places them under heavy responsibilities. It is not from women that any serious opposition to it will proceed. Wise education will show them its value to themselves personally, as a safeguard against unworthy suitors. But, important as the rule is, it should not be legally enforced until it has become established on its own merits as a general custom, which every one has felt to conduce to the healthy organization of the Family as here described.

Coming now to the subject of female educa- The education of women should be identical with that of men. tion, we have only to make a further application of the theory which has guided us hitherto.

Since the vocation assigned by our theory to women is that of educating others, it is clear that the educational system which we have proposed in the last chapter for the working classes, applies to them as well as to the other sex with very slight alterations. Unencumbered as it is with specialities, it will be found, even in its more scientific parts, as suitable for the sympathetic element of the moderating power, as to the synergic element. We have spoken of the necessity of diffusing sound historical views among the working classes ; and the same necessity applies to women ; for social sympathy can never be perfectly developed, without a sense of the continuity of the Past, as well as of the solidarity of the Present. Since then both sexes alike need historical instruction as a basis for the systematization of moral truth, both should alike pass through the scientific training which prepares the way for social studies, and which moreover has as intrinsic a value for women as for men. Again, since the first or systematic stage of education is entirely to be left to women, it is most desirable that they should themselves have passed through the second or systematic stage. The only department with which they need not concern themselves, is what is called professional education. But this, as I have before observed, is not susceptible of regular organization. Professional skill can only be acquired by careful practice and experience, resting upon a sound basis of theory. In all other respects women, philosophers, and working men will receive the same education.

But while I would place the sexes on a level in this respect, I do not take the view of my eminent predecessor Condorcet, that they should be taught together. On moral grounds, which of course are the most important consideration, it is obvious that such a plan would be equally prejudicial to both. In the church, in the club, in the salon, they may associate freely at every period of life. But at school such intercourse would be premature; it would check the natural development of character, not to say that it would obviously have an unsettling influence upon study. Until the feelings on both sides are sufficiently matured, it is of the greatest importance that the relations of the two sexes should not be too intimate, and that they should be superintended by the watchful eye of their mothers.

As, however, the subjects of study are to be the same for both, the necessity of separating the sexes does not imply that there should be special teachers for women. Not to speak of the increased expenditure that would thus be incurred, it would inevitably lower the standard of female education. It would always be presumed that their teachers were men of inferior attainments. To ensure that the instruction given is the same for both sexes, the instructors must be the same, and must give their lectures alternately to each sex. These conditions are perfectly compatible with the scheme described in the last chapter. It was there mentioned that each philosopher would be expected to give one, or, in some cases, two lectures every week. Now supposing this were doubled, it would still come far short of the intolerable burdens which are imposed upon teachers in the present

day. Moreover, as the Positivist educator will pass successively through the seven stages of scientific instruction, he
will be able so to regulate his work as to avoid wearisome
repetition of the same lectures in each year. Besides, the
distinguished men to whom our educational system will be
entrusted will soon discover that their two audiences require some difference in the manner of teaching, and that
this may be done without in any way lowering the uniform
standard which their method and their doctrines require.

But independently of the importance to female education of this identity of teachers, it will react beneficially
on the intellectual and moral character of the philosopher
who teaches. It will preclude him from entering into
useless details, and will keep him involuntarily to the
broad principles of his subject. By coming into contact
simultaneously with two natures, in one of which thought,
and in the other emotion, is predominant, he will gain
clearer insight into the great principle of subordinating
the intellect to the heart. The obligation of teaching both
sexes will complete that universality of mind which is to
be required of the new school of philosophers. To treat
with equal ability of all the various orders of scientific
conceptions, and to interest two audiences of so different
a character, is a task which will demand the highest personal qualifications. However, as the number required by
the conditions is not excessive, it will not be impossible to
find men fit for the purpose, as soon as the proper means
are taken to procure their services, and to guarantee their
material subsistence. It must be borne in mind, too, that
the corporation of teachers is not to be recruited from
any one nation for itself, but from the whole of Western
Europe; so that the Positivist educator will change his
residence, when required, even more frequently than the
priests of the Middle Ages. Putting these considerations

together, we shall find that Positivist education for both
sexes may be organized on a sufficient scale for the whole
of Western Europe, with less than the useless, or worse
than useless, expenditure incurred by the clergy of the
Anglican church.   This would give each functionary an
adequate maintenance, though none of them would be
degraded by wealth.   A body of twenty thousand philosophers would be enough now, and probably would always
suffice, for the spiritual wants of the five Western nations.
This would imply the establishment of the septennial system of instruction in two thousand stations.   The influence
of women and of working men will never become so systematic as to enable them to dispense with philosophic
assistance altogether.   But in proportion as they become
more effectually incorporated as elements of the spiritual
power, the necessity of enlarging the purely speculative
class will diminish.   Under theological systems it has been
far too numerous.   The privilege of living in comfort
without productive labour will be ultimately so rare and
so dearly earned, that no rational ground of objection to
it will be left.   It will be generally felt that the cost of
maintaining these philosophic teachers, like that of maintaining women, is no real burden to the productive classes ;
on the contrary, that it conduces to their highest interest,
by ensuring the performance of intellectual and moral functions which are the noblest characteristics of Humanity.

It appears, then, that the primary principle laid down
at the beginning of this chapter enables us to solve all the
problems that offer themselves on the subject of Woman.
Her function in society is determined by the constitution
of her nature.   She is spontaneously the organ of Feeling,
on which the unity of human nature entirely depends.
And she constitutes the purest and most natural element
of the moderating power ; which, while avowing its own

subordination to the material forces of society, purposes to direct them to higher uses. As mother and as wife, it is her office to conduct the moral education of Humanity. In order the more perfectly to fulfil this mission, her life must be connected even more closely than it has been with the Family. At the same time she must participate, to the full extent that is possible, in the general system of instruction.

A few remarks on the privileges which the fulfilment of this vocation will bring, will complete this part of my subject.   *Women's privileges. Their mission is in itself a privilege.*

Women's mission is a striking illustration of the truth that happiness consists in doing the work for which we are naturally fitted. That mission is always the same; it is summed up in one word, Love. But Love is a work in which there can never be too many workers; it grows by co-operation; it has nothing to fear from competition. Women are charged with the education of Sympathy, the source of human unity; and their highest happiness is reached when they have the full consciousness of their vocation, and are free to follow it. It is the admirable feature of their social mission, that it invites them to cultivate qualities which are natural to them; to call into exercise emotions which all allow to be the most pleasurable. All that is required for them in a better organization of society are certain improvements in their external condition. They must be relieved from out-door labour; and other means must be taken to prevent their moral influence from being impaired. Both objects are contemplated in the material, intellectual, and moral ameliorations which Positivism is destined to effect in female life.

But besides the pleasure inherent in their vocation, Positivism offers a recompense for their services, which Catholic Feudalism fore-   *They will receive honour and worship from men.*

shadowed but could not realise. As men become more and more grateful for the blessing of their moral influence, they will give expression to this feeling in a systematic form. In a word the new doctrine will institute the Worship of Woman, publicly and privately, in a far more perfect way than has ever before been possible. It is the first permanent step towards the worship of Humanity; which, as the concluding chapter of this introductory work will show, is the central principle of Positivism, viewed either as a Philosophy or as a Polity.

Development of mediæval chivalry.   Our ancestors in chivalrous times made noble efforts in this direction, which, except by women, are now no longer appreciated. But these efforts, however admirable, were inadequate; partly owing to the military spirit of society in those times, partly because their religious doctrines had not a sufficiently social character. Nevertheless, they have left memories which will not perish. The refinement of life in Western Europe is in great part due to them, although much of it is already effaced by the anarchy of the present time.

Chivalry, if we are to believe the negative philosophers of the last century, can never revive; because the religious beliefs with which it was connected have become obsolete. But the connection was never very profound, and there is no reason whatever for its continuance. Far too much has been made of it by recent apologists for Catholicism; who, while laying great stress on the sanction which Theology gave to Chivalry, have failed to appreciate the sympathies to which this admirable institution is really due. The real source of Chivalry lies most unquestionably in the feudal spirit. Theological sanction for it was afterwards sought for, as the only systematic basis that offered itself at that time. But the truth is that Theology and Chivalry were hardly compatible. Theology fixed men's thoughts upon a visionary future; Chivalry concentrated his energies upon the world around him. The knight of the Middle Ages had always to choose between his God and his Lady; and could therefore never attain that concentrated unity of purpose, without which the full result of his mission, so generously undertaken, could never be realised.

Placed as we are now, near the close of the revolutionary period, we are beginning to see that Chivalry is not destined to extinction; that, on the contrary, when modern life has assumed its normal character, its influence will be greater than ever, because it will operate on a more pacific society, and will be based on a more practical religion. For Chivalry satisfies an essential want of society, a want which becomes more urgent as civilization advances; it institutes a voluntary combination of the strong for the protection of the weak. The period of transition from the offensive military system of Rome to the defensive system of Feudalism, was naturally the time of its first appearance, and it received the sanction of the religion then dominant. But society is now entering upon a period of permanent peace; and when this, the most striking political feature of modern times, has become firmly established, the influence of Chivalry will be greater than ever. Its procedure will be different, because the modes of oppression are happily not now what they were formerly. The instruments of material force are now not arms, but riches. It is no longer the person that is attacked, but his means of subsistence. The advantages of the change are obvious: the danger is less serious, and protection from it is easier and more effectual. But it will always remain most desirable that protectors should come forward, and that they should form an organized association. The destructive instinct will always show itself in various ways, wherever there is the means of indulging it. And therefore as an adjunct to the spiritual organization, Positivism will encourage a systematic manifestation of chivalrous feeling among the leaders of industry. Those among them who feel animated with the noble spirit of the heroes of the Middle Ages, will devote not their sword, but their wealth, their time, and, if need be, their whole energies to the defence of the oppressed in all classes. The objects of their generosity will principally be found, as in the Middle Ages, among the classes specially exposed to material suffering, that is to say, among women, philosophers, and working men. It would be strange indeed for a system like Positivism, the main object of which is to strengthen the social spirit, not to appropriate the institution which is the noblest product of that spirit.

So far, then, the restoration of Chivalry is merely a reconstruction of the mediæval institution in a shape adapted to the altered state of ideas and feelings. In modern as in mediæval times, devotion of the strong to the weak follows as a natural consequence from the subordination of Politics to Morals. Now, as then, the spiritual power will be nobly seconded by members of the governing class in the attempt to bring that class to a stricter sense of social duty. But besides this, Feudal Chivalry had a deeper and more special purpose in reference to women. And in this respect the superiority of Positivism is even more complete and obvious.

Feudalism introduced for the first time the worship of Woman. But in this it met with little support from Catholicism, and was in many respects thwarted by it. The habits of Christianity were in themselves adverse to real tenderness of heart; they only strengthened it indirectly, by promoting one of the indispensable conditions of true affection, purity of life. In all other respects Chivalry was constantly opposed by the Catholic system;

which was so austere and anti-social, that it could not
sanction marriage except as an infirmity which it was
necessary to tolerate, but which was hazardous to personal
salvation. Even its rules of purity, valuable as they
were, were often weakened by interested motives which
seriously impaired their value. Consequently, notwithstanding all the noble and long-continued efforts of our
mediæval ancestors, the institution of the worship of
Woman was very imperfectly effected, especially in its
relation to public life. Whatever Catholic apologists may
say, there is every reason to believe that if Feudalism
could have arisen before the decline of Polytheism, the
influence of Chivalry would have been greater.

It was reserved for the more comprehensive system of
Positivism, in which sound practice is always supported
by sound theory, to give full expression to the feeling of
veneration for women. In the new religion, tenderness
of heart is looked upon as the first of Woman's attributes.
But purity is not neglected. On the contrary its true
source and its essential value, as the first condition of happiness and of moral growth, are pointed out more distinctly
than before. The shallow and sophistical views of marriage maintained in these unsettled times by men of
narrow minds and coarse feelings, will be easily refuted
by a more careful study of human nature. Even the
obstacles presented by scientific materialism will rapidly
disappear before the spread of Positivist morality. A
physician of great sagacity, Hufeland, has remarked, with
truth, that the well-known vigour of the knights of old
times was a sufficient answer to men who talked of the
physical dangers of continence. Positivism, dealing with
this question in all its aspects, teaches that while the
primary reason for insisting on purity is that it is essential
to depth of affection, it has as close a connection with the

physical and intellectual improvement of the individual and the race as with our moral progress.

Positivism then, as the whole tendency of this chapter indicates, encourages, on intellectual as well as on moral grounds, full and systematic expression of the feeling of veneration for Women, in public as well as in private life, collectively as well as individually. Born to love and to be loved, relieved from the burdens of practical life, free in the sacred retirement of their homes, the women of the West will receive from Positivists the tribute of deep and sincere admiration which their life inspires. They will feel no scruple in accepting their position as spontaneous priestesses of Humanity; they will fear no longer the rivalry of a vindictive Deity. From childhood each of us will be taught to regard their sex as the principal source of human happiness and improvement, whether in public life or in private.

The treasures of affection which our ancestors wasted upon mystical objects, and which these revolutionary times ignore, will then be carefully preserved and directed to their proper purpose. The enervating influence of chimerical beliefs will have passed away; and men in all the vigour of their energies, feeling themselves the masters of the known world, will feel it their highest happiness to submit with gratitude to the beneficent power of womanly sympathy. In a word, Man will in those days kneel to Woman, and to Woman alone.

The source from which these reverential feelings for the sympathetic sex proceed, is a clear appreciation in the other sex of benefits received, and a spirit of deep thankfulness for them. The Positivist will never forget that moral perfection, the primary condition of public and private happiness, is principally due to the influence of Woman over Man, first as mother, then as wife. Such a conviction cannot fail to arouse feelings of loving veneration for those with whom, from their position in society, he is in no danger of rivalry in the affairs of life. When the mission of Woman is better understood, and is carried out more fully, she will be regarded by Man as the most perfect impersonation of Humanity.

Originating in spontaneous feelings of grati- *The practice of Prayer, so far from disappearing, is purified and strengthened in Positive religion.* tude, the worship of Woman, when it has assumed a more systematic shape, will be valued for its own sake as a new instrument of happiness and moral growth. Inert as the tender sympathies are in Man, it is most desirable to strengthen them by such exercise as the public and private institution of this worship will afford. And here it is that Positivists will find all the elevating influences which Catholicism derived from Prayer.

It is a common but very palpable error to imagine that Prayer is inseparable from the chimerical motives of self-interest in which it first originated. In Catholicism there was always a tendency to rise above these motives, so far at least as the principles of theology admitted. From St. Augustine downwards, all the nobler spirits have felt more and more strongly, notwithstanding the self-absorbing tendencies of Christian doctrine, that Prayer did not necessarily imply petition. When sounder views of human nature have become prevalent, the value of this important function will be more clearly appreciated; and it will ultimately become of greater importance than ever, because founded on a truer principle. In the normal state of Humanity, the moral efficacy of Prayer will no longer be impaired by thoughts of personal recompense. It will be simply a solemn out-pouring, whether in private or in public, of men's nobler feelings, inspiring them with larger and more comprehensive thoughts. As a daily practice, it is inculcated by Positivism as the best preservative against the selfish and narrow views which are so apt to arise in the ordinary avocations of life. To men its value is even greater than to women; their life being less favourable to large views and generous sympathies, it is the more important to revive them at regular periods.

But Prayer would be of little value unless the mind could form a clear conception of its object. The worship of Woman satisfies this condition, and is so far of greater efficacy than the worship of God. True, the ultimate object of Positivist Prayer, as shown in the concluding chapter of this volume, is Humanity. But some of its best moral effects would hardly be realised, if it were at once and exclusively directed to an object so difficult to conceive clearly. It is possible that Women with their stronger sympathies may be able to reach this stage without intermediate steps. However this may be, men certainly would not be able to do so; even the intellectual class, with all its powers of generalization, would find it impossible. The worship of Woman, begun in private, and afterwards publicly celebrated, is necessary in man's case to prepare him for any effectual worship of Humanity.

No one can be so unhappy as not to be able to find some woman worthy of his peculiar love, whether in the relation of wife or of mother; some one who in his solitary prayer may be present to him as a fixed object of devotion. Nor will such devotion, as might be thought, cease with death; rather, when its object has been rightly chosen, death strengthens it by making it more pure. The principle upon which Positivism insists so strongly, the union of the Present with the Past, and even with the Future, is not limited to the life of Society. It is a doctrine which unites all individuals and all generations; and when it has become more familiar to us, it will stimulate every one to call his dearest memories to life; the

spirit of the system being that the private life of the very
humblest citizen has a close relation to his public duty.
We all know how intellectual culture enables us to live
with our great predecessors of the Middle Ages and of
Antiquity, almost as we should do with absent friends.
And if Intellect can do so much, will it not be far easier
for the strong passion of Love to effect this ideal resurrec-
tion? We have already many instances where whole
nations have shown strong sympathies or antipathies to
great historical names, especially when their influence was
still sensibly felt. There is no reason why a private life
should not produce the same effect upon those who have
been brought into contact with it. Moral culture has
been conducted hitherto on such unsatisfactory principles,
that we can hardly form an adequate notion of its results
when Positivism has regenerated it, and has concentrated
the affections as well as the thoughts of Man upon human
life. To live with the dead is the peculiar privilege of
Humanity, a privilege which will extend as our conceptions widen and our thoughts become more pure. Under
Positivism the impulse to it will become far stronger, and
it will be recognised as a systematic principle in private
as well as in public life. Even the Future is not excluded
from its application. We may live with those who are
not yet born; a thing impossible only till a true theory of
history had arisen, of scope sufficient to embrace at one
glance the whole course of human destiny. There are
numberless instances to prove that the heart of Man is
capable of emotions which have no outward basis, except
what Imagination has supplied. The familiar spirits of
the Polytheist, the mystical desires of the Monotheist, all
point to a general tendency in the Past, which, with our
better principles, we shall be able in the Future to direct
to a nobler and more real purpose. And thus even those

who may be so unfortunate as to have no special object of love need not, on that account, be precluded from the act of worship: they may choose from the women of the past some type adapted to their own nature. Men of powerful imagination might even form their own more perfect ideal, and thus open out the path of the future. This, indeed, is what was often done by the knights of chivalrous times, simple and uninstructed as they were. Surely then we, with our fuller understanding and greater familiarity with the Past, should be able to idealise more perfectly. But whether the choice lie in the Past or in the Future, its efficacy would be impaired unless it remained constant to one object; and fixed principles, such as Positivism supplies, are needed to check the natural tendency to versatility of feeling.

The worship of Woman a preparation for the worship of Humanity.   I have dwelt at some length upon the personal adoration of Woman under its real or ideal aspects, because upon it depends nearly all the moral value of any public celebration. Public assemblage in the temples of Humanity may strengthen and stimulate feelings of devotion, but cannot originate them. Unless each worshipper has felt in his own person deep and reverential love for those to whom our highest affections are due, a public service in honour of women would be nothing but a repetition of unmeaning formulas. But those whose daily custom it has been to give expression to such feelings in secret, will gain, by assembling together, all the benefit of more intense and more exalted sympathy. In my last letter to her who is for ever mine, I said: "Amidst the heaviest anxieties which Love can bring, I have never ceased to feel that the one thing essential to happiness is that the heart shall be always nobly occupied." And now that we are separated by Death, daily experience confirms this truth, which is moreover

in exact accordance with the Positive theory of human
nature. Without personal experience of Love no public
celebration of it can be sincere.

In its public celebration the superiority of the new Religion is even more manifest than in the private worship.
A system in which the social spirit is uniformly preponderant, is peculiarly adapted to render homage for the
social services of the sympathetic sex. When the knights
of the Middle Ages met together, they might give vent to
their personal feelings, and express to one another the
reverence which each felt for his own mistress; but farther
than this they could not go. And such personal feelings
will never cease to be necessary. Still the principal object
of public celebration is to express gratitude on the part of
the people for the social blessings conferred by Woman, as
the organ of that element in our nature on which its unity
depends, and as the original source of moral power. In
the Middle Ages such considerations were impossible, for
want of a rational theory embracing the whole circle of
social relations. Indeed the received faith was incompatible with any such conception, since God in that faith
occupied the place really due to Humanity.

There are women whose career has been alto- Exceptional
women. Joan
gether exceptional; and these, like the rest, of Arc.
meet with their due tribute of praise in the Positive system. The chief motive, doubtless, for public and private
veneration is the mission of sympathy, which is Woman's
peculiar vocation. But there have been remarkable instances of women whose life has been one of speculation,
or even, what is in most cases still more foreign to their
nature, of political activity. They have rendered real service to Humanity, and they should receive the honour that
is due to them. Theology, from its absolute character,
could not make such concessions; they would have weak-

ened the efficiency of its most important social rules.
Consequently, Catholicism was compelled, though at first
with sincere regret, to leave some of the noblest women
without commemoration. A signal instance is the Maid
of Orleans, whose heroism saved France in the fourteenth
century. Our great king Louis XI. applied very properly to the Pope for her canonization, and no objection
was made to his request. Yet, practically, it was never
carried into effect. It was gradually forgotten ; and the
clergy soon came to feel a sort of dislike to her memory,
which reminded them of nothing but their own social
weakness. It is easy to account for this result ; nor is
any one really to blame for it. It was feared, not without
reason, that to consider Joan of Arc as a saint might have
the effect of spreading false and dangerous ideas of feminine duty. The difficulty was insuperable for any absolute
system, in which to sanction the exception is to compro-
mise the rule. But in a relative system the case is different. It is even more inconsistent with Positive principles
than it is with Catholic, for women to lead a military life,
a life which of all others is the least compatible with their
proper functions. And yet Positivists will be the first to
do justice to this extraordinary heroine, whom theologians
have been afraid to recognise, and whom metaphysicians,
even in France, have had the hardihood to insult. The
anniversary of her glorious martyrdom will be a solemn
festival, not only for France, but for Western Europe.
For her work was not merely of national importance : the
enslavement of France would have involved the loss of all
the influence which France has exercised as the centre of
the advanced nations of Europe. Moreover, as none of
them are altogether clear from the disgrace of detracting,
as Voltaire has done, from her character, all should aid in
the reparation of it which Positivism proposes to institute.

So far from her apotheosis having an injurious effect on
female character, it will afford an opportunity of pointing
out the anomalous nature of her career, and the rarity of
the conditions which alone could justify it. It is a fresh
proof of the advantages accruing to Morality from the
relative character of Positivism, which enables it to appreciate exceptional cases without weakening the rules.

The subject of the worship of Woman by Man raises a
question of much delicacy; how to satisfy analogous feelings of devotion in the other sex. We have seen its
necessity for men as an intermediate step towards the
worship of Humanity; and women, stronger though their
sympathies are, stand, it may be, in need of similar preparation. Yet certainly the direction taken should be somewhat different. What is wanted is that each sex should
strengthen the moral qualities in which it is naturally
deficient. Energy is a characteristic feature of Humanity
as well as Sympathy; as is well shown by the double meaning of the word *Heart*. In Man Sympathy is the weaker
element, and it requires constant exercise. This he gains
by expression of his feelings of reverence for Woman.
In Woman, on the other hand, the defective quality is
Energy; so that, should any special preparation for the
worship of Humanity be needed, it should be such as to
strengthen courage rather than sympathy. But my sex
renders me incompetent to enter farther into the secret
wants of Woman's heart. Theory indicates a blank hitherto
unnoticed, but does not enable me to fill it. It is a problem for women themselves to solve; and I had reserved
it for my noble colleague, for whose premature death I
would fain hope that my own grief may one day be
shared by all.

Throughout this chapter I have been keenly sensible of
the philosophic loss resulting from our objective separation.

True, I have been able to show that Positivism is a matter of the deepest concern to women, since it incorporates them in the progressive movement of modern times. I have proved that the part allotted to them in this movement is one which satisfies their highest aspirations for the Family or for Society. And yet I can hardly hope for much support from them until some woman shall come forward to interpret what I have said into language more adapted to their nature and habits of thought. Till then it will always be taken for granted that they are incapable even of understanding the new philosophy, notwithstanding all the natural affinities for it which I have shown that they possess.

All these difficulties had been entirely removed by the noble and loving friend to whom I dedicate the treatise to which this work is introductory. The dedication is unusual in form, and some may think it overstrained. But my own fear is rather, now that five years have past, that my words were too weak for the deep gratitude which I now feel for her elevating influence. Without it the moral aspects of Positivism would have lain very long latent.

Clotilde de Vaux was gifted equally in mind and heart : and she had already begun to feel the power of the new philosophy to raise feminine influence from the decline into which it had fallen, under the revolutionary influences of modern times. Misunderstood everywhere, even by her own family, her nature was far too noble for bitterness. Her sorrows were as exceptional as they were undeserved ; but her purity was even more rare than her sorrow ; and it preserved her unscathed from all sophistical attacks on marriage, even before the true theory of marriage had come before her. In the only writing which she published, there is a beautiful remark, which to those who know the history of her life is deeply affecting : " Great

natures should always be above bringing their own sorrows
upon others." In this charming story, written before she
knew anything of Positivism, she expressed herself most
characteristically on the subject of Woman's vocation :
" Surely the true sphere of Woman is to provide Man
with the comforts and delights of home, receiving in exchange from him the means of subsistence earned by his
labours. I would rather see the mother of a poor family
washing her children's linen, than see her earning a
livelihood by her talents away from home. Of course I
do not speak of women of extraordinary powers whose
genius leads them out of the sphere of domestic duty. Such
natures should have free scope given to them : for great
minds are kindled by the exhibition of their powers."
These words coming from a young lady distinguished
no less for beauty than for worth, show her antipathy to
the subversive ideas so prevalent in the present day.
But in a large work which she did not live to finish, she
had intended to refute the attacks upon marriage, contained in the works of George Sand, to whom she was
intellectually no less than morally superior. Her nature
was of rare endowment, moved by noble impulse, and yet
allowing its due influence to reason. When she was
beginning to study Positivism she wrote to me : " No one
knows better than myself how weak our nature is, unless
it has some lofty aim beyond the reach of passion." A
short time afterwards, writing with all the graceful freedom of friendship, she let fall a phrase of deep meaning,
almost unawares : " Our race is one which must have
duties, in order to form its feelings."

With such a nature my Saint Clotilda was, as may be
supposed, fully conscious of the moral value of Positivism,
though she had only one year to give to its study. A
few months before her death, she wrote to me : " If I

were a man, I should be your enthusiastic disciple; as a woman, I can but offer you my cordial admiration." In the same letter she explains the part which she proposed to take in diffusing the principles of the new philosophy: "It is always well for a woman to follow modestly behind the army of renovators, even at the risk of losing a little of her own originality." She describes our intellectual anarchy in this charming simile: "We are all standing as yet with one foot in the air over the threshold of truth."

It is for women to introduce Positivism into the Southern nations.   With such a colleague, combining as she did qualities hitherto shared amongst the noblest types of womanhood, it would have been easy to induce her sex to co-operate in the regeneration of society. For she gave a perfect example of that normal reaction of Feeling upon Reason which has been here set forward as the highest aim of Woman's efforts. When she had finished the important work on which she was engaged, I had marked out for her a definite yet spacious field of co-operation in the Positivist cause: a field which her intellect and character were fully competent to occupy. I mention it here, to illustrate the mode in which women may help to spread Positivism through the West; giving thus the first example of the social influence which they will afterwards exert permanently. What I say has special reference to Italy and to Spain. In other countries it only applies to individuals who, though living in an atmosphere of free thought, have not themselves ventured to think freely. Success in this latter case is so frequent, as to make me confident that the agencies of which I am about to speak may be applied collectively with the same favourable result.

The intellectual freedom of the West began in England and Germany; and it had all the dangers of original efforts for which at that time no systematic basis could be found. With the legal establishment of Protestantism, the metaphysical movement stopped. Protestantism, by consolidating it, seriously impeded subsequent progress, and is still, in the countries where it prevails, the chief obstacle to all efficient renovation. Happily France, the normal centre of Western Europe, was spared this so-called Reformation. She made up for the delay, by passing at one stride, under the impulse given by Voltaire, to a state of entire freedom of thought; and thus resumed her natural place as leader of the common movement of social regeneration. But the French, while escaping the inconsistencies and oscillations of Protestantism, have been exposed to all the dangers resulting from unqualified acceptance of revolutionary metaphysics. Principles of systematic negation have now held their ground with us too long. Useful as they once were in preparing the way for social reconstruction, they are now a hindrance to it. It may be hoped that when the movement of free thought extends, as it assuredly will, to the two Southern nations, where Catholicism has been more successful in resisting Protestantism and Deism, it will be attended with less injurious consequences. If France was spared the Calvinistic stage, there seems no reason why Italy and even Spain should not be spared Voltairianism. As a compensation for this apparent stagnation, they might pass at once from Catholicism to Positivism, without halting for any length of time at the negative stage. These countries could not have originated the new philosophy, owing to their insufficient preparation; but as soon as it has taken root in France, they will probably accept it with extreme rapidity. Direct attacks upon Catholicism will not be necessary. The new religion will simply put itself into competition with the old by performing in a better way the same functions that Catholicism fulfils now, or has fulfilled in past times.

All evidence, especially the evidence of the poets, goes to prove that before Luther's time, there was less belief in the South of Europe, certainly less in Italy, than in the North. And Catholicism, with all its resistance to the progress of thought, has never been able really to revive the belief in Christianity. We speak of Italy and Spain as less advanced; but the truth is that they only cling to Catholicism because it satisfies their moral and social wants better than any system with which they are acquainted. Morally they have more affinity to Positivism than other nations; because their feelings of fraternity have not been weakened by the industrial development which has done so much harm in Protestant countries. Intellectually, too, they are less hostile to the primary principle of Positive Polity; the separation of spiritual and temporal power. And therefore they will welcome Positivism as soon as they see that in all essential features it equals and surpasses the mediæval Church. Now as this question is almost entirely a moral one, their convictions in this respect will depend far more upon feeling than upon argument. Consequently, the work of converting them to Positivism is one for which women are peculiarly adapted. Positivism has been communicated to England by men. Holland, too, which has been the vanguard of Germany ever since the Middle Ages, has been initiated in the same way still more efficiently. But its introduction in Italy and Spain will depend upon the women of those countries; and the appeal to them must come, not from a Frenchman, but from a Frenchwoman; for heart must speak to heart. Would that these brief remarks might enable others to appreciate the inestimable worth of the colleague whom I had intended to write such an appeal;

and that they might stimulate some one worthy to take her place !

Already, then, there is ground for encouragement. Already we have one striking instance of a woman ready to co-operate in the philosophical movement, which assigns to her sex a mission of the highest social consequence as the prelude to the function for which in the normal state they are destined. Such an instance, though it may seem now exceptional, does but anticipate what will one day be universal. Highly gifted natures pass through the same phases as others; only they undergo them earlier, and so become guides for the rest. The sacred friend of whom I speak had nothing that specially disposed her to accept Positivism, except the beauty of her mind and character, prematurely ripened by sorrow. Had she been an untaught working woman, it would perhaps have been still easier for her to grasp the general spirit of the new philosophy and its social purpose.

The result of this chapter is to show the affinity of the systematic element of the modifying power, as represented by philosophers, with women who form its sympathetic element; an affinity not less close than that with the people, who constitute its synergic element. The organization of moral force is based on the alliance of philosophers with the people; but the adhesion of women is necessary to its completion. With the union of all three, the regeneration of society begins, and the revolution is brought to a close. But more than this: their union is at once an inauguration of the final order of society. Each of these three elements will be acting as it will be called upon to act in the normal state, and will be occupying its permanent position relatively to the temporal power. The philosophic class whose work it is to combine the action of the other two classes, will find valuable assistance from women in

19

every family, as well as powerful co-operation from the people in every city. The result will be a union of all who are precluded from political administration, instituted for the purpose of judging all practical measures by the fixed rules of universal morality. Exceptional cases will arise when moral influence is insufficient: in these it will be necessary for the people to interfere actively. But philosophers and women are dispensed from such interference. Direct action would be most injurious to their powers of sympathy or meditation. They can only preserve these powers by keeping clear of all positions of political authority.

But while the moral force resulting from the combined action of Women and of the People, will be more efficient than that of the Middle Ages, the systematic organs of that force will find their work one of great difficulty. High powers of intellect are required; and a heart worthy of such intellect. To secure the support of women, and the co-operation of the people, they must have the sympathy and purity of the first, the energy and disinterestedness of the second. Such natures are rare; yet without them the new spiritual power cannot obtain that ascendency over society to which Positivism aspires. And with all the agencies, physical or moral, which can be brought to bear, we shall have to acknowledge that the exceeding imperfections of human nature form an eternal obstacle to the object for which Positivism strives, the victory of social sympathy over self-love.

CHAPTER V.

THE RELATION OF POSITIVISM TO ART.

THE essential principles and the social pur- *Positivism when complete is as favourable to Imagination, as, when incomplete, it was unfavourable to it.* pose of the only philosophy by which the revolution can be brought to a close, are now before us. We have seen too that energetic support from the People and cordial sympathy from Women are necessary to bring this philosophic movement to a practical result. One further condition yet remains. The view here taken of human life as regenerated by this combination of efforts, would be incomplete if it did not include an additional element, with which Positivism, as I have now to show, is no less competent to deal. We have spoken already of the place which Reason occupies in our nature; its function being to subordinate itself to Feeling for the better guidance of the Active powers. But in the normal state of our nature it has also another function; that of regulating and stimulating Imagination, without yielding passive obedience to it. The esthetic faculties are far too important to be disregarded in the normal state of Humanity; therefore they must not be omitted from the system which aims to introduce that state. There is a strong but groundless prejudice that in this respect at least Positivism will be found wanting. Yet it furnishes, as may readily be shown, the only true foundation of modern Art, which, since the Middle Ages, has been cultivated without fixed principles or lofty purpose.

The reproach that Positivism is incompatible with Art arises simply from the fact that almost every one is in the habit of confounding the philosophy itself with the scientific studies on which it is based.   The charge only applies to the Positive spirit in its preliminary phase of disconnected specialities, a phase which scientific men of the present day are making such mischievous efforts to prolong.   Nothing can be more fatal to the fine arts than the narrow views, the overstraining of analysis, the abuse of the reasoning faculty, which characterize the scientific investigation of the present day; to say nothing of their injurious effects upon moral progress, the first condition of esthetic development.   But all these defects necessarily disappear when the Positive spirit becomes more comprehensive and systematic; which is the case as soon as it embraces the higher subjects in the encyclopedic scale of sciences.   When it reaches the study of Society, which is its true and ultimate sphere, it has to deal with the conceptions of Poetry, as well as with the operations of Feeling: since its object must then be to give a faithful and complete representation of human nature under its individual, and still more under its social, aspects.   Hitherto Positive Science has avoided these two subjects: but their charm is such that, when the study of them has been once begun, it cannot fail to be prosecuted with ardour; and their proper place in the constitution of Man and of Society will then be recognised.   Reason has been divorced for a long time from Feeling and Imagination.   But with the more complete and systematic culture here proposed they will be re-united.

To those who have studied the foregoing chapters with attention, the view that the new philosophy is unfavourable to Art, will be obviously unjust.   Supposing even that there were no important functions specially assigned to the fine arts in the Positive system, yet indirectly, the leading principles of the system, its social purpose, and the influences by which it is propagated, are all most conducive to the interests of Art. To demonstrate, as Positivism alone of all philosophies has done, the subordination of the intellect to the heart, and the dependence of the unity of human nature upon Feeling, is to stimulate the esthetic faculties, because Feeling is their true source. To propound a social doctrine by which the Revolution is brought to a close, is to remove the principal obstacle to the growth of Art, and to open a wide field and a firm foundation for it, by establishing fixed principles and modes of life; in the absence of which Poetry can have nothing noble to narrate or to inspire. To exhort the working classes to seek happiness in calling their moral and mental powers into constant exercise, and to give them an education, the principal basis of which is esthetic, is to place Art under the protection of its natural patrons.

But one consideration is of itself sufficient for our purpose. We have but to look at the influence of Positivism upon Women, at its tendency to elevate the social dignity of their sex, and at the same time to strengthen all family ties. Now of all the elements of which society is constituted, Woman certainly is the most esthetic, alike from her nature and her position; and both her position and her nature are raised and strengthened by Positivism. We receive from women, not only our first ideas of Goodness, but our first sense of Beauty; for their own sensibility to it is equalled by their power of imparting it to others. We see in them every kind of beauty combined; beauty of mind and character as well as of person. All their actions, even those which are unconscious, exhibit a spontaneous striving for ideal perfection. And their life at home, when free from the necessity of labouring for a livelihood, favours this tendency. Living as they do for affection, they cannot fail to feel aspirations for all that is highest, in the world around them first, and then also in the world of imagination. A doctrine, then, which regards women as the originators of moral influence in society, and which places the groundwork of education under their charge, cannot be suspected of being unfavourable to Art.

Leaving these prejudices, we may now examine the mode in which the incorporation of Art into the modern social system will be promoted by Positivism. In the first place systematic principles of Art will be laid down, and its proper function clearly defined. The result of this will be to call out new and powerful means of expression, and also new organs. I may observe that the position which Art will occupy in the present movement of social regeneration is already an inauguration of its final function; as we saw in the analogous cases of the position of women and of the working classes.

Esthetic talent is for the adornment of life, not for its government. But before touching on this question, it will be well to rectify a prevalent misconception on the subject, one of the many consequences of our mental and moral anarchy. I refer to the exaggeration of the influence of Art; an error which, if uncorrected, would vitiate all our views with regard to it.

All poets of real genius, from Homer to Corneille, have always considered their work to be that of beautifying human life, and so far, of elevating it. Government of human life they had never supposed to fall within their province. Indeed no sane man would lay it down as a proposition that Imagination should control the other mental faculties. It would imply that the normal condition of the intellect was insanity; insanity being definable as that state of mind in which subjective inspirations are stronger than objective judgments. It is a static law of our nature, which has never been permanently suspended, that the faculties of Representation and Expression should be subordinate to those of Conception and Co-ordination. Even in cerebral disturbances the law holds good. The relation with the external world is perverted, but the original correlation of the internal mental functions remains unaffected.

The foolish vanity of the later poets of antiquity led some of them into errors much resembling those which now prevail on this point. Still in Polytheistic society artists were at no time looked upon as the leading class, notwithstanding the esthetic character of Greek and Roman religion. If proofs were necessary, Homer's poem, especially the Odyssey, would show how secondary the influence of the fine arts was upon society, even when the priesthood had ceased to control them. Plato's Utopia, written when Polytheism was in its decline, represented a state in which the interference of poets was systematically prevented. Medieval Monotheism was still less disposed to overrate the importance of Art, though its true value was recognised more generally than it had ever been before. But with the decline of Catholicism, germs of errors showed themselves, from which even the extraordinary genius of Dante was not free. The revolutionary influences of the last five centuries have developed these errors into the delirium of self-conceit exhibited by the poets and literary men of our time. Theology having arrived at its extreme limits, and no conception having yet arisen of the Positive state, the negative condition of the Western Republic became aggravated to an unheard-of extent. Rules and institutions which had formerly controlled the most headstrong ambition, fell rapidly into discredit. And as the principles of social order disappeared, artists, and especially poets, the leading class among them, stimulated by the applause

which they received from their uninstructed audience, fell
into the error of seeking political influence.   Incompatible
as all mere criticism must be with true poetry, modern Art
since the fourteenth century has participated more and
more actively in the destruction of the old system.   Until,
however, Negativism had received its distinct shape and
character from the revolutions of the sixteenth and seventeenth centuries, the influence of Art for destructive purposes was secondary to that exercised by metaphysicians
and legists.   But in the eighteenth century, when negativism began to be propagated boldly in a systematic form,
the case was changed, and literary ambition asserted itself
more strongly.   The men of learning who had hitherto
formed the vanguard of the destructive movement, were
replaced by mere litterateurs, men whose talents were of a
poetical rather than philosophical kind, but who had, intellectually speaking, no real vocation.   When the crisis
of the Revolution came, this heterogeneous class took the
lead in the movement, and naturally stepped into all political offices; a state of things which will continue until
there is a more direct and general movement of reorganization.

The political
influence of
literary men a
deplorable sign
and source of
anarchy.
This is the historical explanation, and at the
same time the refutation, of the subversive
schemes so prevalent in our time, of which the
object is to establish a sort of aristocracy of
literary pedants.   Such day-dreams of unbridled self-conceit find favour only with the metaphysical minds who
cannot sanction exceptional cases without making them
into an absolute rule.   If philosophers are to be excluded
from political authority, there is still greater reason for
excluding poets.   The mental and moral versatility which
makes them so apt in reflecting the thoughts and feelings
of those around them, utterly unfits them for being our

guides. Their natural defects are such as nothing but
rigorous and systematic education can correct; they are,
therefore, certain to be peculiarly prominent in times like
these when deep convictions of any kind are so rare.
Their real vocation is to assist the spiritual power as
accessory members; and this involves their renouncing all
ideas of government, even more strictly than philosophers
themselves. Philosophers, though not themselves engaging in politics, are called upon to lay down the principles
of political action; but the poet has very little to do with
either. His special function is to idealise and to stimulate; and to do this well, he must concentrate his energies
exclusively upon it. It is a large and noble field, amply
sufficient to absorb men who have a real vocation for it.
Accordingly, in the great artists of former times we see
comparatively few traces of this extravagant ambition.
It comes before us in a time when, owing to the absence of
regular habits of life and fixed convictions, art of the
highest order is impossible. The poets of our time either
have not realised or have mistaken their vocation. When
Society is again brought under the influence of a universal
doctrine, real poetry will again become possible; and such
men as those we have been speaking of, whether spoilt
poets or merely poetasters, will turn their energies in a
different direction. Till then they will continue to waste
their efforts and ruin their character in worthless political
agitation, a state of things in which mediocrity shines and
real genius is left in the background.

In the normal state of human nature, Imagination is
subordinate to Reason as Reason is to Feeling. Any prolonged inversion of this natural order is both morally and
intellectually dangerous. The reign of Imagination would
be still more disastrous than the reign of Reason; only
that it is even more incompatible with the practical con-

ditions of human life. But chimerical as it is, the mere
pursuit of it may do much individual harm by substituting
artificial excitement, and in too many cases affectation of
feeling, in the place of deep and spontaneous emotion.
Viewed politically, nothing can be worse than this undue
preponderance of esthetic considerations caused by the uncontrolled ambition of artists and litterateurs. The true
object of Art, which is to charm and elevate human life,
is gradually lost sight of. By being held out as the aim
and object of existence, it degrades the artist and the
public equally, and is therefore certain to degenerate. It
loses all its higher tendencies, and is reduced either to a
sensuous pleasure, or to a mere display of technical skill.
Admiration for the arts, which when kept in its proper
place has done so much for modern life, may become a
deeply corrupting influence, if it becomes the paramount
consideration. It is notorious what an atrocious custom
prevailed in Italy for several centuries, simply for the
sake of improving men's voices. Art, the true purpose of
which is to strengthen our sympathies, leads when thus
degraded to a most abject form of selfishness ; in which
enjoyment of sounds or forms is held out as the highest
happiness, and utter apathy prevails as to all questions of
social interest. So dangerous is it intellectually, and still
more so morally, for individuals, and above all, for
societies to allow esthetic considerations to become un-
duly preponderant ; even when they spring from a genuine
impulse. But the invariable consequence to which this
violation of the first principles of social order leads, is the
success of mediocrities who acquire technical skill by long
practice.

Thus it is that we have gradually fallen under the
discreditable influence of men who were evidently not
competent for any but subordinate positions, and whose

preponderance has proved as injurious to Art as it has been to Philosophy and Morality. A fatal facility of giving expression to what is neither believed nor felt, gives temporary reputation to men who are as incapable of originality in Art as they are of grasping any new principle in science. It is the most remarkable of all the political anomalies caused by our revolutionary position; and the moral results are most deplorable, unless when, as rarely happens, the possessor of these undeserved honours has a nature too noble to be injured by them. Poets are more exposed to these dangers than other artists, because their sphere is more general and gives wider scope for ambition. But in the special arts we find the same evil in a still more degrading form; that of avarice, a vice by which so much of our highest talent is now tainted. Another signal proof of the childish vanity and uncontrolled ambition of the class is, that those who are merely interpreters of other men's productions claim the same title as those who have produced original works.

Such are the results of the extravagant pretentions which artists and literary men have gradually developed during the last five centuries. I have dwelt upon them because they constitute at present such impediments to all sound views of the nature and purposes of Art. My strictures will not be thought too severe by really esthetic natures, who know from personal experience how fatal the present system is to all talent of a high order. Whatever the outcry of those personally interested, it is certain that in the true interest of Art the suppression of mediocrity is at least as important as the encouragement of talent. True taste always implies distaste. The very fact that the object is to foster in us the sense of perfection, implies that all true connoisseurs will feel a thorough dislike for feeble work. Happily there is this privilege in all masterpieces, that the admiration aroused by them endures in its full strength for all time ; so that the plea which is often put forward of keeping up the public taste by novelties which in reality injure it, falls to the ground. To mention my own experience, I may say that for thirteen years I have been induced alike from principle and from inclination, to restrict my reading almost entirely to the great Occidental poets, without feeling the smallest curiosity for the works of the day which are brought out in such mischievous abundance.

Theory of Art. Guarding ourselves, then, against errors of this kind, we may now proceed to consider the esthetic character of Positivism. In the first place, it furnishes us with a satisfactory theory of Art ; a subject which has never been systematically explained ; all previous attempts to do so, whatever their value, having viewed the subject incompletely. The theory here offered is based on the subjective principle of the new philosophy, on its objective dogma, and on its social purpose ; as set forward in the two first chapters of this work.

Art is the idealized representation of Fact. Art may be defined as an ideal representation of Fact ; and its object is to cultivate our sense of perfection. Its sphere therefore is coextensive with that of Science. Both deal in their own way with the world of Fact ; the one explains it, the other beautifies it. The contemplations of the artist and of the man of science follow the same encyclopedic law ; they begin with the simple objects of the external world ; they gradually rise to the complicated facts of human nature. I pointed out in the second chapter that the scientific scale, the scale, that is, of the True, coincided with that of the Good : we now see that it coincides with that of the Beautiful. Thus between these three great creations of

Humanity, Philosophy, Polity, and Poetry, there is the most perfect harmony. The first elements of Beauty, that is to say, Order and Magnitude, are visible in the inorganic world, especially in the heavens; and they are there perceived with greater distinctness than where the phenomena are more complete and less uniform. The higher degrees of Beauty will hardly be recognised by those who are insensible to this its simplest phase. But as in Philosophy we only study the inorganic world as a preliminary to the study of Man; so, but to a still greater extent, is it with Poetry. In Polity the tendency is similar, but less apparent. Here we begin with Material progress; we proceed to Physical and subsequently to Intellectual progress; but it is long before we arrive at the ultimate goal, Moral progress. Poetry passes more rapidly over the three preliminary stages, and rises with less difficulty to the contemplation of moral beauty. Feeling, then, is essentially the sphere of Poetry. And it supplies not the end only, but the means. Of all the phenomena which relate to man, human affections are the most modifiable, and therefore the most susceptible of idealization. Being more imperfect than any other, by virtue of their higher complexity, they allow greater scope for improvement. Now the act of expression, however imperfect, reacts powerfully upon these functions, which from their nature are always seeking some external vent. Every one recognizes the influence of language upon thoughts: and surely it cannot be less upon feelings, since in them the need of expression is greater. Consequently all esthetic study, even if purely imitative, may become a useful moral exercise, by calling sympathies and antipathies into healthy play. The effect is far greater when the representation, passing the limits of strict accuracy, is suitably idealised. This indeed is the characteristic mission of

Art. Its function is to construct types of the noblest kind, by the contemplation of which our feelings and thoughts may be elevated. That the portraiture should be exaggerated follows from the definition of Art; it should surpass realities so as to stimulate us to amend them. Great as the influence is of these poetic emotions on individuals, they are far more efficacious when brought to bear upon public life; not only from the greater importance of the subject matter, but because each individual impression is rendered more intense by combination.

Poetry is intermediate between Philosophy and Polity. Thus Positivism explains and confirms the view ordinarily taken of Poetry, by placing it midway between Philosophy and Polity; issuing from the first, and preparing the way for the second.

Even Feeling itself, the highest principle of our existence, accepts the objective dogma of Philosophy, that Humanity is subject to the order of the external world. And Imagination on still stronger grounds must accept the same law. The ideal must always be subordinate to the real; otherwise feebleness as well as extravagance is the consequence. The statesman who endeavours to improve the existing order, must first study it as it exists. And the poet, although his improvements are but imagined, and are not supposed capable of realization, must do likewise. True, in his fictions he will transcend the limits of the possible, while the statesman will keep within those limits; but both have the same points of departure; both begin by studying the actual facts with which they deal. In our artificial improvements we should never aim at anything more than wise modification of the natural order; we should never attempt to subvert it. And though Imagination has a wider range for its pictures, they are yet subject to the same fundamental law, imposed by Phi-

losophy upon Polity and Poetry alike.   Even in the most
poetic ages this law has always been recognised, only the
external world was interpreted then in a way very differently from ours.   We see the same thing every day in
the mental growth of the child.   As his notions of fact
change, his fictions are modified in conformity with these
changes.

But while Poetry depends upon Philosophy for the
principles on which its types are constructed, it influences
Polity by the direction which it gives to those types.   In
every operation that man undertakes, he must imagine
before he executes, as he must observe before he imagines.
He can never produce a result which he has not conceived
first in his own mind.   In the simplest application of
mechanics or geometry he finds it necessary to form a
mental type, which is always more perfect than the reality
which it precedes and prepares.   Now none but those who
confound poetry with verse-making can fail to see that this
conception of a type is the same thing as esthetic imagination, under its simplest and most general aspect.   Its
application to social phenomena, which constitute the chief
sphere both of Art and of Science, is very imperfectly
understood as yet, and can hardly be said to have begun,
owing to the want of any true theory of society.   The
real object of so applying it is, that it should regulate the
formation of social Utopias ; subordinating them to the laws
of social development as revealed by history.   Utopias are
to the Art of social life what geometrical and mechanical
types are to their respective arts.   In these their necessity is universally recognised ; and surely the necessity
can not be less in problems of such far greater intricacy.
Accordingly we see that, notwithstanding the empirical
condition in which political art has hitherto existed, every
great change has been ushered in, one or two centuries

beforehand, by an Utopia bearing some analogy to it. It was the product of the esthetic genius of Humanity working under an imperfect sense of its conditions and requirements. Positivism, far from laying an interdict on Utopias, tends rather to facilitate their employment and their influence, as a normal element in society. Only, as in the case of all other products of imagination, they must always remain subordinated to the actual laws of social existence. And thus by giving a systematic sanction to this the Poetry, as it may be called, of Politics, most of the dangers which now surround it will disappear. Its extravagances arise simply from the absence of some philosophical principle to control it, and therefore there is no reason for regarding them with great severity.

The whole of this theory may be summed up in the double meaning of the word so admirably chosen to designate our esthetic functions. The word *Art* is a remarkable instance of the popular instinct from which language proceeds, and which is far more enlightened than educated persons are apt to suppose. It indicates, however vaguely, a sense of the true position of Poetry, midway between Philosophy and Polity, but with a closer relation to the latter. True, in the case of the technical arts the improvements proposed are practically realised, while those of the fine arts remain imaginary. Poetry, however, does produce one result of an indirect but most essential kind ; it does actually modify our moral nature. If we include oratory, which is only Poetry in a simpler phase, though often worthless enough, we find its influence exerted in a most difficult and critical task, that of arousing or calming our passions ; and this not arbitrarily, but in accordance with the fixed laws of their action. Here it has been always recognised as a moral agency of great power. On every ground, then, Poetry seems more closely related to prac-

tical than to speculative life.   For its practical results are
of the most important and comprehensive nature.   Whatever the utility of other arts, material, physical, or intellectual, they are only subsidiary or preparatory to that
which in Poetry is the direct aim, moral improvement.·
In the Middle Ages it was common in all Western languages to speak of it as a Science, the proper meaning
of the word Science being then very imperfectly understood.   But as soon as both artistic and scientific genius
had become more fully developed, their distinctive features
were more clearly recognised, and finally the name of Art
was appropriated to the whole class of poetic functions.
The fact is, at all events, an argument in favour of the
Positive theory of idealization, as standing midway between
theoretical inquiry and practical result.

Evidently, then, it is in Art that the unity of   Art calls each
element of our
human nature finds its most complete and most   nature   into
harmonious
natural representation.   For Art is in direct   action.
relation with the three orders of phenomena by which
human nature is characterised; Feelings, Thoughts, and
Actions.   It originates in Feeling; the proof of this is
even more obvious than in the case of Philosophy and
Polity.   It has its basis in Thought, and its end is Action.
Hence its power of exerting an influence for good alike
on every phase of our existence, whether personal or
social.   Hence too its peculiar attribute of giving equal
pleasure to all ranks and ages.   Art invites the thinker
to leave his abstractions for the study of real life; it
elevates the practical man into a region of thought where
self-love has no place.   By its intermediate position it
promotes the mutual reaction of Affection and Reason.
It stimulates feeling in those who are too much engrossed
with intellectual questions: it strengthens the contem-
plative faculty in natures whose sympathy predominates.

It has been said of Art that its province is to hold a
mirror to nature. The saying is usually applied to social
life where its truth is most apparent. But it is no less true
of every aspect of our existence ; for under every aspect
it may be a source of Art, and may be represented and
modified by it. Turning to Biology for the cause of this
sociological relation, we find it in the relation of the muscular and nervous systems. Our motions, involuntary at
first, and then voluntary, indicate internal impressions,
moral impressions more especially ; and as they proceed
from them, so they react upon them. Here we find the
first germ of a true theory of Art. Throughout the animal
kingdom language is simply gesticulation of a more or
less expressive kind. And with man esthetic development
begins in the same spontaneous way.

Three stages
in the esthetic
process.: Imi-
tation, Ideal-
ization, Ex-
pression.
With this primary principle we may now
complete our statical theory of Art, by indicating in it three distinct degrees or phases.
The fine arts have been divided into imitative
and inventive ; but this distinction has no real foundation.
Art always imitates, and always idealizes. True, as the
real is in every case the source of the ideal, art begins at
first with simple Imitation. In the childhood, whether of
man or of the race, as also with the lower animals, servile
imitation and that of the most insignificant actions, is
the only symptom of esthetic capacity. No representation, however, has at present any claim to the title of
Art (although from motives of puerile vanity the name
is often given to it), except so far as it is made more
beautiful, that is to say, more perfect. The representation thus becomes in reality more faithful, because the
principal features are brought prominently forward, instead of being obscured by a mass of unmeaning detail.
This it is which constitutes Idealization ; and from the

time of the great master-pieces of antiquity, it has become more and more the characteristic feature of esthetic productions.   But in recognising the superiority of Idealization as the second stage of Art, we must not forget the necessity of its first stage, Imitation.   Without it neither the origin nor the nature of Art could be correctly understood.

In addition to the creative process, which is the chief characteristic of Art, there is a third function which, though not absolutely necessary in its imitative stage, becomes so in its ideal stage.   I mean the function of Expression strictly so called, without which the product of imagination could not be communicated to others.   Language, whether it be the language of sound or of form, is the last stage of the esthetic operation, and it does not always bear a due proportion to the inventive faculty.   When it is too defective, the sublimest creations may be ranked lower than they deserve, owing to the failure of the poet to communicate his thought completely.   Great powers of style may, on the other hand, confer unmerited reputation, which however does not endure.   An instance of this is the preference that was given for so long a time to Racine over Corneille.

So long as Art is confined to Imitation, no special language is required; imitation is itself the substitute for language.   But as soon as the representation has become idealized by heightening some features and suppressing or altering others, it ceases to have any existence except in the mind of its composer; and its communication to the world requires additional labour devoted exclusively to Expression.   In this final process, so necessary to the complete success of his work, the poet moulds his signs upon his inward type; just as he began at first by adapting them to external facts.   So far there is some truth in Grétry's principle that song is derived from speech by the intermediate stage of declamation. The same principle has been applied to all the special arts : it might also be applied to Poetry, oratory being the link between verse and prose. These views, however, are somewhat modified by the historical spirit of Positive Philosophy. We must invert Grétry's relation of cause and effect ; at least when we are considering those primitive times, when Art and Language first arose together.

In their origin all our faculties of expression had an esthetic character. The only expressions were those that resulted from intense feeling. Feeling had, in primitive times at all events, far more to do with these faculties than Thought, being a far stronger stimulant to external demonstration. Even in the most highly wrought languages, where, in consequence of social requirements, reason has to a great extent encroached upon emotion, we see evidence of this truth.. There is a musical element in the most ordinary conversation. Listening carefully to a lecture on the most abstruse mathematical problem, we shall hear intonations which proceed obviously from the heart rather than the head, and which are indications of character even in the most unimpassioned speaker. Biology at once explains this law, by teaching that the stimulus to the muscles used in expression, whether vocal or gesticulatory, comes principally from the affective region of the brain; the speculative region being too inert to produce muscular contractions for which there is no absolute necessity. Accordingly, Sociology regards every language as containing in its primitive elements all that is spontaneous and universal in the esthetic development of Humanity; enough, that is, to satisfy the general need of communicating emotion. In this common field the special arts commence, and they ultimately widen it. But the operation is the same in its nature, whether carried on by popular instinct or by individuals. The final result is always more dependent on feeling than on reason, even in times like these, when the intellect has risen in revolt against the heart. Song, therefore, comes before Speech; Painting before Writing; because the first things we express are those which move our feelings most. Subsequently the necessities of social life oblige us to employ more frequently, and ultimately to develope, those elements in painting or in song, which relate to our practical wants and to our speculative faculties so far as they are required for supplying them; these forming the topics of ordinary communication. Thus the emotion from which the sign had originally proceeded becomes gradually effaced; the practical object is alone thought of, and expression becomes more rapid and less emphatic. The process goes on until at last the sign is supposed to have originated in arbitrary convention; though, if this were the case, its universal and spontaneous adoption would be inexplicable. Such, then, is the sociological theory of Language, on which I shall afterwards dwell more fully. I connect it with the whole class of esthetic functions, from which in the lower animals it is not distinguished. For no animal idealizes its song or gesture so far as to rise to anything that can properly be called Art.

To complete our examination of the philosophy of Art, statically viewed, we have now only to speak of the order in which the various arts should be classified. Placed as Art is midway *Classification of the arts on the principle of decreasing generality, and increasing intensity.* between Theory and Practice, it is classified on the same principle, the principle, that is, of decreasing generality, which I have long ago shown to be applicable to all Positive classifications of whatever kind. We have already obtained from it a scale of the Beautiful, answering in

most points to that which was first laid down for the True,
and which we applied afterwards to the Good. By following it in the present instance, we shall be enabled to
range the arts in the order of their conception and succession, as was done in my Treatise on Positive Philosophy
for the various branches of Science and Industry.

The arts, then, should be classified by the decreasing
generality and the increasing intensity, which involves
also increasing technicality, of their modes of expression.
In its highest term the esthetic scale connects itself with
the scientific scale ; and in its lowest, with the industrial
scale. This is in conformity with the position assigned to
Art intermediate between Philosophy and Practical life.
Art, never becomes disconnected from human interests ;
but as it becomes less general and more technical, its relation with our higher attributes becomes less intimate, and
it is more dependent on inorganic Nature, so that at last
the kind of beauty depicted by it is merely material.

Poetry.   On these principles of classification we must
give the first place to Poetry properly so called, as being
the most general and least technical of the arts, and as
being the basis on which all the rest depend. The impressions which it produces are less intense than those of
the rest, but its sphere is evidently wider, since it embraces
every side of our existence, whether individual, domestic,
or social. Poetry, like the special arts, has a closer relation with actions and impulses than with thoughts. Yet
the most abstract conceptions are not excluded from its
sphere ; for not merely can it improve the language in
which they are expressed, but it may add to their intrinsic
beauty. It is, on the whole, the most popular of all the
arts, both on account of its wider scope, and also because,
its instruments of expression being taken directly from
ordinary language, it is more generally intelligible than

any other.   True, in the highest kind of poetry versifica-
tion is necessary ; but this cannot be called a special art.
The language of Poetry, although distinct in form, is in
reality nothing but the language of common men more
perfectly expressed.   The only technical element in it,
prosody, is easily acquired by a few days' practice..   A
proof of the identity of the language of Poetry with that
of common life, is the fact that no poet has ever been
able to write with effect in a foreign or a dead language.
And not only is this noblest of Arts more comprehensive,
more spontaneous, more popular than the rest, but it surpasses them in that which is the characteristic feature of
all art, Ideality.   Poetry is the art which idealises the
most, and imitates the least.   For these reasons it has
always held the first place among the arts ; a view which
will be strengthened in proportion as we attach greater
importance to idealization and less to mere expression.
In expression it is inferior to the other arts, which represent such subjects as fall within their compass with greater
intensity.   But it is from Poetry that these subjects are
usually borrowed.

The first term of the series being thus deter-   Music.
mined, the other arts may at once be ranked according to
the degree of their affinity with Poetry.   Let us begin by
distinguishing the different senses to which they appeal ;
and we shall find that our series proceeds on the principle
which biologists, since Gall's time, have adopted for the
classification of the special senses, the principle of decreasing sociability.   There are only two senses which can be
called esthetic ; namely, Sight and Hearing : the others
having no power of raising us to Idealization.   The sense
of smell can, it is true, enable us to associate ideas ; but in
man it exists too feebly for artistic effects.   Hearing and
Sight correspond to the two modes of natural language,

voice and gesture. From the first arises the art of Music; the second, which however is less esthetic, includes the three arts of form. These are more technical than Music; their field is not so wide, and morever they stand at a greater distance from poetry; whereas Music remained for a long time identified with it. Another distinction is that the sense to which music appeals performs its function involuntarily; and this is one reason why the emotions which it calls forth are more spontaneous and more deep, though less definite, than in the case where it depends on the will whether we receive the impression or not. Again, the difference between them answers to the distinction of Time and Space. The art of sound represents succession; the arts of form, coexistence. On all these grounds music should certainly be ranked before the other special arts, as the second term of the esthetic series. Its technical difficulties are exaggerated by pedants, whose interest it is to do so; in reality, special training is less needed for its appreciation, and even for its composition, than in the case of either painting or sculpture. Hence it is in every respect more popular and more social.

Painting.
Sculpture.
Architecture. Of the three arts which appeal to the voluntary sense of sight, and which present simultaneous impressions, Painting, on the same principle of arrangement, holds the first rank, and Architecture the last; Sculpture being placed between them. Painting alone employs all the methods of visual expression, combining the effects of colour with those of form. Whether in public or private life, its sphere is wider than that of the other two. More technical skill is required in it than in music, and it is harder to obtain; but the difficulty is less than in Sculpture or in Architecture. These latter idealise less, and imitate more. Of the two, Architecture is the less esthetic. It is far more dependent on technical

processes; and indeed most of its productions are rather works of industry than works of art. It seldom rises above material beauty : moral beauty it can only represent by artifices, of which the meaning is often ambiguous. But the impressions conveyed by it are so powerful and so permanent, that it will always retain its place among the fine arts, especially in the case of great public buildings, which stand out as the most imposing record of each successive phase of social development. Never has the power of Architecture been displayed to greater effect than in our magnificent cathedrals, in which the spirit of the Middle Ages has been idealised and preserved for posterity. They exhibit in a most striking manner the property which Architecture possesses of bringing all the arts together into a common centre.

These brief remarks will illustrate the method adopted by the new philosophy in investigating a systematic theory of Art under all its statical aspects. *The conditions favourable to Art have never yet been combined.* We have now to speak of its action upon social life, whether in the final state of Humanity, or in the transitional movement through which that state is to be reached.

The Positive theory of history shows us at once, in spite of strong prejudices to the contrary, that up to the present time the progress achieved by Art has been, like that of Science and Industry, only preparatory; the conditions essential to its full development never having yet been combined.

Too much has been made of the esthetic tendencies of the nations of antiquity, owing to *Neither in Polytheism,* the free scope that was given to Imagination in constructing their doctrines. In fact, Polytheism, now that the belief in its principles exists no longer, has been regarded as simply a work of art. But the long duration of its principles would be sufficient proof that they were not created by the poets, but that they emanated from the philosophic genius of Humanity working spontaneously, as explained in my theory of human development, in the only way that was then possible. All that Art did for Polytheism was to perform its proper function of clothing it in a more poetic form. It is quite true that the peculiar character of Polytheistic philosophy gave greater scope for the development of Art than has been afforded by any subsequent system. It is to this portion of the theological period that we must attribute the first steps of esthetic development, whether in society or in the individual. Yet Art was never really incorporated into the ancient order. Its free growth was impossible so long as it remained under the control of Theocracy, which made use of it as an instrument, but which, from the stationary character of its dogmas, shackled its operations. Moreover, the social life of antiquity was highly unfavourable to Art. The sphere of personal feelings and domestic affections was hardly open to it. Public life in ancient times had certainly more vigorous and more permanent features, and here there was a wider field. Yet even in such a case as that of Homer, we feel that he would hardly have spent his extraordinary powers upon descriptions of military life, had there been nobler subjects for his genius. The only grand aspect, viewed socially, that war could offer, the system of incorporation instituted by Rome after a succession of conquests, could not then be foreseen. When that period arrived, ancient history was drawing to a close, and the only poetical tribute to this nobler policy was contained in a few beautiful lines of Virgil's Æneid, ending with the remarkable expression,

" Pacisque imponere morem."
(Impose the law of peace.)

Mediæval society, notwithstanding irra- tional prejudices to the contrary, would have been far more favourable to the fine arts, could it have continued longer. I do not speak, indeed, of its dogmas; which were so incompatible with Art, as to lead to the strange inconsistency of giving a factitious sanction to Paganism in the midst of Christianity. By holding personal and chimerical objects before us as the end of life, Monotheism discouraged all poetry, except so far as it related to our individual existence. This, however, was idealised by the mystics, whose beautiful compositions penetrated into our inmost emotions, and wanted nothing but greater perfection of form. All that Catholicism effected for Art in other respects was to secure a better position for it, as soon as the priesthood became strong enough to counteract the intellectual and moral defects of Christian doctrine. But the social life of the Middle Ages was far more esthetic than that of antiquity. War was still the prevailing occupation; but by assuming a defensive character, it had become far more moral, and therefore more poetic. Woman had acquired a due measure of freedom; and the free development of home affections was thus no longer restricted. There was a consciousness of personal dignity hitherto unknown, and yet quite compatible with social devotion, which elevated individual life in all its aspects. All these qualities were summed up in the noble institution of Chivalry; and Chivalry gave a strong stimulus to Art throughout Western Europe, and diffused it more largely than in any former period. This movement was in reality, though the fact is not recognised as it should be, the source of modern Art. The reason for its short duration is to be found in the essentially transient and provisional character of mediæval society under all its aspects. By the time that its lan-

guages and habits had become sufficiently stable for the
esthetic spirit to produce works of permanent value, Catholic Feudalism was already undermined by the growing
force of the negative movement. The beliefs and modes
of life offered for idealization were seen to be declining :
and neither the poet nor his readers could feel those deep
convictions which the highest purposes of Art require.

Much less in   During the decline of Chivalry, Art received
modern times.   indirectly an additional impulse from the movement of social decomposition which has been going on
rapidly for the last five centuries. In this movement all
mental and social influences gradually participated. Negativism, it is true, is not the proper province of Art; but
the dogmas of Christianity were so oppressive to it, that
its efforts to shake off the yoke were of great service to
the cause of general emancipation. Dante's incomparable
work is a striking illustration of this anomalous combination of contradictory influences. It was a situation unfavourable for art, because every aspect of life was rapidly
changing and losing its character before there was time to
idealize it. Consequently the poet had to create his own
field artificially from ancient history, which supplied him
with those fixed and definite modes of life which he could
not find around him. Thus it was that for several centuries the Classical system became the sole source of esthetic culture; the result being that Art lost much of the
originality and popularity which had previously belonged
to it. That great master-pieces should have been produced
at all under such unfavourable circumstances is the best
proof of the spontaneous character of our esthetic faculties.
The value of the Classical system has been for some time
entirely exhausted; and now that the negative movement
has reached its extreme limits, there only remained one
service (a service of great temporary importance) for Art

to render, the idealization of Doubt itself.   Such a phase
of course admitted of but short duration.   The best examples of it are the works of Byron and Göthe, the
principal value of which has been, that they have initiated
Protestant countries into the unrestricted freedom of
thought which emanated originally from French philosophy.

Thus history shows that the esthetic development of
Humanity has been the result of spontaneous tendencies
rather than of systematic guidance.   The mental conditions most favourable to it have never been fulfilled simultaneously with its social conditions.   At the present time
both are alike wanting.   Yet there is no evidence that our
esthetic faculties are on the decline.   Not only has the
growth of art proceeded in spite of every obstacle, but it
has become more thoroughly incorporated into the life of
ordinary men.   In ancient times it was cultivated only by
a small class.   So little was it recognised as a component
part of social organization, that it did not even enter into
men's imaginary visions of a future existence.   But in the
Middle Ages the simplest minds were encouraged to cultivate the sense of beauty as one of the purest delights of
human life ; and it was held out as the principal occupation of the celestial state.   From that time all classes of
European society have taken an increasing interest in
these elevating pleasures, beginning with poetry, and
thence passing to the special arts, especially music, the
most social of all.   The influence of artists, even when
they had no real claim to the title, has been on the increase ; until at last the anarchy of the present time
has introduced them to political power, for which they
are utterly unqualified.

All this would seem to show that the greatest
epoch of Art has yet to come.   In this respect,

Under Posi-
tivism the con-
ditions will all
be favourable.

There will be fixed principles, and a nobler moral culture.

as in every other, the Past has but supplied the necessary materials for future reconstruction. What we have seen as yet is but a spontaneous and immature prelude; but in the manhood of our moral and mental powers, the culture of Art will proceed on principles as systematic as the culture of Science and of Industry, both of which at present are similarly devoid of organization. The regeneration of society will be incomplete until Art has been fully incorporated into the modern order. And to this result all our antecedents have been tending. To renew the esthetic movement so admirably began in the Middle Ages, but interrupted by classical influences, will form a part of the great work which Positivism has undertaken, the completion and re-establishment of the Mediæval structure upon a firmer intellectual basis. And when Art is once restored to its proper place, its future progress will be unchecked, because, as I shall now proceed to show, all the influences of the final order, spontaneous or systematic, will be in every respect favourable to it. If this can be made clear, the poetic capabilities of Positive Philosophy will require no further proof.

As being the only rallying point now possible for fixed convictions, without which life can have no definite or permanent character, Positivism is on this ground alone indispensable to all further development of modern Art. If the poet and his readers are alike devoid of such convictions, no idealization of life, whether personal, domestic, or social, is in any true sense possible. No emotions are fit subjects for Art unless they are felt deeply, and unless they come spontaneously to all. When society has no marked intellectual or moral feature, Art, which is its mirror, can have none either. And although the esthetic faculty is so innate in us that it never can remain inactive, yet its culture becomes in this case vague and objectless. The fact therefore that Positivism terminates the Revolution by initiating the movement of organic growth is of itself enough to prove its beneficial influence upon Art.

Art, indeed, would profit by any method of re-organization, whatever its nature. But the principle on which Positivism proposes to reconstruct is peculiarly favourable to its growth. The opinions and the modes of life to which that principle conducts are precisely those which are most essential to esthetic development.

A more esthetic system cannot be imagined than one which teaches that Feeling is the basis on which the unity of human nature rests ; and which assigns as the grand object of man's existence, progress in every direction, but especially moral progress. It may seem at first as if the tendency of the new philosophy was merely to make us more systematic. And systematization is assuredly indispensable ; but the sole object of it is to increase our sympathy and our synergic activity by supplying that fixity of principle which alone can lead to energetic practice. By teaching that the highest happiness is to aid in the happiness of others, Positivism invites the poet to his noblest function, the culture of generous sympathies, a subject far more poetic than the passions of hatred and oppression which hitherto have been his ordinary theme. A system which regards such culture as the highest object cannot fail to incorporate Poetry as one of its essential elements, and to give to it a far higher position than it has ever held before. Science, although it be the source from which the Positive system emanates, will be restricted to its proper function of supplying the objective basis for human prevision ; thus giving to Art and Industry, which must always be the principal

objects of our attention, the foundation they require.
Positivism, substituting in every subject the relative point
of view for the absolute, regarding, that is, every subject
in its relation to Humanity, would not prosecute the study
of the True beyond what is required for the development
of the Good and the Beautiful. Beyond this point, scientific
culture is a useless expenditure of time, and a diversion
from the great end for which Man and Society exist. Subordinate as the ideal must ever be to the real, Art will
yet exercise a most salutary influence upon Science, as
soon as we cease to study Science in an absolute spirit.
In the very simplest phenomena, after reaching the degree
of exactness which our wants require, there is always a
certain margin of liberty for the imagination ; and advantage may very well be taken of this to make our conceptions more beautiful and so far more useful. Still
more available is this influence of the Beautiful on the
True in the highest subjects, that is, in those which concern Humanity. Minute accuracy being here more difficult and at the same time less important, more room is
left for esthetic considerations. In representing the great
historical types, for instance, Art has its place as well as
Science. A society which devotes all its powers to
making every aspect of life as perfect as possible, will
naturally give preference to that kind of intellectual culture which is of all others the best calculated to heighten
our sense of perfection.

Predisposing influence of Education. The tendency of Positivism to favour these
the most energetic of our intellectual faculties
and the most closely related to our moral nature, is apparent throughout its educational system. The reader
will have seen in the third chapter that in Positive education more importance is attached to Art than to Science,
as the true theory of human development requires. Science

intervenes only to put into systematic shape what Art, operating under the direct influence of affection, has spontaneously begun.   As in the history of mankind esthetic development preceded scientific development, so it will be with the individual, whose education on the Positive method is but a reproduction of the education of the race.   The only rational principle of our absurd classical system is its proposed tendency to encourage poetical training.   The futility, however, of this profession is but too evident: the usual result of the system being to implant erroneous notions of all the fine arts, if not utter distaste for them.   A striking illustration of its worthlessness is the idolatry with which for a whole century our French pedants regarded Boileau; a most skilful versifier, but of all our poets perhaps the least gifted with true poetic feeling.   Positivist education will effect what classical education has attempted so imperfectly.   It will familiarise the humblest working man or woman from childhood with all the beauties of the best poets; not those of his own nation merely, but of all the West.   To secure the genuineness and efficiency of esthetic development, attention must first be given to the poets who depict our own modern society.   Afterwards, as I have said, the young Positivist will be advised to complete his poetical course, by studying the poets who have idealised antiquity.   But his education will not be limited to poetry, it will embrace the special arts of sound and form, by which the principal effects of poetry are reproduced with greater intensity.   Thus the contemplation and meditation suggested by Art, besides their own intrinsic charm, will prepare the way for the exercise of similar faculties in Science.   For with the individual, as with the species, the combination of images will assist the combination of signs; signs in their origin being images which have lost their vividness.   As the sphere of Art includes every subject of human interest, we shall become familiarised, during the esthetic period of education, with the principal conceptions that are afterwards to be brought before us systematically in the scientific period.   Especially will this be true of historical studies.   By the time that the pupil enters upon them, he will be already familiar with poetic descriptions of the various social phases, and of the men who played a leading part in them.

Relation of Art to Religion.   And if Art is of such importance in the education of the young, it is no less important in the afterwork of education ; the work of recalling men or classes of men to those high feelings and principles which, in the daily business of life, are so apt to be forgotten.   In the solemnities, private or public, appointed for this purpose, Positivism will rely far more on impressions such as poetry can inspire, than on scientific explanations.   Indeed the preponderance of Art over Science will be still greater than in education properly so called.   The scientific basis of human conduct having been already laid down, it will not be necessary to do more than refer to it.   The philosophic priesthood will in this case be less occupied with new conceptions, than with the enforcement of truth already known, which demands esthetic rather than scientific talent.

A vague presentiment of the proper function of Art in regulating public festivals was shown empirically by the Revolutionists.   But all their attempts in this direction proved notorious failures ; a signal proof that politicians should not usurp the office of spiritual guides.   The intention of a festival is to give public expression to deep and genuine feeling ; spontaneousness therefore is its first condition.   Hence it is a matter with which political rulers are incompetent to deal ; and even the spiritual power should only act as the systematic organ of impulses which already exist. Since the decline of Catholicism we have had no festivals worthy of the name; nor can we have them until Positivism has become generally accepted. All that governments could do at present is to exhibit unmeaning and undignified shows before discordant crowds, who are themselves the only spectacle worth beholding. Indeed the usurpation of this function by government is in many cases as tyrannical as it is irrational; arbitrary formulas are often imposed, which answer to no pre-existing feeling whatever. Evidently the direction of festivals is a function which more than any other belongs exclusively to the spiritual power, since it is the spiritual power which regulates the tendencies of which these festivals are the manifestation. Here its work is essentially esthetic. A festival even in private, and still more in public life, is or should be a work of art; its purpose being to express certain feelings by voice or gesture, and to idealise them. It is the most esthetic of all functions, since it involves usually a complete combination of the four special arts, under the presidence of the primary art, Poetry. On this ground governments have in most cases been willing. to waive their official authority in this matter, and to be largely guided by artistic counsel, accepting even the advice of painters and sculptors in the default of poets of real merit.

The esthetic tendencies of Positivism, with regard to institutions of this kind, are sufficiently evident in the worship of Woman, spoken of in the preceding chapter, and in the worship of Humanity, of which I shall speak more particularly afterwards. From these, indeed, most Positivist festivals, private or public, will originate. But this subject has been already broached, and will be discussed in the next chapter with as much detail as the limits of this introductory work allow.

While the social value of Art is thus enhanced by the importance of the work assigned to it, new and extensive fields for its operation are opened out by Positivism. Chief amongst these is History, regarded as a continuous whole; a domain at present almost untouched.

Idealization of historical types.

Modern poets, finding little to inspire them in their own times, and driven back into ancient life by the classical system, have already idealised some of the past phases of Humanity. Our great Corneille, for instance, is principally remembered for the series of dramas in which he has so admirably depicted various periods of Roman history. In our own times where the historical spirit has become stronger, novelists, like Scott and Manzoni, have made similar though less perfect attempts to idealize later periods. Such examples, however, are but spontaneous and imperfect indications of the new field which Positivism now offers to the artist; a field which extends over the whole region of the Past and even of the Future. Until this vast domain had been conceived of as a whole by the philosopher, it would have been impossible to bring it within the compass of poetry. Now theological and metaphysical philosophers were prevented by the absolute spirit of their doctrines from understanding history in all its phases, and were totally incapable of idealizing them as they deserved. Positivism, on the contrary, is always relative; and its principal feature is a theory of history which enables us to appreciate and become familiar with every mode in which human society has formed itself. No sincere Monotheist can understand and represent with fairness the life of Polytheists or Fetichists. But the Positivist poet, accustomed to look upon all past historical stages in their proper filiation, will be able so thoroughly to identify himself with all, as to awaken our sympathies for them, and revive the traces which each individual may recognise of corresponding phases in his own history. Thus we shall be able thoroughly to enter into the esthetic beauty of the Pagan creeds of Greece and Rome, without any of the scruples which Christians could not but feel when engaged on the same subject. In the Art of the Future all phases of the Past will be recalled to life with the same distinctness with which some of them have been already idealized by Homer and Corneille. And the value of this new source of inspiration is the greater that, at the same time that it is being opened out to the artist, the public is being prepared for its enjoyment. An almost exhaustless series of beautiful creations in epic or dramatic art may be produced, which, by rendering it more easy to comprehend and to glorify the Past in all its phases, will form an essential element, on the one hand, of our educational system, and on the other, of the worship of Humanity.

Lastly, not only will the field for Art become wider, but its organs will be men of a higher stamp. The present system, in which the arts are cultivated by special classes, must be abolished, as being wholly alien to that synthetic spirit which always characterises the highest poetic genius.

Art requires the highest education; but little special instruction.

Real talent for Art cannot fail to be called out by the educational system of Positivism, which, though intended for the working classes, is equally applicable to all others. We can only idealize and portray what has become familiar to us; consequently poetry has always rested upon some system of belief, capable of giving a fixed direction to our thoughts and feelings. The greatest poets, from Homer to Corneille, have always participated largely in the best education of which their times admitted. The artist must have clear conceptions before he can exhibit true pictures. Even in these anarchic times, when the system of specialities is being carried to such an irrational extent, the so-called poets who imagine that they can save themselves the trouble of philosophical training, have in reality to borrow a basis of belief from some worn-out metaphysical or theological creed. Their special education, if it can be called so, consists merely in cultivating the talent for expression, and is equally injurious to their intellect and their heart. Incompatible with deep conviction of any kind, while giving mechanical skill in the technical department of Art, it impairs the far more important faculty of idealization. Hence it is that we are at present so deplorably over-stocked with verse-makers and literary men, who are wholly devoid of real poetic feeling, and are fit for nothing but to disturb society by their reckless ambition. As for the four special arts, the training for them at present given, being still more technical, is even more hurtful in every respect to the student whose education does not extend beyond it. On every ground, then, artists of whatever kind should begin their career with the same education as the rest of society. The necessity for such an education in the case of women has been already recognised; and it is certainly not less desirable for artists and poets.

Indeed, so esthetic is the spirit of Positive education, that no special training for Art will be needed, except that which is given spontaneously by practice. There is no other profession which requires so little direct instruction; the tendency of it in Art being to destroy originality, and to stifle the fire of genius with technical erudition. Even for the special arts no professional education is needed. These, like industrial arts, should be acquired by careful practice under the guidance of good masters. The notorious failure of public institutions established for the purpose of forming musicians and painters, makes it unneces-

sary to dwell further upon this point. Not to speak of
their injurious effects upon character, they are a positive
impediment to true genius. Poets and artists, then, require no education beyond that which is given to the
public, whose thoughts and emotions it is their office to
represent. Its want of speciality makes it all the more
fit to develop and bring forward real talent. It will
strengthen the love of all the fine arts simultaneously ;
for the connection between them is so intimate that those
who make it a boast that their talent is for one of them
exclusively will be strongly suspected of having no real
vocation for any. Ths greatest masters even in modern
times have all shown this universality of taste. Its
absence in the present day is but a fresh proof that
esthetic genius does not and cannot exist in times like
these, when Art has no social purpose and rests on no
philosophic principles. If even amateurs are expected
to enjoy Art in all its forms, is it likely that composers of
real genius will restrict their admiration to their own
special mode of idealization and expression ?

Positivism then, while infusing a profoundly
esthetic spirit into general education, would
suppress all special schools of Art on the ground
that they impede its true growth, and simply
promote the success of mediocrities. When
this principle is carried out to its full length, we shall no
longer have any special class of artists. The culture of
Art, especially of poetry, will be a spontaneous addition to
the functions of the three classes which constitute the
moral power of society.

Artists as a class will disappear. Their function will be appropriated by the philosophic priesthood.

Under theocracy, the system by which the evolution of
human society was inaugurated, the speculative class absorbed all functions except those relating to the common
business of life. No distinction was made between esthetic

and scientific talent. Their separation took place afterwards : and though it was indispensable to the full development of both, yet it forms no part of the permanent order
of society, in which the only well-marked division is that
between Theory and Practice. Ultimately all theoretic
faculties will be again combined even more closely than
in primitive times. So long as they are dispersed, their
full influence on practical life cannot be realized. Only
it was necessary that they should remain dispersed until
each constituent element had attained a sufficient degree
of development. For this preliminary growth the long
period of time that has elapsed since the decline of theocracy was necessary. Art detached itself from the theoretical system before Science, because its progress was more
rapid, and from its nature it was more independent. The
priesthood had lost its hold of Art, as far back as the time
of Homer : but it still continued to be the depositary of
science, until it was superseded at first by philosophers
strictly so called, afterwards by mathematicians and astronomers. So it was that Art first, and subsequently Science,
yielded to the specializing system which, though normal
for Industry, is in their case abnormal. It stimulated the
growth of our speculative faculties at the time of their
escape from the yoke of theocracy ; but now that the need
for it no longer exists, it is the principal obstacle to the
final order, towards which all their partial developments
have been tending. To recombine these special elements
on new principles is at present the primary condition of
social regeneration.

Looking at the two essential functions of the spiritual
power, education and counsel, it is not difficult to see that
what they require is a combination of poetic feeling with
scientific insight. We look for a measure of both these
qualities in the public ; therefore men who are devoid of

either of them cannot be fit to be its spiritual guides. That they take the name of philosophers in preference to that of poets, is because their ordinary duties are more connected with Science than with Art; but they ought to be equally interested in both. Science requires systematic teaching, whereas Art is cultivated spontaneously, with the exception of the technical branches of the special arts. It must be remembered that the highest esthetic functions are not such as can be performed continuously. It is only works of rare excellence which are in the highest sense useful: these, once produced, supply an unfailing source of idealization and expression for our emotions, whether in public or in private. It is enough, if the interpreter of these works and his audience have been so educated as to appreciate what is perfect, and reject mediocrity. Organs of unusual power will arise occasionally, as in former times, from all sections of society, whenever the need of representing new emotions may be felt. But they will come more frequently from the philosophic class, in whose character, when it is fully developed, Sympathy will be as prominent a feature as System.

There is, in truth, no organic distinction be- *Identity of esthetic and scientific genius.* tween scientific and poetic genius. The difference lies merely in their combinations of thought, which are concrete and ideal in the one case, abstract and real in the other. Both employ analysis at starting; both alike aim ultimately at synthesis. The erroneous belief in their incompatibility proceeds merely from the absolute spirit of metaphysical philosophy, which so often leads us to mistake a transitory phase for the permanent order. If it is the fact, as appears, that they have never been actually combined in the same person, it is merely because the two functions cannot be called into action at the same moment. A state of society that calls

for great philosophical efforts cannot be favourable to
poetry, because it involves a new elaboration of first principles ; and it is essential to Art that these should have
been already fixed.   This is the reason why in history we
find periods of esthetic growth succeeding periods of great
philosophical change, but never coexisting.   If we look at
instances of great minds who were never able to find their
proper sphere, we see at once that had they risen at some
other time, they might have cultivated either poetry or
philosophy, as the case might be, with equal success.
Diderot would no doubt have been a great poet in a time
more favourable to art ; and Göthe, under different political influences, might have been an eminent philosopher.
All scientific discoverers in whom the inductive faculty
has been more active than the deductive, have given manifest proof of poetic capacity.   Whether the powers of
invention take an abstract or a concrete direction, whether
they are employed in discovering truth or in idealizing it,
the cerebral function is always essentially the same.   The
difference is merely in the objects aimed at ; and as these
alternate according to the circumstances of the time, they
cannot both be pursued simultaneously.   The remarkably
synthetic character of Buffon's genius may be looked on
historically as an instance of fusion of the scientific and
esthetic spirit.   Bossuet is even a more striking instance
of a mind equally capable of the deepest philosophy and
of the sublimest poetry, had the circumstances of his life
given him a more definite impulse in either direction.

It is, then, not unreasonable to expect, notwithstanding
the opinion usually maintained, that the philosophical class
will furnish poets of the highest rank when the time calls
for them.   To pass from scientific thought to esthetic
thought will not be difficult for minds of the highest
order ; for in such minds there is always a natural incli-

nation towards the work which is most urgently required by their age.   To meet the technical conditions of the arts of sound and form, it will be necessary to provide a few special masters, who, in consideration of the importance of their services to general education, will be looked upon as accessory members of the new spiritual power. But even here the tendency to specialities will be materially restricted.   This exceptional position will only be given to men of sufficient esthetic power to appreciate all the fine arts ; and they should be capable of practising at least the three arts of form simultaneously, as was done by Italian painters in the sixteenth century.

As an ordinary rule, it is only by their appreciation and power of explaining ideal Art in all its forms that our philosophers will exhibit their esthetic faculty.   They will not be actively engaged in esthetic functions, except in the arrangement of public festivals.   But when the circumstances of the time are such as to call for great epic or dramatic works, which implies the absence of any philosophical question of the first importance, the most powerful minds among them will become poets in the common sense of the word.   As the work of Co-ordination and that of Idealization will for the future alternate with greater rapidity, we might conceive them, were man's life longer, performed by the same organ.   But the shortness of life, and the necessity of youthful vigour for all great undertakings, excludes this hypothesis.   I only mention it to illustrate the radical identity of two forms of mental activity which are often supposed incompatible.

An additional proof of the esthetic capacity *Women's poetry.* of the moderating power in works of less difficulty, but admitting of greater frequency, will be furnished by its feminine element.   In the special arts, or at least in the arts of form, but little can be expected of them, because these demand more technical knowledge than they can well acquire, and, moreover, the slow process of training would spoil the spontaneousness which is so admirable in them. But for all poetic composition which does not require intense or prolonged effort, women of genius are better qualified than men. This they should consider as their proper department intellectually, since their nature is not well adapted for the discovery of scientific truth. When women have become more systematically associated with the general movement of society under the influence of the new system of education, they will do much to elevate that class of poetry which relates to personal feelings and to domestic life. Women are already better judges of such poetry than men ; and there is no reason why they should not excel them in composing it. For the power of appreciating and that of producing are in reality identical ; the difference is in degree only, and it depends greatly upon culture. The only kind of composition which seems to me to be beyond their powers is epic or dramatic poetry in which public life is depicted. But in all its other branches, poetry would seem their natural field of study ; and one which, regarded always as an exceptional occupation, is quite in keeping with the social duties assigned to them. The affections of our home life cannot be better portrayed than by those in whom they are found in their purest form, and who, without training, combine talent and expression with the tendency to idealize. Under a more perfect organization, then, of the esthetic world than prevails at present, the larger portion of poetical and perhaps also of musical productions, will pass into the hands of the more loving sex. The advantage of this will be that the poetry of private life will then rise to that high standard of moral purity of which it so peculiarly admits, but which our coarser sex can never attain without struggles which injure its spontaneity. The simple grace of Lafontaine and the delicate sweetness of Petrarch will then be found united with deeper and purer sympathies, so as to raise lyrical poetry to a degree of perfection that has never yet been attained.

The popular element of the spiritual power **People's poetry.** has not so well marked an aptitude for art, since the active nature of their occupations hardly admits of the same degree of intellectual life. But there is a minor class of poems, where energy of character and freedom from worldly cares are the chief sources of inspiration, for which working men are better adapted than women, and far more so than philosophers. When Positivist education has extended sufficiently to the People of the West, poets and musicians will spontaneously arise, as in many cases they have already arisen, to give expression to its own special aspirations. But independently of what may be due to individual efforts, the People as a whole has an indirect but most important influence upon the progress of Art, from the fact of being the principal source of language.

Such, then, is the position which Art will finally assume in the Positive system. There will be no class, as at present, exclusively devoted to it, with the exception of a few special masters. But there will be a general education, enabling every class to appreciate all the modes of idealization, and encouraging their culture among the three elements which constitute the moral force of society and which are excluded from political government. Among these there will be a division of esthetic labour. Poetry descriptive of public life will emanate from the philosophic class. The poetry of personal or domestic life will be written by women or working men, according as affection or energy may be the source of inspiration. Thus the mental exer-

cise for which our faculties are best qualified will be fully
developed with those classes in which the various features
of our nature are most prominently exhibited. The only
classes who cannot participate in this pleasant task are
those whose life is occupied by considerations of power or
wealth, and whose enjoyment of Art, though heightened
by the education which they in common with others will
receive, must remain essentially passive. Our idealizing
powers will henceforth be directly concentrated on a work
of the highest social importance, the purification of our
moral nature. The speciality by which so much of the
natural charm of Art was lost will cease, and the moral
dangers of a life exclusively devoted to the faculty of
expression, will exist no longer.

Value of Art in the present crisis.   I have now shown the position which Art
will occupy in the social system as finally con-
stituted. I have yet to speak of its influence in the actual
movement of regeneration which Positivism is inaugurating. We have already seen that each of the three classes
who participate in this movement, assumes functions similar to those for which it is ultimately destined, performing
them in a more strenuous, though less methodic way.
This is obviously true of the philosophic class who head
the movement; nor is it less true of the proletariate, from
whom it derives its vigour, or of women, whose support
gives it a moral sanction. It is, therefore, at first sight
probable that the same will hold good of the esthetic conditions which are necessary to the completeness of these
three functions of the social organism. On closer examination we shall find that this is the case.

Construction of normal types on the basis furnished by philosophy.   The principal function of Art is to construct
types on the basis furnished by Science. Now
this is precisely what is required for inaugurating the new social system. However perfectly its first

principles may be elaborated by thinkers, they will still be not sufficiently definite for the practical result. Systematic study of the Past can only reveal the Future in general outline. Even in the simpler sciences perfect distinctness is impossible without overstepping the limits of actual proof. Still more, therefore, in Sociology will the conclusions of Science fall always far short of that degree of precision and clearness, without which no principle can be thoroughly popularised. But at the point where Philosophy must always leave a void, Poetry steps in and stimulates to practical action. In the early periods of Polytheism, Poetry repaired the defects of the system viewed dogmatically. Its value will be even greater in idealizing a system founded, not upon imagination, but upon observation of fact. In the next chapter I shall dwell at greater length on the service which Poetry will render in representing the central conception of Positivism. It will be easy to apply the same principle to other cases.

In his efforts to accomplish this object, the *Pictures of the Future of Man.* Positivist poet will naturally be led to form prophetic pictures of the regeneration of Man, viewed in every aspect that admits of being ideally represented. And this is the second service which Art will render to the cause of social renovation; or rather it is an extension of the first. Systematic formation of Utopias will in fact become habitual; on the distinct understanding that, as in every other branch of art, the ideal shall be kept in subordination of the real. The unlimited license which is apparently given to Utopias by the unsettled character of the time is in reality a bar to their practical influence, since even the wildest dreamers shrink from extravagance that oversteps the ordinary conditions of mental sanity. But when it is once understood that the sphere of Imagi-

nation is simply that of explaining and giving life to the
conclusions of Reason, the severest thinkers will welcome
its influence ; because, so far from obscuring truth, it will
give greater distinctness to it than could be given by
Science unassisted. Utopias have, then, their legitimate
purpose, and Positivism will strongly encourage their
formation. They form a class of poetry which, under
sound sociological principles, will prove of material service in leading the people of the West towards the normal
state. Each of the five modes of Art may participate in
this salutary influence ; each in its own way may give a
foretaste of the beauty and greatness of the new life that
is now offered to the individual, to the family, and to
society.

Contrasts with the Past. From this second mode in which Art assists
the great work of reconstruction we pass natur-
ally to a third, which at the present time is of equal
importance. To remove the spell under which the Western nations are still blinded to the Future by the decayed
ruins of the Past, all that is necessary is to bring these
ruins into comparison with the prophetic pictures of which
we have been speaking. Since the decline of Catholicism
in the fourteenth century, Art has exhibited a critical
spirit alien to its true nature, which is essentially synthetic. Henceforth it is to be constructive rather than
critical ; yet this is not incompatible with the secondary
object of contending against opinions, and still more
against modes of life, which ought to have died out with
the Catholic system, or with the revolutionary period
which followed it. But resistance to some of the most
deeply-rooted errors of the Past will not interfere with the
larger purpose of Positivist Art. No direct criticism will
be needed. Whether against theological or against metaphysical dogmas, argument is henceforth needless, even in

a philosophical treatise, much more so in poetry. All that is needed is simple contrast, which in most cases would be implied rather than expressed, of the procedure of Positivism and Catholicism in reference to similar social and moral problems. The scientific basis of such a contrast is already furnished; it is for Art to do the rest, since the appeal should be to Feeling rather than to Reason. At the close of the last chapter I mentioned the principal case in which this comparison would have been of service, the introduction, namely, of Positivism to the two Southern nations. It was the task that I had marked out for my saintly fellow-worker, for it is one in which the esthetic powers of women would be peculiarly available.

In this the third of its temporary functions, Positivist Art approximates to its normal character. We have spoken of its idealization of the Future, but here it will idealize the Past also. Positivism cannot be accepted until it has rendered the fullest and most scrupulous justice to Catholicism. Our poets, so far from detracting from the moral and political worth of the mediæval system, will begin by doing all the honour to it that is consistent with philosophical truth, as a prelude to the still higher beauty of the system which supersedes it. It will be the inauguration of their permanent office of restoring the Past to life. For it is equally in the interest of systematic thought and of social sympathy that the relation of the Past to the Future should be deeply impressed upon all.

But these three steps towards the incorporation of Art into the final order, though not far distant, cannot be taken immediately. They presuppose a degree of intellectual preparation which is not yet reached either by the public or by its esthetic teachers. The present generation under which, in France, the great revolution is now peacefully entering upon its second phase, may diffuse Positivism largely, not merely amongst qualified thinkers, but among the people of Paris, who are entrusted with the destinies of Western Europe, and among women of nobler nature. The next generation, growing up in the midst of this movement, may, before the expiration of a century from the date of the Convention, complete spontaneously the moral and mental inauguration of the new system, by exhibiting the new esthetic features which Humanity in her regenerate condition will assume.

Let us now sum up the conclusions of this chapter. We have found Positive Philosophy peculiarly favourable to the continuous development of all the fine arts. A doctrine which encourages Humanity to strive for perfection of every kind, cannot but foster and assimilate that form of mental activity by which our sense of perfection is so highly stimulated. It controls the Ideal, indeed, by systematic study of the Real; but only in order to furnish it with an objective basis, and so to secure its coherence and its moral value. Placed on this footing, our esthetic faculties are better adapted than the scientific, both to the nature and range of our understanding, and also to that which is the object of all intellectual effort, the organization of human unity. For they are more immediately connected with Feeling, on which the unity of our nature must rest. Next to direct culture of the heart, it is in ideal Art that we shall find the best assistance in our efforts to become more loving and more noble.

Logically, Art should have a salutary influence upon our intellectual faculties, because it familiarises us from childhood with the features by which all constructive efforts of man should be characterised. Science has for a long time preferred the analytic method, whereas Art, even in these times of anarchy, always aims at Synthesis, which is the final goal of all intellectual activity. Even when Art, contrary to its nature, undertakes to destroy, it cannot do its work, whatever it be, without constructing. Thus, by implanting a taste and faculty for ideal construction, Art enables us to build with greater effect than ever upon the more stubborn soil of reality.

On all these grounds Art, in the Positive system, becomes the primary basis of general education. In a subsequent stage education assumes a more scientific character, with the object of supplying systematic notions of the external world. But in after life Art resumes its original position. There the ordinary functions of the spiritual power will be esthetic rather than scientific. The three elements of which the modifying power is composed will become spontaneously the organs of idealization, a function which will henceforth never be dissociated from the power of philosophic synthesis.

Such a combination implies that the new philosophers shall have a true feeling for all the fine arts. In ordinary times passive appreciation of them will suffice; but there will occasionally be periods where philosophic effort ceases to be necessary, and which call rather for the vigour of the poet; and at these times the more powerful minds among them should be capable of rising to the loftiest creative efforts. Difficult as the condition may be, it is essential to the full degree of moral influence of which their office admits and which their work requires. The priest of Humanity will not have attained his full measure of superiority over the priest of God, until, with the intellect of the Philosopher, he combines the enthusiasm of the Poet, as well as the tenderness of Woman, and the People's energy.

CHAPTER VI.

CONCLUSION. THE RELIGION OF HUMANITY.

Recapitulation of the results obtained.   LOVE, then, is our principle; Order our basis; and Progress our end.   Such, as the preceding chapters have shown, is the essential character of the system of life which Positivism offers for the definite acceptance of society; a system which regulates the whole course of our private and public existence, by bringing Feeling, Reason, and Activity into permanent harmony.   In this final synthesis, all essential conditions are far more perfectly fulfilled than in any other.   Each special element of our nature is more fully developed, and at the same time the general working of the whole is more coherent.   Greater distinctness is given to the truth that the affective element predominates in our nature.   Life in all its actions and thoughts is brought under the control and inspiring influence of Social Sympathy.

By the supremacy of the Heart, the Intellect, so far from being crushed, is elevated; for all its powers are consecrated to the service of the social instincts, with the purpose of strengthening their influence and directing their employment.   By accepting its subordination to Feeling, Reason adds to its own influence.   To it we look for the revelation of the laws of nature, of the established Order which dictates the inevitable conditions of human life.   The objective basis thus discovered for human effort reacts most beneficially on our moral nature.   Forced as we are to accept it, it controls the fickleness to which our affections are liable, and acts as a direct stimulus to social sympathy. Concentrated on so high an office, the intellect will be preserved from useless digression; and will yet find a boundless field for its operations in the study of all the natural laws by which human destinies are affected, and especially those which relate to the constitution of man or of society. The fact that every subject is to be regarded from the sociological point of view, so far from discouraging even the most abstract order of speculations, adds to their logical coherence as well as to their moral value, by introducing the only principle by which they can be co-ordinated into a whole.

And whilst Reason is admitted to its due share of influence on human life, Imagination is also strengthened and called into constant exercise. Henceforth it will assume its proper function, the idealization of truth. For the objective basis of our conceptions scientific investigation is necessary. But this basis once obtained, the constitution of our mind is far better adapted to esthetic than to scientific study, provided always that imagination never disregard the truths of science, and degenerate into extravagance. Subject to this condition, Positivism gives every encouragement to esthetic studies, being as they are so closely related to its guiding principle and to its practical aim, to Love namely, and to Progress. Art will enter largely into the social life of the Future, and will be regarded as the most pleasurable and most salutary exercise of our intellectual powers, because it leads them in the most direct manner to the culture and improvement of our moral nature.

Originating in the first instance from practical life, Positivism will return thither with increased force, now that its long period of scientific preparation is accomplished, and that it has occupied the field of moral truth, which henceforth will be its principal domain. Its principle of sympathy, so far from relaxing our efforts, will stimulate all our faculties to universal activity by urging them onwards towards perfection of every kind. The obligation of scientific study of the natural Order is to enable us to direct all the forces of Man and of Society to its improvement by artificial effort. Hitherto this aim has hardly been recognised, even with regard to the material world, and but a very small proportion of our energies has been spent upon it. Yet the aim is high, provided always that the view taken of human progress extend beyond its lower and more material stages. Our theoretical powers once concentrated on the moral problems which form their principal field, our practical energies will not fail to take the same direction, devoting themselves to that portion of the natural Order which is most imperfect, and at the same time most modifiable. With these larger and more systematic views of human life, its best efforts will be given to the improvement of the mind, and still more to the improvement of the character and to the increase of affection and courage. Public and private life are now brought into close relation by the identity of their principal aims, which, being kept constantly in sight, ennobles every action in both. Practical questions must ever continue to preponderate, as before, over questions of theory; but this condition, so far from being adverse to speculative power, concentrates it upon the most difficult of all problems, the discovery of moral and social laws, our knowledge of which will never be fully adequate to our practical requirements. Mental and practical activity of this kind can never result in hardness of feeling. On the contrary, it impresses us more strongly with the conviction that Sympathy is not merely our highest happiness, but the most effectual of all our means of improvement; and that without it, all other means can be of little avail.

Thus it is that in the Positive system, the Heart, the Intellect, and the Character mutually strengthen and develope one another, because each is systematically directed to the mode of action for which it is by nature adapted. Public and private life are brought into a far more harmonious relation than in any former time, because the purpose to which both are consecrated is identical, the difference being merely in the range of their respective powers. The aim in both is to secure, to the utmost possible extent, the victory of Social feeling over Self-love; and to this aim all our powers, whether of affection, thought, or action, are in both unceasingly directed.

This, then, is the shape in which the great human problem comes definitely before us. Its solution demands all the appliances of Social Art. The primary principle on which the solution rests, is the separation of the two elementary powers of society; the moral power of counsel, and the political power of command. The necessary preponderance of the latter, which rests upon material force, corresponds to the fact that in our imperfect nature, where the coarser wants are the most pressing and the most continuously felt, the selfish instincts are naturally stronger than the unselfish. In the absence of all compulsory authority, our action even as individuals would be feeble and purposeless, and social life still more certainly would lose its character and its energy. Moral force, therefore, by which is meant the force of conviction and persuasion, is to be regarded simply as a modifying influence, not as a means of authoritative direction.

Moral force originates in Feeling and in Reason. It represents the social side of our nature, and to this its direct influence is limited. Indeed by the very fact that it is the expression of our highest attributes, it is precluded from that practical ascendancy which is possessed by faculties of a lower but more energetic kind. Inferior to material force in power, though superior to it in dignity, it contrasts and opposes its own classification of men according to the standard of moral and intellectual worth, to the classification by wealth and worldly position which actually prevails. True, the higher standard will never be adopted practically, but the effort to uphold it will react beneficially on the natural order of society. It will inspire those larger views, and reanimate that sense of duty, which are so apt to become obliterated in the ordinary current of life.

The means of effecting this important result, the need of which is so generally felt, will not be wanting, when the moderating power enters upon its characteristic function of preparing us for practical life by a rational system of education, throughout which, even in its intellectual department, moral considerations will predominate. This power will therefore concentrate itself upon theoretical and moral questions; and it can only maintain its position as the recognised organ of social sympathy, by invariable abstinence from political action. It will be its first duty to contend against the ambitious instincts of its own members. True, such instincts, in spite of the impurity of their source, may be of use in those natures who are really destined for the indispensable business of government. But for a spiritual power formal renunciation of wealth and rank is at the very root of its influence; it is the first of the conditions which justify it in resisting the encroachments to which political power is always tempted. Hence the classes to whose natural sympathies it looks for support are those who, like itself, are excluded from political administration.

Women, from their strongly sympathetic nature, were the original source of all moral influence; and they are peculiarly qualified by the passive character of their life to assist the action of the spiritual power in the family. In its essential function of education, their co-operation is of the highest importance. The education of young children is entrusted to their sole charge; and the education of more advanced years simply consists in giving a more systematic shape to what the mother has already inculcated in childhood. As a wife, too, Woman assumes still more distinctly the spiritual function of counsel; she softens by persuasion where the philosopher can only influence by conviction. In social meetings, again, the only mode of public life in which women can participate, they assist the spiritual power in the formation of Public Opinion, of which it is the systematic organ, by applying the principles which it inculcates to the case of particular actions or persons. In all these matters their influence will be far more effectual, when men have done their duty to women by setting them free from the necessity of gaining their own livelihood; and when women on their side have renounced both power and wealth, as we see so often exemplified among the working classes.

The affinity of the People with the philosophic power is less direct and less pure; but it will prove a vigorous ally in meeting the obstacles which the temporal power will inevitably oppose. The working classes having but little spare time and small individual influence, cannot, except on rare occasions, participate in the practical administration of government, since all efficient government involves concentration of power. Moral force, on the contrary, created as it is by free convergence of opinion, admits of, and indeed requires, the widest ramification. Working men, owing to their freedom from practical responsibilities and their unconcern for personal aggrandisement, are better disposed than their employers to broad views and to generous sympathies, and will therefore naturally associate themselves with the spiritual power. It is they who will furnish the basis of a true public opinion, so soon as they are enabled by Positive education, which is specially framed with a view to their case, to give greater definiteness to their aspirations. Their wants and their sympathies will alike induce them to support the philosophic priesthood as the systematic guardian of their interests against the governing classes. In return for such protection they will bring the whole weight of their influence to assist the priesthood in its great social mission, the subordination of Politics to Morals. In those exceptional cases where it becomes necessary for the moderating power to assume political functions, the popular element will of itself suffice for the emergency, thus exempting the philosophic element from participating in an anomaly from which its character could hardly fail to suffer, as would be the case also in a still higher degree with the feminine character.

The direct influence of Reason over our imperfect nature is so feeble that the new priesthood could not of itself ensure such respect for its theories as would bring them to any practical result. But the sympathies of women and of the people operating as they will in every town and in every family, will be sufficient to ensure its efficacy in organizing that legitimate degree of moral pressure which the poor may bring to bear upon the rich. Moreover, we may look, as one of the results of our common system of education, for additional aid in the ranks of the governing classes themselves; for some of their noblest members will volunteer their assistance to the spiritual power, forming, so to speak, a new order of chivalry. And yet, with all this, comprehensive as our organization

of moral force may be, so great is the innate strength of
the selfish instincts, that our success in solving the great
human problem will always fall short of what we might
legitimately desire.   To this conclusion we must come, in
whatever way we regard the destiny of Man ; but it should
only encourage us to combine our efforts still more strongly
in order to ameliorate the order of Nature in its most important, that is, in its moral aspects, these being at once
the most modifiable and the most imperfect.

The highest progress of man and of society consists in
gradual increase of our mastery over all our defects, especially the defects of our moral nature.   Among the nations
of antiquity the progress in this direction was but small ;
all that they could do was to prepare the way for it by
certain necessary phases of intellectual and social development.   The whole tendency of Greek and Roman society
was such as made it impossible to form a distinct conception of the great problem of our moral nature.   In fact,
Morals were with them invariably subordinate to Politics.
Nevertheless, it is moral progress which alone can satisfy
our nature ; and in the Middle Ages it was recognised as
the highest aim of human effort, notwithstanding that its
intellectual and social conditions were as yet very imperfectly realised.   The creeds of the Middle Ages were too
unreal and imperfect, the character of society was too
military and aristocratic, to allow Morals and Politics to
assume permanently their right relation.   The attempt
was made, however ; and, inadequate as it was, it was
enough to allow the people of the West to appreciate the
fundamental principle involved in it, a principle destined
to survive the opinions and the habits of life from which
it arose.   Its full weight could never be felt until the
Positive spirit had extended beyond the elementary subjects to which it had been so long subjected, to the sphere

of social truth; and had thus reached the position at
which a complete synthesis became possible. Equally
essential was it that in those countries which had been
incorporated into the Western Empire, and had passed
from it into Catholic Feudalism, war should be definitely
superseded by industrial activity. In the long period of
transition which has elapsed since the Middle Ages, both
these conditions have been fulfilled, while at the same
time the old system has been gradually decomposed.
Finally the great crisis of the Revolution has stimulated
all advanced minds to reconsider, with better intellectual
and social principles, the same problem that Christianity
and Chivalry had attempted. The radical solution of it
was then begun, and it is now completed and enunciated
in a systematic form by Positivism.

Humanity is   All essential phases in the evolution of society
the centre to
which every as- answer to corresponding phases in the growth
pect of Positiv-
ism converges. of the individual, whether it has proceeded
spontaneously or under systematic guidance, supposing
always that his development be complete. But it is not
enough to prove the close connection which exists between
all modes and degrees of human regeneration. We have
yet to find a central point round which all will naturally
meet. In this point consists the unity of Positivism as a
system of life. Unless it can be thus condensed round
one single principle, it will never wholly supersede the
synthesis of Theology, notwithstanding its superiority in
the reality and stability of its component parts, and in
their homogeneity and coherence as a whole. There
should be a central point in the system, towards which
Feeling, Reason, and Activity alike converge. The proof
that Positivism possesses such a central point will remove
the last obstacle to its complete acceptance, as the guide
of private or of public life.

Such a centre we find in the great conception of Humanity, towards which every aspect of Positivism naturally converges. By it the conception of God will be entirely superseded, and a synthesis be formed, more complete and permanent than that provisionally established by the old religions. Through it the new doctrine becomes at once accessible to men's hearts in its full extent and application. From their hearts it will penetrate their minds, and thus the immediate necessity of beginning with a long and difficult course of study is avoided, though this must of course be always indispensable to its systematic teachers.

This central point of Positivism is even more moral than intellectual in character ; it represents the principle of Love upon which the whole system rests. It is the peculiar characteristic of the Great Being who is here set forth, to be compounded of separable elements. Its existence depends therefore entirely upon mutual Love knitting together its various parts. The calculations of self-interest can never be substituted as a combining influence for the sympathetic instincts.

Yet the belief in Humanity while stimulating Sympathy, at the same time enlarges the scope and vigour of the Intellect. For it requires high powers of generalization to conceive clearly of this vast organism, as the result of spontaneous co-operation, abstraction made of all partial antagonisms. Reason, then, has its part in this central dogma as well as Love. It enlarges and completes our conception of the Supreme Being, by revealing to us the external and internal conditions of its existence.

Lastly, our active powers are stimulated by it no less than our feelings and our reason. For since Humanity is so far more complex than any other organism, it will react more strongly and more continuously on its environment, submitting to its influence and so modifying it.

Hence results Progress, which is simply the development of Order under the influence of Love.

Thus, in the conception of Humanity, the three essential aspects of Positivism, its subjective principle, its objective dogma, and its practical object, are united. Towards Humanity, who is for us the only true Great Being, we, the conscious elements of whom she is composed, shall henceforth direct every aspect of our life, individual or collective. Our thoughts will be devoted to the knowledge of Humanity, our affections to her love, our actions to her service.

Positivists then may, more truly than theological believers of whatever creed, regard life as a continuous and earnest act of worship; worship which will elevate and purify our feelings, enlarge and enlighten our thoughts, ennoble and invigorate our actions. It supplies a direct solution, so far as a solution is possible, of the great problem of the Middle Ages, the subordination of Politics to Morals. For this follows at once from the consecration now given to the principle that social sympathy should preponderate over self-love.

Thus Positivism becomes, in the true sense of the word, a Religion; a religion more real and more complete than any other, and therefore destined to replace all imperfect and provisional systems resting on the primitive basis of theology.

For even the synthesis established by the old theocracies of Egypt and India was insufficient, because, being based on purely subjective principles, it could never embrace practical life, which must always be subordinated to the objective realities of the external world. Theocracy was thus limited at the outset to the sphere of thought and of feeling; and part even of this field was soon lost when Art became emancipated from theocratical control, showing a spontaneous tendency to its natural vocation of idealizing real life. Of science and of morality the priests were still left sole arbiters; but here, too, their influence materially diminished so soon as the discovery of the simpler abstract truths of Positive science gave birth to Greek Philosophy. Philosophy, though as yet necessarily restricted to the metaphysical stage, yet already stood forward as the rival of the sacerdotal system. Its attempts to construct were in themselves fruitless; but they overthrew Polytheism, and ultimately transformed it into Monotheism. In this the last phase of theology, the intellectual authority of the priests was undermined no less deeply than the principle of their doctrine. They lost their hold upon Science, as long ago they had lost their hold upon Art. All that remained to them was. the moral guidance of society; and even this was soon compromised by the progress of free thought; progress really due to the Positive spirit, although its systematic exponents still belonged to the metaphysical school.

When Science had expanded sufficiently to exist apart from Philosophy, it showed a rapid tendency towards a synthesis of its own, alike incompatible with metaphysics and with theology. It was late in appearing, because it required a long series of preliminary efforts; but as it approached completion, it gradually brought the *With the discovery of sociological laws, a synthesis on the basis of Science becomes possible, science being now concentrated on the study of Humanity.* Positive spirit to bear upon the organization of practical life, from which that spirit had originally emanated. But thoroughly to effect this result was impossible until the science of Sociology had been formed; and this was done by my discovery of the law of historical development. Henceforth all true men of science will rise to the higher dignity of philosophers, and by so doing will necessarily assume something of the sacerdotal character, because the final result to which their researches tend is the subordination of every subject of thought to the moral principle ; a result which leads us at once to the acceptance of a complete and homogeneous synthesis. Thus the philosophers of the future become priests of Humanity, and their moral and intellectual influence will be far wider and more deeply rooted than that of any former priesthood. The primary condition of their spiritual authority is exclusion from political power, as a guarantee that theory and practice shall be systematically kept apart. A system in which the organs of counsel and those of command are never identical cannot possibly degenerate into any of the evils of theocracy.

By entirely renouncing wealth and worldly position, and that not as individuals merely, but as a body, the priests of Humanity will occupy a position of unparalleled dignity. For with their moral influence they will combine what since the downfall of the old theocracies has always been separated from it, the influence of superiority in art and science. Reason, Imagination, and Feeling will be brought into unison : and so united, will react strongly on the imperious conditions of practical life ; bringing it into closer accordance with the laws of universal morality, from which it is so prone to deviate. And the influence of this new modifying power will be the greater that the synthesis on which it rests will have preceded and prepared the way for the social system of the future ; whereas theology could not arrive at its central principle, until the time of its decline was approaching. All functions, then, that co-operate in the elevation of man will be regenerated by the Positive priesthood. Science, Poetry, Morality, will be devoted to the study, the praise, and the love of Humanity, in order that under their combined influence, our political action may be more unremittingly given to her service.

With such a mission, Science acquires a position of unparalleled importance, as the sole means through which we come to know the nature and conditions of this Great Being, the worship of whom should be the distinctive feature of our whole life. For this all-important knowledge, the study of Sociology would seem to suffice : but Sociology itself depends upon preliminary study, first of the outer world, in which the actions of Humanity take place ; and secondly, of Man, the individual agent.

The object of Positivist worship is not like that of theological believers, an absolute, isolated, incomprehensible Being, whose existence admits of no demonstration, or comparison with anything real. The evidence of the Being here set forward is spontaneous, and is shrouded in no mystery. Before we can praise, love, and serve Humanity as we ought, we must know something of the laws which govern her existence, an existence more complicated than any other of which we are cognizant.

And by virtue of this complexity, Humanity possesses the attributes of vitality in a higher degree than any other organization ; that is to say, there is at once more intimate harmony of the component elements, and more complete subordination to the external world. Immense as is the magnitude of this organism measured both in Time and Space, yet each of its parts carefully examined will show the general consensus of the whole. At the same time it is more dependent than any other upon the conditions of the outer world ; in other words, upon the sum of the laws that regulate inferior phenomena. Like other vital organisms, it submits to mathematical, astronomical, physical, chemical, and biological conditions ; and, in addition to these, is subject to special laws of Sociology with which lower organisms are not concerned. But as a further result of its higher complexity it reacts upon the world more powerfully; and is indeed in a true sense its chief. Scientifically defined, then, it is truly the Supreme Being: the Being who manifests to the fullest extent all the highest attributes of life.

But there is yet another feature peculiar to Humanity, and one of primary importance. That feature is, that the elements of which she is composed must always have an independent existence. In other organisms the parts have no existence when severed from the whole; but this, the greatest of all organisms, is made up of lives which can really be separated. There is, as we have seen, harmony of parts as well as independence, but the last of these conditions is as indispensable as the first. Humanity would cease to be superior to other beings were it possible for her elements to become inseparable. The two conditions are equally necessary: but the difficulty of reconciling them is so great as to account at once for the slowness with which this highest of all organisms has been developed. It must not, however, be supposed that the new Supreme Being is, like the old, merely a subjective result of our powers of abstraction. Its existence is revealed to us, on the contrary, by close investigation of objective fact. Man indeed, as an individual, cannot properly be said to exist, except in the exaggerated abstractions of modern metaphysicians. Existence in the true sense can only be predicated of Humanity; although the complexity of her nature prevented men from forming a systematic conception of it, until the necessary stages of scientific initiation had been passed. Bearing this conclusion in mind, we shall be able now to distinguish in Humanity two distinct orders of functions: those by which she acts upon the world, and those which bind together her component parts. Humanity cannot herself act otherwise than by her separable members; but the efficiency of these members depends upon their working in co-operation, whether instinctively or with design. We find, then, external functions relating principally to the material existence of this organism; and internal functions by which its moveable elements are combined. This distinction is but an application of the great theory, due to Bichat's genius, of the distinction between the life of nutrition and the life of relation which we find in the individual organism. Philosophically it is the source from which we derive the great social principle of separation of spiritual from temporal power. The temporal power governs: it originates in the personal instincts, and it stimulates activity. On it depends social Order. The spiritual power can only moderate: it is the exponent of our social instincts, and it promotes co-operation, which is the guarantee of Progress. Of these functions of Humanity the first corresponds to the function of nutrition, the second to that of innervation in the individual organism.

Having now viewed our subject statically, we may come to its dynamical aspect; reserving *Dynamical aspects.* more detailed discussion for the third volume of this treatise, which deals with my fundamental theory of human development. The Great Being whom we worship is not immutable any more than it is absolute. Its nature is relative; and, as such, is eminently capable of growth. In a word it is the most vital of all living beings known to us. It extends and becomes more complex by the continuous successions of generations. But in its progressive changes as well as in its permanent functions, it is subject to invariable laws. And these laws considered, as we may now consider them, as a whole, form a more sublime object of contemplation than the solemn inaction of the old Supreme Being, whose existence was passive except when interrupted by acts of arbitrary and unintelligible volition. Thus it is only by Positive science that we can appreciate this highest of all destinies to which all the fatalities of individual life are subordinate. It is with this as with subjects of minor importance : systematic study of the Past is necessary in order to determine the Future, and so explain the tendencies of the Present. Let us then pass from the conception of Humanity as fully developed, to the history of its rise and progress ; a history in which all other modes of progress are included. In ancient times it was incompatible both with the theological spirit and also with the military character of society, which involved the slavery of the productive classes. The feeling of Patriotism, restricted as it was at first, was the only prelude that was then possible to the recognition of Humanity. From this narrow nationality there arose in the Middle Ages the feeling of universal brotherhood, as soon as military life had entered on its defensive phase, and all supernatural creeds had spontaneously merged into a monotheistic form common to the whole West. The growth of Chivalry, and the attempt made to effect a permanent separation of the two social powers, announced already the subordination of Politics to Morals, and thus showed that the conception of Humanity was in direct course of preparation. But the unreal and anti-social nature of the mediæval creed, and the military and aristocratic character of feudal society, made it impossible to go very far in this direction. The abolition of personal slavery was the most essential result of this important period. Society could now assume its industrial character ; and feelings of fraternity were encouraged by modes of life in which all classes alike participated. Meanwhile,

the growth of the Positive spirit was proceeding, and preparing the way for the establishment of Social Science, by
which alone all other Positive studies could be systema-
tized. This being done, the conception of the Great
Being became possible. It was with reference to subjects
of a speculative and scientific nature that the conception
first arose in a distinct shape. As early as two centuries
ago, Pascal spoke of the human race as one Man.* Amidst
the inevitable decline of the theological and military
system, men became conscious of the movement of society,
which had now advanced through so many phases; and
the notion of Progress as a distinctive feature of Humanity
became admitted. Still the conception of Humanity as
the basis for a new synthesis was impossible until the
crisis of the French Revolution. That crisis on the one
hand proved the urgent necessity for social regeneration,
and on the other gave birth to the only philosophy capable
of effecting it. Thus our consciousness of the new Great
Being has advanced co-extensively with its growth. Our
present conception of it is as much the measure of our
social progress as it is the summary of Positive knowledge.

In speaking of the dignity of Science when
regenerated by this lofty application of it, I do
not refer solely to the special science of Social
phenomena, but also to the preliminary studies
of Life and of the Inorganic World, both of
which form an essential portion of Positive doctrine. A
social mission of high importance will be recognised in
the most elementary sciences, whether it be for the sake
of their method or for the value of their scientific results.
True, the religion of Humanity will lead to the entire

*Inorganic and organic sci-
ences elevated by their connection with the supreme
science of Hu-
manity.*

---

* Toute la suite des hommes, pendant le cours de tant de siècles, doit être
considérée comme un même homme qui subsiste toujours et qui apprend con-
tinuellement.—Pascal, Pensées, Part 1., Art. 1.

abolition of scientific Academies, because their tendency, especially in France, is equally hurtful to science and morality. They encourage mathematicians to confine their attention exclusively to the first step in the scientific scale; and biologists to pursue their studies without any solid basis or definite purpose. Special studies carried on without regard for the encyclopedic principles which determine the relative value of knowledge, and its bearing on human life, will be condemned by all men of right feeling and good sense. Such men will feel the necessity of resisting the morbid narrowness of mind and heart to which the anarchy of our times inevitably leads. But the abolition of the Academic system will only ensure a larger measure of respect for all scientific researches of real value, on whatever subject. The study of Mathematics, the value of which is at present negatived by its hardening tendency, will now manifest its latent moral efficacy, as the only sure basis for firm conviction; a state of mind that can never be perfectly attained in more complex subjects of thought, except by those who have experienced it in the simpler subjects. When the close connection of all scientific knowledge becomes more generally admitted, Humanity will reject political teachers who are ignorant of Geometry, as well as geometricians who neglect Sociology. Biology meanwhile will lose its dangerous materialism, and will receive all the respect due to its close connection with social science and its important bearing on the essential doctrines of Positivism. To attempt to explain the life of Humanity without first examining the lower forms of life, would be as serious an error as to study Biology without regard to the social purpose which Biology is intended to serve. Science has now become indispensable to the establishment of moral truth, and at the same time its subordination to the inspirations of the heart is fully recognised; thus it takes its place henceforward among the most essential functions of the priesthood of Humanity. The supremacy of true Feeling will strengthen Reason, and will receive in turn from Reason a systematic sanction. Natural philosophy, besides its evident value in regulating the spontaneous action of Humanity, has a direct tendency to elevate human nature; it draws from the outer world that basis of fixed truth which is so necessary to control our various desires.

The study of Humanity therefore, directly or indirectly, is for the future the permanent aim of Science; and Science is now in a true sense consecrated, as the source from which the universal religion receives its principles. It reveals to us not merely the nature and conditions of the Great Being, but also its destiny and the successive phases of its growth. The aim is high and arduous; it requires continuous and combined exertion of all our faculties; but it ennobles the simplest processes of scientific investigation by connecting them permanently with subjects of the deepest interest. The scrupulous exactness and rigorous caution of the Positive method, which when applied to unimportant subjects seem almost puerile, will be valued and insisted on when seen to be necessary for the efficacy of efforts relating to our most essential wants. Rationalism, in the true sense of the word, so far from being incompatible with right feeling, strengthens and develops it, by placing all the facts of the case, in social questions especially, in their true light.

But, however honourable the rank which Science when regenerated will hold in the new religion, the sanction given to Poetry will be even direct and unqualified, because the function assigned to it is one which is more practical and which touches us more nearly. Its function will be the praise of Humanity.

The new religion is even more favourable to Art than to Science.

All previous efforts of Art have been but the prelude to this, its natural mission ; a prelude often impatiently performed, since Art threw off the yoke of theocracy at an earlier period than Science. Polytheism was the only religion under which it had free scope : there it could idealize all the passions of our nature, no attempt being made to conceal the similarity of the gods to the human type. The change from Polytheism to Monotheism was unacceptable to Art, because it narrowed its field ; but towards the close of the Middle Ages it began to shake off the influence of obscure and chimerical beliefs, and to take possession of its proper sphere. The field that now lies before it in the religion of Humanity is inexhaustible. It is called upon to idealize the social life of Man, which, in the time of the nations of antiquity, had not been sufficiently developed to inspire the highest order of poetry.

Poetic por- In the first place it will be of the greatest
traiture of the service in enabling men to realize the concep-
new Supreme
Being, and con- tion of Humanity, subject only to the condi-
trast with the
old. tion of not overstepping the fundamental truths
of Science. Science unassisted cannot define the nature and destinies of this Great Being with sufficient clearness. In our religion the object of worship must be conceived distinctly, in order to be ardently loved and zealously served. Science, especially in subjects of this nature, is confined within narrow limits ; it leaves inevitable deficiencies which esthetic genius must supply. And there are certain qualities in Art as opposed to Science, which specially qualify it for the representation of Humanity. For Humanity is distinguished from other forms of life by the combination of independence with co-operation, attributes which also are natural to Poetry. For while Poetry is more sympathetic than Science, its productions have far more individuality ; the genius of their author is

more strongly marked in them, and the debt to his predecessors and contemporaries is less apparent.   Thus the synthesis on which the inauguration of the final religion depends, is one in which Art will participate more than Science, Science furnishing merely the necessary basis. Its influence will be even greater than in the times of Polytheism ; for powerful as Art appeared to be in those times, it could in reality do nothing but embellish the fables to which the confused ideas of theocracy had given rise.   By its aid we shall for the first time rise at last to a really human point of view, and be enabled distinctly to understand the essential attributes of the Great Being of whom we are members.   The material power of Humanity, and the successive phases of her physical, her intellectual, and, above all, her moral progress, will each in turn be depicted.   Without the difficulties of analytical study, we shall gain a clear knowledge of her nature and her conditions, by the poet's description of her future destiny, of her constant struggle against painful fatalities, which have at last become a source of happiness and greatness, of the slow growth of her infancy, of her lofty hopes now so near fulfilment.   The history of universal Love, the soul by which this Great Being is animated ; the history, that is, of the marvellous advance of man, individually or socially, from brutish appetite to pure unselfish sympathy, is of itself an endless theme for the poetry of the Future.

Comparisons, too, may be instituted, in which the poet, without specially attacking the old religion, will indicate the superiority of the new.   The attributes of the new Great Being may be forcibly illustrated, especially during the time of transition, by contrast with the inferiority of her various predecessors.   All theological types are absolute, indefinite, and immutable ; consequently in none of them has it been possible to combine to a satisfactory

extent the attributes of goodness, wisdom, and power.
Nor can we conceive of their combination, except in a
Being whose existence is a matter of certainty, and who is
subject to invariable laws. The gods of Polytheism were
endowed with energy and sympathy, but possessed neither
dignity nor morality. They were superseded by the sublime deity of Monotheism, who was sometimes represented
as inert and passionless, sometimes as impenetrable and
inflexible. But the new Supreme Being, having a real
existence, an existence relative and modifiable, admits of
being more distinctly conceived than the old; and the
influence of the conception will be equally strong and
far more elevating. Each one of us will recognise in it a
power superior to his own, a power on which the whole
destiny of his life depends, since the life of the individual
is in every respect subordinate to the evolution of the
race. But the knowledge of this power has not the crush-
ing effect of the old conception of omnipotence. For every
great or good man will feel that his own life is an indispensable element in the great organism. The supremacy
of Humanity is but the result of individual co-operation;
her power is not supreme, it is only superior to that of all
beings whom we know. Our love for her is tainted by no
degrading fears, yet it is always coupled with the most
sincere reverence. Perfection is in nowise claimed for
her; we study her natural defects with care, in order to
remedy them as far as possible. The love we bear to her
is a feeling as noble as it is strong; it calls for no degrading expressions of adulation, but it inspires us with unremitting zeal for moral improvement. But these and other
advantages of the new religion, though they can be indicated by the philosopher, need the poet to display them in
their full light. The moral grandeur of man when freed
from the chimeras that oppress him, was foreseen by

Göthe, and still more clearly by Byron. But the work of these men was one of destruction; and their types could only embody the spirit of revolt. Poetry must rise above the negative stage in which, owing to the circumstances of the time, their genius was arrested, and must embrace in the Positive spirit the system of sociological and other laws to which human development is subject, before it can adequately portray the new Man in his relation to the new God.

There is yet another way in which Art may serve the cause of religion; that is, in organizing the festivals, whether private or public, of which, to a great extent, the worship of Humanity will consist. For this purpose esthetic talent is far more required than scientific, the object in view being to reveal the nature of the great Organism more clearly, by presenting all aspects of its existence, static or dynamic, in idealized forms.

Organization of festivals, representing statical and dynamical aspects of Humanity.

These festivals, then, should be of two kinds, corresponding to the two essential aspects of Humanity; the first illustrating her existence, the second her action. Thus we shall stimulate both the elements of true social feeling; the love of Order, namely, and the love of Progress. In our static festivals social Order and the feeling of Solidarity, will be illustrated; the dynamic festivals will explain social Progress, and inspire the sense of historical Continuity. Taken together, their periodic recurrence will form a continuation of Positive education. They will develope and confirm the principles instilled in youth. But there will be nothing didactic in their form; since it is of the essence of Art not to instruct otherwise than by giving pleasure. Of course the regular recurrence of these festivals will not prevent any modifications which may be judged necessary to adapt them to special incidents that may from time to time arise.

The festivals representing Order will necessarily take more abstract and austere forms than those of Progress. It will be their object to represent the statical relations by which the great Organism preserves its unity, and the various aspects of its animating principle, Love. The most universal and the most solemn of these festivals will be the feast of Humanity, which will be held throughout the West at the beginning of the new year, thus consecrating the only custom which still remains in general use to relieve the prosaic dullness of modern life. In this feast, which celebrates the most comprehensive of all unions, every branch of the human race will at some future time participate. In the same month there might be three festivals of a secondary order, representing the minor degrees of association, the Nation, the Province, and the Town. Giving the first month to the direct celebration of the social tie, we might devote the first days of the four succeeding months to the four principal domestic relations, Connubial, Parental, Filial, and Fraternal. In the sixth month, the honourable position of domestic servitude would receive its due measure of respect.

These would be the static festivals; taken together they would form a representation of the true theory of our individual and social nature, together with the principles of moral duty to which that theory gives rise. No direct mention is made of the personal instincts, notwithstanding their preponderance, because it is the main object of Positive worship to bring them under the control of the social instincts. Personal virtues are by no means neglected in Positive education; but to make them the objects of any special celebration, would only stimulate egotistic feeling. Indirectly their value is recognised in every part of our religious system, in the reaction which they exercise upon our generous sympathies. Their omission, therefore, implies no real deficiency in this ideal portraiture of human faculties and duties. Again, no special announcement of the subordination of Humanity to the laws of the External World is needed. The consciousness of this external power pervades every part of the Positive system; it controls our desires, directs our speculations, stimulates our actions. The simple fact of the recurrence of our ceremonies at fixed periods, determined by the Earth's motion, is enough to remind us of our inevitable subjection to the fatalities of the External World.

As the static festivals represent Morality, so the dynamic festivals, those of Progress, will represent History. In these the worship of Humanity assumes a more concrete and animated form; as it will consist principally in rendering honour to the noblest types of each phase of human development. It is desirable, however, that each of the more important phases should be represented in itself, independently of the greatness of any individual belonging to it. Of the months unoccupied by static festivals, three might be given to the principal phases of the Past, Fetichism, Polytheism, and Monotheism; and a fourth to the celebration of the Future, the normal state to which all these phases have been tending.

Forming thus the chain of historical succession, we may consecrate each month to some one of the types who best represent the various stages. I omit, however, some explanations of detail given in the first edition of this Introduction, written at a time when I had not made the distinction between the abstract and concrete worship sufficiently clear. A few months after its publication, in 1848, the circumstances of the time induced me to frame a complete system of commemoration applicable to Western Europe, under the title of "Positivist Calendar." Of this I shall speak more at length in the fourth

volume of the present treatise. Its success has fully justified
me in anticipating this part of my subject. To it I now
refer the reader, recommending him to familiarize himself
with the provisional arrangement of the new Western year
then put forward and already adopted by most Positivists.

Worship of the dead. Commemoration of their service. But the practice need not be restricted to
names of European importance. It is applica-
ble in its degree to each separate province, and
even to private life. Catholicism offers two institutions
in which the religion of the family connects itself with
public worship in its most comprehensive sense. There
is a day appointed in Catholic countries in which all are
in the habit of visiting the tombs of those dear to them;
finding consolation for their grief by sharing it with
others. To this custom Positivists devote the last day of
the year. The working classes of Paris give every year
a noble proof that complete freedom of thought is in no
respect incompatible with worship of the dead, which in
their case is unconnected with any system. Again there
is the institution of baptismal names, which though little
thought of at present, will be maintained and improved
by Positivism. It is an admirable mode of impressing on
men the connection of private with public life, by furnishing every one with a type for his own personal imitation.
Here the superiority of the new religion is very apparent;
since the choice of a name will not be limited to any time
or country. In this as in other cases, the absolute spirit
of Catholicism proved fatal to its prospects of becoming
universal.

These brief remarks will be enough to illustrate the two
classes of festivals instituted by Positivism. In every
week of the year some new aspect of Order or of Progress
will be held up to public veneration; and in each the link
connecting public and private worship will be found in

the adoration of Woman.   In this esthetic side of Positive
religion everything tends to strengthen its fundamental
principle of Love.   All the resources of Poetry, and of
the other arts of sound and form, will be involved to give
full and regular expression to it.   The dominant feeling
is always that of deep reverence proceeding from sincere
acknowledgment of benefits received.   Our worship will
be alike free from mysticism and from affectation.   While
striving to surpass our ancestors, we shall yet render due
honour to all their services and look with respect upon
their systems of life.   Influenced no longer by chimeras
which though comforting to former times are now degrading, we have now no obstacle to becoming as far as
possible incorporate with the Great Being whom we worship.   By commemoration of past services we strengthen
the desire inherent in all of us to prolong our existence in
the only way which is really in our power.   The fact that
all human affairs are subject to one fundamental law, as
soon as it becomes familiarly known, enables and encourages each one of us to live in a true sense in the Past and
even in the Future ; as those cannot do who attribute the
events of life to the agency of an arbitrary and impenetrable Will.   The praise given to our predecessors will stimulate a noble rivalry ; inspiring all with the desire
to become themselves incorporate into this mighty Being
whose life endures through all time, and who is formed of
the dead far more than the living.   When the system of
commemoration is fully developed, no worthy co-operator
will be excluded, however humble his sphere ; whether
limited to his family or town, or extending to his country
or to the whole West.   The education of Positivists will
soon convince them that such recompense for honourable
conduct is ample compensation for the imaginary hopes
which inspired their predecessors.

To live in others is, in the truest sense of the word, life. Indeed the best part of our own life is passed thus. As yet this truth has not been grasped firmly, because the social point of view has never yet been brought systematically before us. But the religion of Humanity, by giving an esthetic form to the Positivist synthesis, will make it intelligible to minds of every class : and will enable us to enjoy the untold charm springing from the sympathies of union and of continuity when allowed free play. To prolong our life indefinitely in the Past and Future, so as to make it more perfect in the Present, is abundant compensation for the illusions of our youth which have now passed away for ever. Science which deprived us of these imaginary comforts, itself in its maturity supplies the solid basis for consolation of a kind unknown before; the hope of becoming incorporate into the Great Being whose static and dynamic laws it has revealed. On this firm foundation Poetry raises the structure of public and private worship; and thus all are made active partakers of this universal life, which minds still fettered by theology cannot understand. Thus Imagination, while accepting the guidance of Reason, will exercise a far more efficient and extensive influence than in the days of Polytheism. For the priests of Humanity the sole purpose of Science is to prepare the field for Art, whether esthetic or industrial. This object once attained, poetic study or composition will form the chief occupation of our speculative faculties. The poet is now called to his true mission, which is to give beauty and grandeur to human life, by inspiring a deeper sense of our relation to Humanity. Poetry will form the basis of the ceremonies in which the new priesthood will solemnise more efficiently than the old, the most important events of private life: especially Birth, Marrriage, and Death ; so as to impress the family as well as the state with the sense of this relation. Forced as we are henceforth to concentrate all our hopes and efforts upon the real life around us, we shall feel more strongly than ever that all the powers of Imagination as well as those of Reason, Feeling, and Activity, are required in its service.

Poetry once raised to its proper place, the arts of sound and form, which render in a more vivid way the subjects which Poetry has suggested, will soon follow. *All the arts may co-operate in the service of religion.* Their sphere, like that of Poetry, will be the celebration of Humanity; an exhaustless field, leaving no cause to regret the chimeras which, in the present empirical condition of these arts, are still considered indispensable. Music in modern times has been limited almost entirely to the expression of individual emotions. Its full power has never been felt in public life, except in the solitary instance of the *Marseillaise,* in which the whole spirit of our great Revolution stands recorded. But in the worship of Humanity, based as it is on Positive education, and animated by the spirit of poetry, Music, as the most social of the special arts, will aid in the representation of the attributes and destinies of Humanity, and in the glorification of great historical types. Painting and Sculpture will have the same object; they will enable us to realise the conception of Humanity with greater clearness and precision than would be possible for Poetry, even with the aid of Music. The beautiful attempts of the artists of the sixteenth century, men who had very little theological belief, to embody the Christian ideal of Woman, may be regarded as an unconscious prelude to the representation of Humanity, in the form which of all others is most suitable. Under the impulse of these feelings, the sculptor will overcome the technical difficulties of representing figures in groups, and will adopt such subjects by preference. Hitherto this has only been effected

in bas-reliefs, works which stand midway between painting and sculpture.   There are, however, some splendid
exceptions from which we can imagine the scope and
grandeur of the latter art, when raised to its true position.   Statuesque groups, whether the figures are joined
or, as is preferable, separate, will enable the sculptor to
undertake many great subjects from which he has been
hitherto debarred.

In Architecture the influence of Positivism will be felt
less rapidly; but ultimately, this art, like the rest, will
be made available for the new religion.   The buildings
erected for the service of God may for a time suffice for
the worship of Humanity, in the same way that Christian
worship was carried on at first in Pagan temples as they
were gradually vacated.   But ultimately buildings will be
required more specially adapted to a religion in which all
the functions connected with education and worship are
so entirely different.   What these buildings will be it
would be useless at present to enquire.   It is less easy to
foresee the Positivist ideal in Architecture than in other
arts.   And it must remain uncertain until the new principles of education have been generally spread, and until
the Positive religion, having received all the aid that
Poetry, Music, and the arts of Form can give, has become
the accepted faith of Western Europe.   When the more
advanced nations are heartily engaged in the cause, the
true temples of Humanity will soon arise.   By that time
mental and moral regeneration will have advanced far
enough to commence the reconstruction of all political
institutions.   Until then the new religion will avail itself
of Christian churches as these gradually become vacant.

Positivism is
the successor
of Christianity,
and surpasses
it.

Art, then, as well as Science, partakes in the
regenerating influence which Positivism derives
from its synthetic principle of Love.   Both are

called to their proper functions, the one to contemplate, the other to glorify, Humanity, in order that we may love and serve her more perfectly.   Yet while the intellect is thus made the servant of the heart, far from being weakened by this subordinate position, it finds in it an exhaustless field, in which the value of its labours is amply recognised.   Each of its faculties is called directly into play, and is supplied with its appropriate employment. Poetry institutes the forms of the worship of Humanity; Science supplies the principles on which those forms are framed, by connecting them with the laws of the external world.   Imagination, while ceasing to usurp the place of Reason, yet enhances rather than diminishes its original influence, which the new philosophy shows to be as beneficial as it is natural.   And thus human life at last attains that state of perfect harmony which has been so long sought for in vain, and which consists in the direction of all our faculties to one common purpose under the supremacy of Affection.   At the same time all former efforts of Imagination and Reason, even when they clashed with each other, are fully appreciated; because we see that they developed our powers, that they taught us the conditions of their equilibrium, and made it manifest that nothing but that equilibrium was wanting to allow them to work together for our welfare.   Above all do we recognise the immense value of the mediæval attempt to form a complete synthesis, although, notwithstanding all the results of Greek and Roman civilization, the time was not yet ripe for it.   To renew that attempt upon a sounder basis, and with surer prospects of success, is the object of those who found the religion of Humanity.   Widely different as are their circumstances and the means they employ, they desire to regard themselves as the successors of the great men who conducted the progressive movement of Catholicism. For those alone are worthy to be called successors, who continue or carry into effect the undertakings which former times have left unfinished; the title is utterly unmerited by blind followers of obsolete dogmas, which have long ceased to bear any relation to their original purpose, and which their very authors, if now living, would disavow.

But while bearing in mind our debt to Catholicism, we need not omit to recognise how largely Positivism gains by comparison with it. Full justice will be done to the aims of Catholicism, and to the excellence of its results. But the whole effect of Positivist worship will be to make men feel clearly how far superior in every respect is the synthesis founded on the Love of Humanity to that founded on the Love of God.

Christianity satisfied no part of our nature fully, except the affections. It rejected Imagination, it shrank from Reason; and therefore its power was always contested, and could not last. Even in its own sphere of affection, its principles never lent themselves to that social direction which the Catholic priesthood, with such remarkable persistency, endeavoured to give to them. The aim which it set before men, being unreal and personal, was ill-suited to a life of reality and of social sympathy. It is true that the universality of this supreme affection was indirectly a bond of union; but only when it was not at variance with true social feeling. And from the nature of the system, opposition between these two principles was the rule, and harmony the exception; since the Love of God, even as viewed by the best Catholic types, required in almost all cases the abandonment of every other passion. The moral value of such a synthesis consisted solely in the discipline which it established; discipline of whatever kind being preferable to anarchy, which would have given

free scope to all the lowest propensities. But notwithstanding all the tender feeling of the best mystics, the affection which to them was supreme admitted of no real reciprocity. Moreover, the stupendous nature of the rewards
and penalties by which every precept in this arbitrary
system was enforced, tended to weaken the character and
to taint our noblest impulses. The essential merit of the
system was that it was the first attempt to exercise systematic control over our moral nature. The discipline of
Polytheism was usually confined to actions : sometimes it
extended to habits; but it never touched the affections
from which both habits and actions spring. Christianity
took the best means of effecting its purpose that were then
available; but it was not successful, except so far as it
gave indirect encouragement to our higher feelings. And
so vague and absolute were its principles, that even this
would have been impossible, but for the wisdom of the
priesthood, who for a long time saved society from the
dangers incident to so arbitrary a system. But at the
close of the Middle Ages, when the priesthood became
retrograde, and lost at once their morality and their
freedom, the doctrine was left to its own impotence, and
rapidly degenerated till it became a chronic source of
degradation and of discord.

But the synthesis based upon Love of Humanity has
too deep a foundation in Positive truth to be liable to
similar decline; and its influence cannot but increase so
long as the progress of our race endures. The Great
Being, who is its object, tolerates the most searching enquiry, and yet does not restrict the scope of Imagination.
The laws which regulate her existence are now known to
us ; and the more deeply her nature is investigated, the
stronger is our consciousness of her reality and of the
greatness of her benefits. The thought of her stimulates

all the powers of Imagination, and thus enables us to participate in a measure in the universality of her life, throughout the whole extent of Time and Space of which we have any real knowledge. All our intellectual results, whether in art or science, are alike co-ordinated by the religion of Humanity; for it furnishes the sole bond of connection by which permanent harmony can be established between our thoughts and our feelings. It is the only system which without artifice and without arbitrary restriction, can establish the preponderance of Affection over Thought and Action. It sets forth social feeling as the first principle of morality; without ignoring the natural superiority in strength of the personal instincts. To live for others it holds to be the highest happiness. To become incorporate with Humanity, to sympathize with all her former phases, to foresee her destinies in the future, and to do what lies in us to forward them; this is what it puts before us as the constant aim of life. Self-love in the Positive system is regarded as the great infirmity of our nature : an infirmity which unremitting discipline on the part of each individual and of society may materially palliate, but will never radically cure. The degree to which this mastery over our own nature is attained is the truest standard of individual or social progress, since it has the closest relation to the existence of the Great Being, and to the happiness of the elements that compose it.

Inspired as it is by sincere gratitude, which increases the more carefully the grounds for it are examined, the worship of Humanity raises Prayer for the first time above the degrading influence of self-interest. We pray to the Supreme Being; but only to express our deep thankfulness for her present and past benefits, which are an earnest of still greater blessings in the future. Doubtless it is a fact of human nature, that habitual expression of such feelings reacts beneficially on our moral nature; and so far we, too, find in Prayer a noble recompense. But it is one that can suggest to us no selfish thoughts, since it cannot come at all unless it come spontaneously. Our highest happiness consists in Love; and we know that more than any other feeling Love may be strengthened by exercise; that alone of all feelings it admits of, and increases with, simultaneous expansion in all. Humanity will become more familiar to us than the old gods were to the Polytheists, yet without the loss of dignity which, in their case, resulted from familiarity. Her nature has in it nothing arbitrary, yet she co-operates with us in the worship that we render, since in honouring her we receive back " grace for grace." Homage accepted by the Deity of former times laid him open to the charge of puerile vanity. But the new Deity will accept praise only where it is deserved, and will derive from it equal benefit with ourselves. This perfect reciprocity of affection and of influence is peculiar to Positive religion, because in it alone the object of worship is a Being whose nature is relative, modifiable, and perfectible; a Being of whom her own worshippers form a part, and the laws of whose existence, being more clearly known than theirs, allow her desires and her tendencies to be more distinctly foreseen.

The morality of Positive religion combines all the advantages of spontaneousness with those of demonstration. *Superiority of Positive morality.* It is so thoroughly human in all its parts, as to preclude all the subterfuges by which repentance for transgression is so often stifled or evaded. By pointing out distinctly the way in which each individual action reacts upon society, it forces us to judge our own conduct without lowering our standard. Some might think it too gentle, and not sufficiently vigorous; yet the love by which it is inspired is no passive feeling, but a principle which strongly stimulates our energies to the full extent compatible with the attainment of that highest good to which it is ever tending. Accepting the truths of science, it teaches that we must look to our own unremitting activity for the only providence by which the rigour of our destiny can be alleviated. We know well that the great Organism, superior though it be to all beings known to us, is yet under the dominion of inscrutable laws, and is in no respect either absolutely perfect or absolutely secure from danger. Every condition of our existence, whether those of the external world or those of our own nature, might at some time be compromised. Even our moral and intellectual faculties, on which our highest interests depend, are no exception to this truth. Such contingencies are always possible, and yet they are not to prevent us from living nobly ; they must not lessen our love, our thought, or our efforts for Humanity ; they must not overwhelm us with anxiety, nor urge us to useless complaint. But the very principles which demand this high standard of courage and resignation, are themselves well calculated to maintain it. For by making us fully conscious of the greatness of man, and by setting us free from the degrading influences of fear, they inspire us with keen interest in our efforts, inadequate though they be, against the pressure of fatalities which are not always beyond our power to modify. And thus the reaction of these fatalities upon our character is turned at last to a most beneficial use. It prevents alike overweening anxiety for our own interests and dull indifference to them ; whereas, in theological and metaphysical systems, even when inculcating self-denial, there is always a dangerous tendency to concentrate thought on personal considerations. Dignified resignation to evils which cannot be resisted, wise and energetic action where modification of them is possible ; such is the moral standard which Positivism puts forward for individuals and for society.

Catholicism, notwithstanding the radical defects of its doctrine, has unconsciously been influenced by the modern spirit; and at the close of the Middle Ages was tending in a direction similar to that here described, although its principles were inconsistent with any formal recognition of it. It is only in the countries that have been preserved from Protestantism that any traces are left of these faint efforts of the priesthood to rise above their own theories. The Catholic God would gradually change into a feeble and imperfect representation of Humanity, were not the clergy so degraded socially as to be unable to participate in the spontaneous feelings of the community. It is a tendency too slightly marked to lead to any important result; yet it is a striking proof of the new direction which men's minds and hearts are unconsciously taking in countries which are often supposed to be altogether left behind in the march of modern thought. The clearest indication of it is in their acceptance of the worship of Woman, which is the first step towards the worship of Humanity. Since the twelfth century, the influence of the Virgin, especially in Spain and Italy, has been constantly on the increase. The priesthood have often protested against it, but without effect; and sometimes they have found it necessary to sanction it, for the sake of preserving their authority. The special and privileged adoration which this beautiful creation of Poetry has received, could not but produce a marked change in the spirit of Catholicism. It may serve as a connecting link between the religion of our ancestors and that of our descendants, the Virgin becoming gradually regarded as a personification of Humanity. Little, however, will be done in this direction by the established priesthood,

whether in Italy or Spain. We must look to the purer
agency of women, who will be the means of introducing
Positivism among our Southern brethren.

All the points, then, in which the morality of Positive
science excels the morality of revealed religion are summed
up in the substitution of Love of Humanity for Love of
God. It is a principle as adverse to metaphysics as to
theology, since it excludes all personal considerations, and
places happiness, whether for the individual or for society,
in constant exercise of kindly feeling. To love Humanity
may be truly said to constitute the whole duty of Man;
provided it be clearly understood what such love really
implies, and what are the conditions required for maintaining it. The victory of Social Feeling over our innate
Self-love is rendered possible only by a slow and difficult
training of the heart, in which the intellect must co-
operate. The most important part of this training consists in the mutual love of Man and Woman, with all other
family affections which precede and follow it. But every
aspect of morality, even the personal virtues, are included
in love of Humanity. It furnishes the best measure of
their relative importance, and the surest method for laying
down incontestable rules of conduct. And thus we find
the principles of systematic morality to be identical with
those of spontaneous morality, a result which renders
Positive doctrine equally accessible to all.

Rise of the
new Spiritual
power.
Science, therefore, Poetry, and Morality,
will alike be regenerated by the new religion, and will ultimately form one harmonious whole, on which the destinies of Man will henceforth rest. With women, to whom the first germs of
spiritual power are due, this consecration of the rational
and imaginative faculties to the source of feeling has
always existed spontaneously. But to realise it in social

life it must be brought forward in a systematic form as part of a general doctrine. This is what the mediæval system attempted upon the basis of Monotheism. A moral power arose composed of the two elements essential to such a power, the sympathetic influence of women in the family, the systematic influence of the priesthood on public life. As a preliminary attempt the Catholic system was most beneficial; but it could not last, because the synthesis on which it rested was imperfect and unstable. The Catholic doctrine and worship addressed themselves exclusively to our emotional nature, and even from the moral point of view their principles were uncertain and arbitrary. The field of intellect, whether in art or science, as well as that of practical life, would have been left almost untouched but for the personal character of the priests. But with the loss of their political independence, which had been always in danger from the military tendencies of the time, the priesthood rapidly degenerated. The system was in fact premature; and even before the industrial era of modern times had set in, the esthetic and metaphysical growth of the times had already gone too far for its feeble power of control; and it then became as hostile to progress as it had formerly been favourable to it. Moral qualities without intellectual superiority are not enough for a true spiritual power; they will not enable it to modify to any appreciable extent the strong preponderance of material considerations. Consequently it is the primary condition of social reorganization to put an end to the state of utter revolt which the intellect maintains against the heart; a state which has existed ever since the close of the Middle Ages, and the source of which may be traced as far back as the Greek Metaphysicians. Positivism has at last overcome the immense difficulties of this task. Its solution consists in the foundation of social science on the basis of the preliminary sciences, so that at last there is unity of method in our conceptions. Our active faculties have always been guided by the Positive spirit: and by its extension to the sphere of Feeling, a complete synthesis, alike spontaneous and systematic in its nature, is constructed; and every part of our nature is brought under the regenerating influence of the worship of Humanity. Thus a new spiritual power will arise, complete and homogeneous in structure; coherent and at the same time progressive; and better calculated than Catholicism to engage the support of women which is so necessary to its efficient action on society.

Temporal power will always be necessary, but its action will be modified by the spiritual. Were it not for the material necessities of human life, nothing further would be required for its guidance than a spiritual power. such as is here described. We should have in that case no need for any laborious exertion; and universal benevolence would be looked upon as the sovereign good, and would become the direct object of all our efforts. All that would be necessary would be to call our reasoning powers, and still more, our imagination into play, in order to keep this object constantly in view. Purely fictitious as such an hypothesis may be, it is yet an ideal limit, to which our actual life should be more and more nearly approximated. As an Utopia, it is a fit subject for the poet: and in his hands it will supply the new religion with resources far superior to any that Christianity derived from vague and unreal pictures of future bliss. In it we may carry out a more perfect social classification, in which men may be ranked by moral and intellectual merit, irrespectively of wealth or position. For the only standard by which in such a state men could be tried would be their capacity to love and to please Humanity.

Such a standard will of course never be practically

accepted, and indeed the classification in question would be impossible to effect : yet it should always be present to our minds ; and should be contrasted dispassionately with the actual arrangements of social rank, with which power, even where accidentally acquired, has more to do than wealth. The priests of Humanity with the assistance of women will avail themselves largely of this contrast in modifying the existing order. Positivist education will fully explain its moral validity, and in our religious services appeal will frequently be made to it. Although an ideal abstraction, yet being based on reality, except so far as the necessities of daily life are concerned, it will be far more efficacious than the vague and uncertain classification founded on the theological doctrine of a future state. When society learns to admit no other Providence than its own, it will go so far in adopting this ideal classification as to produce a strong effect on the classes who are the best aware of its impracticability. But those who press this contrast must be careful always to respect the natural laws which regulate the distribution of wealth and rank. They have a definite social function, and that function is not to be destroyed, but to be improved and regulated. In order, therefore, to reconcile these conditions, we must limit our ideal classification to individuals, leaving the actual subordination of office and position unaffected. Well-marked personal superiority is not very common, and society would be wasting its powers in useless and interminable controversy if it undertook to give each function to its best organ, thus dispossessing the former functionary without taking into account the conditions of practical experience. Even in the spiritual hierarchy, where it is easier to judge of merit, such a course would be utterly subversive of discipline. But there would be no political danger, and morally there would be great advantage, in pointing out all remarkable cases which illustrate the difference between the order of rank and the order of merit. Respect may be shown to the noblest without compromising the authority of the strongest. St. Bernard was esteemed more highly than any of the Popes of his time; yet he remained in the humble position of an abbot, and never failed to show the most perfect deference for the higher functionaries of the Church. A still more striking example was furnished by St. Paul in recognizing the official superiority of St. Peter, of whose moral and mental inferiority to himself he must have been well aware. All organized corporations, civil or military, can show instances on a less important scale where the abstract order of merit has been adopted consistently with the concrete order of rank. Where this is the case the two may be contrasted without any subversive consequences. The contrast will be morally beneficial to all classes, at the same time that it proves the imperfection to which so complicated an organism as human society must be ever liable.

Thus the religion of Humanity creates an intellectual and moral power, which, could human life be freed from the pressure of material wants, would suffice for its guidance. Imperfect as our nature assuredly is, yet social sympathy has an intrinsic charm which would make it paramount, but for the imperious necessities by which the instincts of self-preservation are stimulated. So urgent are they, that the greater part of life is necessarily occupied with actions of a self-regarding kind, before which Reason, Imagination, and even Feeling, have to give way. Consequently this moral power, which seems so well adapted for the direction of society, must only attempt to act as a modifying influence. Its sympathetic element, in other words, women, accept this necessity without difficulty; for true affection always takes the right course of action, as soon as it is clearly indicated. But the intellect is far more unwilling to take·a subordinate position. Its rash ambition is far more unsettling to the world than the ambition of rank and wealth, against which it so often inveighs. It is the hardest of social problems to regulate the exercise of the intellectual powers, while securing them their due measure of influence; the object being that theoretical power should be able really to modify, and yet should never be permitted to govern. For the nations of antiquity this problem was insoluble; with them the intellect was always either a tyrant or a slave. The solution was attempted in the Middle Ages; but without success, owing to the military and theological character of the times. Positivism relies for solving it on the reality which is one of its principal features, and on the fact that Society has now entered on its industrial phase. Based on accurate inquiry into the past and future destinies of man, its aim is so to regenerate our political action, as to transform it ultimately into a practical worship of Humanity; Morality being the worship rendered by the affections, Science and Poetry that rendered by the intellect. Such is the principal mission of the Occidental priesthood, a mission in which women and the working classes will actively co-operate.

The most important object of this regenerated polity will be the substitution of Duties for Rights; thus subordinating personal to social considerations. The word *Right* should be excluded from political language, as the word *Cause* from the language of philosophy. Both are theological and metaphysical conceptions; and the former is as immoral and subversive as the latter is unmeaning and sophistical. Both are alike incompatible with the final state; and their value during the

Substitution of duties for rights.

revolutionary period of modern history has simply consisted in their solvent action upon previous systems.
Rights, in the strict sense of the word, are possible only
so long as power is considered as emanating from a superhuman will. Rights, under all theological systems, were
divine; but in their opposition to theocracy, the metaphysicians of the last five centuries introduced what they
called the rights of Man; a conception, the value of which
consisted simply in its destructive effects. Whenever it
has been taken as the basis of a constructive policy, its
anti-social character, and its tendency to strengthen individualism have always been apparent. In the Positive
state, where no supernatural claims are admissible, the
idea of *Right* will entirely disappear. Every one has
duties, duties towards all; but Rights in the ordinary
sense can be claimed by none. Whatever security the
individual may require is found in the general acknow-
ledgement of reciprocal obligations; and this gives a
moral equivalent for rights as hitherto claimed, without
the serious political dangers which they involved. In
other words, no one has in any case any Right but that of
doing his Duty. The adoption of this principle is the one
way of realising the grand ideal of the Middle Ages, the
subordination of Politics to Morals. In those times, however, the vast bearings of the question were but very
imperfectly apprehended; its solution is incompatible
with every form of theology, and is only to be found
in Positivism.

The solution consists in regarding our political and social
action as the service of Humanity. Its object should be
to assist by conscious effort all functions, whether relating
to Order or to Progress, which Humanity has hitherto
performed spontaneously. This is the ultimate object of
Positive religion. Without it all other aspects of that

religion would be inadequate, and would soon cease to have any value. True affection does not stop short at desire for good; it strains every effort to attain it. The elevation of soul arising from the act of contemplating and adoring Humanity is not the sole object of religious worship. Above and beyond this there is the motive of becoming better able to serve Humanity; unceasing action on our part being necessary for her preservation and development. This indeed is the most distinctive feature of Positive religion. The Supreme Being of former times had really little need of human services. The consequence was, that with all theological believers, and with monotheists especially, devotion always tends to degenerate into quietism. The danger could only be obviated when the priesthood had sufficient wisdom to take advantage of the vagueness of these theories, and to draw from them motives for practical exertion. Nothing could be done in this direction unless the priesthood retained their social independence. As soon as this was taken from them by the usurpation of the temporal power, the more sincere amongst Catholics lapsed into the quietistic spirit which for a long time had been kept in check. In Positivism, on the contrary, the doctrine itself, irrespective of the character of its teachers, is a direct and continuous incentive to exertion of every kind. The reason for this is to be found in the relative and dependent nature of our Supreme Being, of whom her own worshippers form a part.

In this, which is the essential service of Humanity, and which infuses a religious spirit *Consensus of the social organism.* into every act of life, the feature most prominent is co-operation of effort; co-operation on so vast a scale that less complicated organisms have nothing to compare with it. The consensus of the social organism extends to Time as well as Space. Hence the two distinct aspects of social sympathy: the feeling of Solidarity, or union with the Present; and of Continuity, or union with the Past. Careful investigation of any social phenomenon, whether relating to Order or to Progress, always proves convergence, direct or indirect, of all contemporaries and of all former generations, within certain geographical and chronological limits; and those limits recede as the development of Humanity advances. In our thoughts and feelings such convergence is unquestionable; and it should be still more evident in our actions, the efficacy of which depends on co-operation to a still greater degree. Here we feel how false as well as immoral is the notion of *Right*, a word which, as commonly used, implies absolute individuality. The only principle on which Politics can be subordinated to Morals is, that individuals should be regarded, not as so many distinct beings, but as organs of one Supreme Being. Indeed, in all settled states of society, the individual has always been considered as a public functionary, filling more or less efficiently a definite post, whether formally appointed to it or not. So fundamental a principle has ever been recognised instinctively up to the period of revolutionary transition, which is now at length coming to an end; a period in which the obstructive and corrupt character of organized society roused a spirit of anarchy which, though at first favourable to progress, has now become an obstacle to it. Positivism, however, will place this principle beyond reach of attack, by giving a systematic demonstration of it, based on the sum of our scientific knowledge.

Continuity of the past with the present.   And this demonstration will be the intellectual basis on which the moral authority of the new priesthood will rest. What they have to do is to show the dependence of each important question, as it

arises, upon social co-operation, and by this means to indicate the right path of duty.   For this purpose all their
scientific knowledge and esthetic power will be needed,
otherwise social feeling could never be developed sufficiently to produce any strong effect upon conduct.   It
would never, that is, go further than the feeling of mere
solidarity with the Present, which is only its incipient
and rudimentary form.   We see this unfortunate narrowness of view too often in the best socialists, who, leaving
the Present without roots in the Past, would carry us
headlong towards a Future, of which they have no definite conception.   In all social phenomena, and especially
in those of modern times, the participation of our predecessors is greater than that of our contemporaries.   This
truth is especially apparent in industrial undertakings,
for which the combination of efforts required is so vast.
It is our filiation with the Past, even more than our connection with the Present, which teaches us that the only
real life is the collective life of the race; that individual
life has no existence except as an abstraction.   Continuity
is the feature which distinguishes our race from all others.
Many of the lower races are able to form a union among
their living members; but it was reserved for Man to conceive and realize co-operation of successive generations,
the source to which the gradual growth of civilization
is to be traced.   Social sympathy is a barren and imperfect feeling, and indeed it is a cause of disturbance, so
long as it extends no further than the present time.   It
is a disregard for historical Continuity which induces that
mistaken antipathy to all forms of inheritance which is
now so common.   Scientific study of history would soon
convince those of our socialist writers who are sincere of
their radical error in this respect.   If they were more
familiar with the collective inheritance of society, the

value of which no one can seriously dispute, they would feel less objection to inheritance in its application to individuals or families. Practical experience, moreover, bringing them into contact with the facts of the case, will gradually show them that without the sense of continuity with the Past they cannot really understand their solidarity with the Present. For, in the first place, each individual in the course of his growth passes spontaneously through phases corresponding in a great measure to those of our historical development; and therefore, without some knowledge of the history of society, he cannot understand the history of his own life. Again, each of these successive phases may be found amongst the less advanced nations who do not as yet share in the general progress of Humanity; so that we cannot properly sympathize with these nations, if we ignore the successive stages of development in Western Europe. The nobler socialists and communists, those especially who belong to the working classes, will soon be alive to the error and danger of these inconsistencies, and will supply this deficiency in their education, which at present vitiates their efforts. With women, the purest and most spontaneous element of the moderating power, the priests of Humanity will find it less difficult to introduce the broad principles of historical science. They are more inclined than any other class to recognise our continuity with the Past, being themselves its original source.

Necessity of a spiritual power to study and teach these truths, and thus to govern men by persuasion, instead of by compulsion. Without a scientific basis, therefore, a basis which must itself rest on the whole sum of Positive speculation, it is impossible for our social sympathies to develop themselves fully, so as to extend not to the Present only, but also and still more strongly to the Past. And this is the first motive, a motive founded alike on moral and on intel-

lectual considerations, for the separation of temporal from
spiritual power in the final organization of society.   The
more vigorously we concentrate our efforts upon social progress, the more clearly shall we feel the impossibility of
modifying social phenomena without knowledge of the
laws that regulate them.   This involves the existence of
an intellectual class specially devoted to the study of social
phenomena.   Such a class will be invested with the consultative authority for which their knowledge qualifies
them, and also with the function of teaching necessary for
the diffusion of their principles.   In the minor arts of life
it is generally recognised that principles should be investigated and taught by thinkers who are not concerned
in applying them.   In the art of Social Life, so far more
difficult and important than any other, the separation of
theory from practice is of far greater moment.   The wisdom of such a course is obvious, and all opposition to it
will be overcome, as soon as it becomes generally recognised that social phenomena are subject to invariable laws;
laws of so complicated a character and so dependent upon
other sciences as to make it doubly necessary that minds
of the highest order should be specially devoted to their
interpretation.

But there is another aspect of the question of not less
importance in sound polity.   Separation of temporal from
spiritual power is as necessary for free individual activity
as for social co-operation.   Humanity is characterised by
the independence as well as by the convergence of the
individuals or families of which she is composed.   The
latter condition, convergence, is that which secures Order;
but the former is no less essential to Progress.   Both are
alike urgent: yet in ancient times they were incompatible, for the reason that spiritual and temporal power were
always in the same hands; in the hands of the priests in

some cases, at other times in those of the military chief.
As long as the State held together, the independence of
the individual was habitually sacrificed to the convergence
of the body politic. This explains why the conception
of Progress never arose, even in the minds of the most
visionary schemers. The two conditions were irreconcileable until the Middle Ages, when a remarkable attempt
was made to separate the modifying power from the
governing power, and so to make Politics subordinate to
Morals. Co-operation of efforts was now placed on a
different footing. It was the result of free assent rendered by the heart and understanding to a religious system which laid down general rules of conduct, in which
nothing was arbitrary, and which were applied to governors as strictly as to their subjects. The consequence
was that Catholicism, notwithstanding its extreme defects
intellectually and socially, produced moral and political
results of very great value. Chivalry arose, a type of life,
in which the most vigorous independence was combined
with the most intense devotion to a common cause. Every
class in Western Society was elevated by this union of
personal dignity with universal brotherhood. So well is
human nature adapted for this combination, that it arose
under the first religious system of which the principles
were not incompatible with it. With the necessary decay
of that religion, it became seriously impaired, but yet was
preserved instinctively, especially in countries preserved
from Protestantism. By it the mediæval system prepared
the way for the conception of Humanity ; since it put an
end to the fatal opposition in which the two characteristic
attributes of Humanity, independence and co-operation,
had hitherto existed. Catholicism brought unity into
theological religion, and by doing so, led to its decline;
but it paved the way long beforehand for the more com-

plete and more real principle of unity, on which human society will be finally organised.

But meritorious and useful as this premature attempt was, it was no real solution of the problem. The spirit and temper of the period were not ripe for any definite solution. Theological belief and military life were alike inconsistent with any permanent separation of theoretical and practical powers. It was maintained only for a few centuries precariously and inadequately, by a sort of natural balance or rather oscillation between imperialism and theocracy. But the Positive spirit and the industrial character of modern times tend naturally to this division of power; and when it is consciously recognised as a principle, the difficulty of reconciling co-operation with independence will exist no longer. For in the first place, the rules to which human conduct will be subjected, will rest, as in Catholic times, but to a still higher degree, upon persuasion and conviction, instead of compulsion. Again, the fact of the new faith being always susceptible of demonstration, renders the spiritual system based on it more elevating as well as more durable. The rules of Catholic morality were only saved from being arbitrary by the introduction of a supernatural Will as a substitute for mere human authority. The plan had undoubtedly many advantages; but liberty in the true sense was not secured by it, since the rules remained as before without explanation; it was only their source that was changed. Still less successful was the subsequent attempt of metaphysicians to prove that submission to government was the foundation of virtue. It was only a return to the old system of arbitrary wills, stripped of the theocratic sanction to which all its claims to respect and its freedom from caprice had been due. The only way to reconcile independence with social union, and thereby to reach true liberty, lies in obedience to the objective laws of the world and of human nature; clearing these as far as possible of all that is subjective, and thus rendering them amenable to scientific demonstration. Of such immense consequence to society will it be to extend the scientific method to the complex and important phenomena of human nature. Man will no longer be the slave of man; he yields only to external Law; and to this those who demonstrate it to him are as submissive as himself. In such obedience there can be no degradation even where the laws are inflexible. But, as Positivism shows us, in most cases they are modifiable, and this especially in the case of our mental and moral constitution. Consequently our obedience is here no longer passive obedience: it implies the devotion of every faculty of our nature to the improvement of a world of which we are in a true sense masters. The natural laws to which we owe submission furnish the basis for our intervention; they direct our efforts and give stability to our purpose. The more perfectly they are known, the more free will our conduct become from arbitrary command or servile obedience. True, our knowledge of these laws will very seldom attain such precision as to enable us to do altogether without compulsory authority. When the intellect is inadequate, the heart must take its place. There are certain rules of life for which it is difficult to assign the exact ground, and where affection must assist reason in supplying motives for obedience. Wholly to dispense with arbitrary authority is impossible; nor will it degrade us to submit to it, provided that it be always regarded as secondary to the uniform supremacy of external Laws, and that every step in the development of our mental and moral powers shall restrict its employment. Both conditions are evidently satisfied in the Positive system of life. The tendency of modern industry and science is to make us less dependent on individual caprice, as well as more assimilable to the universal Organism. Positivism therefore secures the liberty and dignity of man by its demonstration that social phenomena, like all others, are subject to natural laws, which, within certain limits, are modifiable by wise action on the part of society. Totally contrary, on the other hand, is the spirit of metaphysical schemes of polity, in which society is supposed to have no spontaneous impulses, and is handed over to the will of the legislator. In these degrading and oppressive schemes, union is purchased, as in ancient times, at the cost of independence.

In these two ways, then, Positive religion influences the practical life of Humanity, in accordance with the natural laws that regulate her existence. First, the sense of Solidarity with the Present is perfected by adding to it the sense of Continuity with the Past; secondly, the co-operation of her individual agents is rendered compatible with their co-operation. Not till this is done can Politics become really subordinate to Morals, and the feeling of Duty be substituted for that of Right. Our active powers will be modified by the combined influence of feeling and reason, as expressed in indisputable rules which it will be for the spiritual power to make known to us. Temporal government, whoever its administrators may be, will always be modified by morality. Whereas in all metaphysical systems of polity nothing is provided for but the modes of access to government and the limits of its various departments; no principles are given to direct its application or to enable us to form a right judgment of it.

From this general view of the practical service of Humanity, we pass now to the two leading divisions of the subject; with the view of completing our conception of the funda-

Nutritive functions of Humanity, performed by Capitalists, as the temporal power.

mental principle of Positive Polity, the separation of
temporal from spiritual power.

The action of Humanity relates either to her external
circumstances, or to the facts of her own nature. Each
of these two great functions involves both Order and
Progress; but the first relates more specially to the preservation of her existence, the second to her progressive
development. Humanity, like every other organism, has
to act unceasingly on the surrounding world in order to
maintain and extend her material existence. Thus the
chief object of her practical life is to satisfy the wants of
our physical nature, wants which necessitate continual
reproduction of materials in sufficient quantities. This
production soon comes to depend more on the co-
operation of successive generations than on that of contemporaries. Even in these lower but indispensable functions, we work principally for our successors, and the
results that we enjoy are in great part due to those that
have gone before us. Each generation produces more
material wealth than is required for its own wants; and
the use of the surplus is to facilitate the labour and prepare the maintenance of the generation following. The
agents in this transmission of wealth naturally take the
lead in the industrial movement; since the possession of
provisions and instruments of production gives an advantage which can only be lost by unusual incapacity.
And this will seldom happen, because capital naturally
tends to accumulate with those who make a cautious and
skilful use of it.

Capitalists then will be the political leaders of modern
society. Their office is consecrated in Positive religion as
that of the nutritive organs of Humanity; organs which
collect and prepare the materials necessary for life, and
which also distribute them, subject always to the in-

fluence of a modifying central organ. The direct and palpable importance of their functions is a stimulus to pride ; and in every respect they are strongly influenced by personal instincts, which are necessary to sustain the vigour of their energies. Consequently, if left to themselves, they are apt to abuse their power, and to govern by the ignoble method of compulsion, disregarding all appeals to reason and to morality. Hence the need of a combination of moral forces to exercise a constant check upon the hardness with which they are so apt to use their authority. And this leads us to the second of the two great functions of Humanity.

This function is analogous to that of Innervation in individuals. Its object is the advancement of Humanity, whether in physical or still more in intellectual and moral aspects.

These are modified by the cerebral functions, performed by the spiritual power.

It might seem at first sight restricted, as in lower organisms, to the secondary office of assisting the nutritive function. Soon however it develops qualities peculiar to itself, qualities on which our highest happiness depends. And thus we might imagine that life was to be entirely given up to the free play of reason, imagination, and feeling, were we not constantly forced back by the necessities of our physical nature to less delightful occupations. Therefore this intellectual and moral function, notwithstanding its eminence, can never be supreme in our nature ; yet independently of its intrinsic charm, it forms our principal means, whether used consciously or otherwise, in controlling the somewhat blind action of the nutritive organs. It is in women, whose function is analogous to that of the affective organs in the individual brain, that we find this modifying influence in its purest and most spontaneous form. But the full value of their influence is not realised until they act in combination with the philosophic class ;

which, though its direct energy is small, is as indispensable to the collective Organism as the speculative functions of the brain are to the individual. Besides these two essential elements of moral power, we find, when Humanity reaches her maturity, a third element which completes the constitution of this power and furnishes a basis for its political action. This third element is the working class, whose influence may be regarded as the active function in the innervation of the social Organism.

It is indeed to the working class that we look for the only possible solution of the great human problem, the victory of Social feeling over Self-love. Their want of leisure, and their poverty, excludes them from political power; and yet wealth, which is the basis of that power, cannot be produced without them. They are allied to the spiritual power by the similarity of their tastes and of their circumstances. Moreover, they look to it for systematic education, of the importance of which not merely to their happiness, but to their dignity and moral culture, they are deeply conscious. The nature of their occupations, though absorbing so large a portion of their time, yet leaves the mind for the most part free. Finding little in the specialities of their work to interest them, they are the more inclined to rise to general principles, provided always that such principles combine utility with reality. Being less occupied than other classes with considerations of rank and wealth, they are the more disposed to give free play to generous feelings, the value and the charm of which is more strongly impressed on them by their experience of life. As their strength lies in numbers, they have a greater tendency to union than capitalists, who, having in their own hands a power which they are apt to suppose resistless, have no such motive for association. They will give their energetic support to the priesthood in its efforts to control the abuse of the power of wealth, and in every respect they are prepared to accept and enforce its moral influence. Being at once special and general, practical and speculative, and at the same time always animated by strong sympathies, they form an intermediate link between the practical and theoretical powers; connected with the one by the need of education and counsel, and with the other by the necessities of labour and subsistence. The people represent the activity of the Supreme Being, as women represent its sympathy, and philosophers its intellect.

But in the organized action of these three organs of innervation upon the organs of social nutrition, it must be borne in mind that the latter are not to be impeded in their functions. The control exercised is to be of a kind that will ennoble them by setting their importance in its true light. True, we are not to encourage the foolish and immoral pride of modern capitalists, who look upon themselves as the creators and sole arbiters of their material power, the foundations of which are in reality due to the combined action of their predecessors and contemporaries. They ought to be regarded simply as public functionaries, responsible for the administration of capital and the direction of industrial enterprise. But at the same time we must be careful not to underrate the immense value of their function, or in any way obstruct its performance. All this follows at once from the policy of Separation of Powers. The responsibility under which it is here proposed to place capitalists is purely moral, whereas metaphysicians of the revolutionary school have always been in favour of political coercion. In cases where the rich neglect their duty, the Positive priesthood will resort in the first instance to every method of conviction and persuasion that can be suggested by the education which the rich have received in common with other classes. Should this course fail, there remains the resource of pronouncing formal condemnation of their conduct ; and supposing this to be ratified by the working men of every city, and the women of every family, its effect will be difficult to withstand. In very heinous cases, it might be necessary to proceed to the extreme length of social excommunication, the efficacy of which, in cases where it deserved and received general assent, would be even greater than in the Middle Ages ; the organization of the spiritual power in those times being very imperfect. But even in this case the means used for repression are of a purely moral kind. The rare cases that call for political measures belong exclusively to the province of the temporal power.

Hereditary transmission of wealth has been strongly condemned by metaphysical writers. But it is after all a natural mode of transmission, and the moral discipline above described will be a sufficient check upon its worst abuses. When the sense of Duty is substituted for the sense of Right, it matters little who may be the possessor of any given power, provided it be well used. Inheritance, as Positivism shows, has great social advantages, especially when applied to functions which require no extraordinary capacity, and which are best learnt in the training of domestic life. Taking the moral point of view, we find that men who have been always accustomed to wealth are more disposed to be generous than those who have amassed it gradually, however honourable the means used. Inheritance was originally the mode in which all functions were transmitted ; and in the case of wealth there is no reason why it should not always continue, since the mere preservation of wealth, without reference to its employment, requires but little special ability. There is no guarantee that, if other guardians of capital were appointed, the public would be better served. Modern industry has long ago proved the administrative superiority of private enterprise in commercial transactions; and all social functions that admit of it will gradually pass into private management, always excepting the great theoretic functions, in which combined action will always be necessary. Declaim as the envious will against hereditary wealth, its possessors, when they have a good disposition moulded by a wise education and a healthy state of public opinion, will in many cases rank amongst the most useful organs of Humanity. It is not the class who constitute the moral force of society, that will give vent to these idle complaints, or at least they will be confined to those individuals among them who fail to understand the dignity and value of their common mission of elevating man's affections, intellect, and energies.

The only cases in which the spiritual power has to interfere specially for the protection of material interests fall under two principles, *Women and priests to have their material subsistence guaranteed.* which are very plainly indicated by the natural order of society. The first principle is, that Man should support Woman; the second, that the Active class should support the Speculative class. The necessity of both these conditions is evident; without them the affective and speculative functions of Humanity cannot be adequately performed. Private and public welfare are so deeply involved in the influence exercised by Feeling over the intellectual and active powers, that we shall do well to secure that influence, even at the cost of removing one half of the race from industrial occupations. Even in the lowest tribes of savages we find the stronger sex recognising some obligations towards the weaker; and it is this which distinguishes human love, even in its coarser forms, from animal appetite. With every step in the progress of

Humanity we find the obligation more distinctly acknowledged, and more fully satisfied. In Positive religion it
becomes a fundamental duty, for which each individual,
or even society, when it may be necessary, will be held
responsible. As to the second principle, it is one which
has been already admitted by former systems ; and, in
spite of the anarchy in which we live, it has never been
wholly discarded, at least in countries which have been
unaffected by the individualist tendencies of Protestantism.. Positivism, however, while adopting the principle
as indispensable to the theoretic functions of Humanity,
will employ it far more sparingly than Catholicism, the
decay of which was very much hastened by its excessive wealth. If temporal and spiritual power are really
to be separated, philosophers should have as little to do
with wealth as with government. Resembling women
in their exclusion from political power, their position
as to wealth should be like that of the working classes,
proper regard being had to the requirements of their
office. By following this course, they may be confident
that the purity of their opinions and advice will never
be called in question.

These two conditions then, Capitalists, as the normal
administrators of the common fund of wealth, will be
expected to satisfy. They must, that is, so regulate the
distribution of wages, that women shall be released from
work ; and they must see that proper remuneration is
given for intellectual labour. To exact the performance
of these conditions seems no easy task ; yet until they are
satisfied, the equilibrium of our social economy will remain
unstable. The institution of property can be maintained
no longer upon the untenable ground of personal right.
Its present possessors may probably decline to accept these
principles. In that case their functions will pass in one

way or another to new organs, until Humanity finds servants who will not shirk their fundamental duties, but who will recognise them as the first condition of their tenure of power. That power, subject to these limitations, will then be regarded with the highest respect, for all will feel that the existence of Humanity depends on it. Alike on intellectual and on moral grounds, society will repudiate the envious passions and subversive views which are aroused at present by the unfounded claims of property, and by its repudiation, since the Middle Ages, of every real moral obligation. Rich men will feel that principles like these, leaving as they do so large a margin of voluntary action to the individual, are the only method of escaping from the political oppression with which they are now threatened. The free concentration of capital will then be readily accepted as necessary to its social usefulness; for great duties imply great powers.

This, then, is the way in which the priests of Humanity may hope to regenerate the material power of wealth, and bring the nutritive *Normal relation of priests, people, and capitalists.* functions of society into harmony with the other parts of the body politic. The contests for which as yet there are but too many motives, will then cease; the People without loss of dignity will give free play to their natural instincts of respect, and will be as willing to accept the authority of their political rulers as to place confidence in their spiritual guides. They will feel that true happiness has no necessary connection with wealth; that it depends far more on free play being given to their intellectual, moral, and social qualities; and that in this respect they are more favourably situated than those above them. They will cease to aspire to the enjoyments of wealth and power, leaving them to those whose political activity requires that strong stimulus. Each man's ambition will be to do his work well; and after it is over, to perform his more general function of assisting the spiritual power, and of taking part in the formation of Public Opinion, by giving his best judgment upon passing events. Of the limits to be observed by the spiritual power the People will be well aware; and they will accept none which does not subordinate the intellect to the heart, and guarantee the purity of its doctrine by strict abstinence from political power. By an appeal to the principles of Positive Polity, they will at once check any foolish yielding on the part of philosophers to political ambition, and will restore the temporal power to its proper place. They will be aware that though the general principles of practical life rest upon Science, it is not for Science to direct their application. The incapacity of theorists to apply their theories practically has long been recognised in minor matters, and it will now be recognised as equally applicable to political questions. The province of the philosopher is education; and as the result of education, counsel: the province of the capitalist is action and authoritative direction. This is the only right distribution of power; and the people will insist on maintaining it in its integrity, seeing, as they will, that without it the harmonious existence of Humanity is impossible.

We are not yet ripe for the normal state. But the revolution of 1848 is a step towards it. From this view of the practical side of the religion of Humanity taken in connection with its intellectual and moral side, we may form a general conception of the final reorganization of political institutions, by which alone the great Revolution can be brought to a close. But the time for affecting this reconstruction has not yet come. There must be a previous reconstruction of opinions and habits of life upon the basis laid down by Positivism; and for this at least one generation is required.

In the interval, all political measures must retain their provisional character, although in framing them the final state is always to be taken into account. As yet nothing can be said to have been established, except the moral principle on which Positivism rests, the subordination of Politics to Morals. For this is in fact implicitly involved in the proclamation of a Republic in France ; a step which cannot now be recalled, and which implies that each citizen is to devote all his faculties to the service of Humanity. But with regard to the social organization, by which alone this principle can be carried into effect, although its basis has been laid down by Positivism, it has not yet received the sanction of the Public. It may be hoped, however, that the motto which I have put forward as descriptive of the new political philosophy, *Order and Progress*, will soon be adopted spontaneously.

In the first or negative phase of the Revolution, all that was done was utterly to repudiate the old political system. No indication whatever was given of the state of things which was to succeed it. The motto of the time, *Liberty and Equality*, is an exact representation of this state of things, the conditions expressed in it being utterly contradictory, and incompatible with organization of any kind. For obviously, Liberty gives free scope to superiority of all kinds, and especially to moral and mental superiority ; so that if a uniform level of Equality is insisted on, freedom of growth is checked. Yet inconsistent as the motto was, it was admirably adapted to the destructive temper of the time ; a time when hatred of the Past compensated the lack of insight into the Future. It had, too, a progressive tendency, which partly neutralised its subversive spirit. It inspired the first attempt to derive true principles of polity from general views of history ; the memorable though un-

First revolutionary motto; Liberty and Equality.

successful essay of my great predecessor Condorcet. Thus
the first intimation of the future influence of the historical
spirit was given at the very time when the anti-historical
spirit had reached its climax.

The long period of reaction which succeeded the first
crisis gave rise to no political motto of any importance.
It was a period for which men of any vigour of thought
and character could not but feel secret repugnance. It
produced, however, a universal conviction that the metaphysical policy of the revolutionists was of no avail for
constructive purposes. And it gave rise to the historical
works of the Neo-Catholic school, which prepared the way
for Positivism by giving the first fair appreciation of the
Middle Ages.

But the Counter-revolution, begun by Robespierre, carried to its full length by Bonaparte,
and continued by the Bourbons, came to an
end in the memorable outbreak of 1830. A neutral period
of eighteen years followed, and a new motto, *Liberty and
Public Order*, was temporarily adopted. This motto was
very expressive of the political condition of the time; and
the more so that it arose spontaneously, without ever
receiving any formal sanction. It expressed the general
feeling of the public, who, feeling that the secret of the
political future was possessed by none of the existing
parties, contented itself with pointing out the two conditions essential as a preparation for it. It was an improvement on the first motto, because it indicated more
clearly that the ultimate purpose of the revolution was
construction. It got rid of the anti-social notion of
Equality. All the moral advantages of Equality without
its political dangers existed already in the feeling of Fraternity, which, since the Middle Ages, has become sufficiently diffused in Western Europe to need no special

Second motto; Liberty and Order.

formula. Again, this motto introduced empirically the great conception of Order; understanding it of course in the limited sense of material order at home and abroad. No deeper meaning was likely to be attached to the word in a time of such mental and moral anarchy.

But with the adoption of the Republican principle in 1848, the utility of this provisional motto ceased. For the Revolution now entered *Third motto; Order and Progress.* upon its positive phase; which indeed, for all philosophical minds, had been already inaugurated by my discovery of the laws of Social Science. But the fact of its having fallen into disuse is no reason for going back to the old motto, Liberty and Equality, which, since the crisis of 1789, has ceased to be appropriate. In the utter absence of social convictions, it has obtained a sort of official resuscitation; but this will not prevent men of good sense and right feeling from adopting spontaneously the motto *Order and Progress*, as the principle of all political action for the future. In the second chapter I dwelt at some length upon this motto, and pointed out its political and philosophical meaning. I have now only to show its connection with the other mottoes of which we have been speaking, and the probability of its adoption. Each of them, like all combinations, whether in the moral or physical world, is composed of two elements; and the last has one of its elements in common with the second, as the second has in common with the first. Moreover, Liberty, the element common to the two first, is in reality contained in the third; since all Progress implies Liberty. But Order is put foremost, because the word is here intended to cover the whole field that properly belongs to it. It includes things private as well as public, theoretical as well as practical, moral as well as political. Progress is put next, as the end for which Order exists, and as the mode in which it should be manifested. This conception, for which the crisis of 1789 prepared the way, will be our guiding principle throughout the constructive phase of the Western Revolution. The reconciliation of Order and Progress, which had hitherto been impossible, is now an accepted fact for all advanced minds. For the public this is not yet the case; but since the close of the Counter-revolution in 1830, all minds have been tending unconsciously in this direction. The tendency becomes still more striking by contrast with an opposite movement, the increasing identity of principles between the reactionary and the anarchist schools.

Provisional policy for the period of transition. But even if we suppose accomplished what is yet only in prospect, even if the fundamental principle of our future polity were accepted and publicly ratified by the adoption of this motto, yet permanent reconstruction of political institutions would still be premature. Before this can be attempted, the spiritual interregnum must be terminated. For this object, in which all hearts and minds, especially among the working classes and among women, must unite their efforts with those of the philosophic priesthood, at least one generation is required. During this period governmental policy should be avowedly provisional; its one object should be to maintain what is so essential to our state of transition, Order, at home and abroad. Here, too, Positivism suffices for the task; by explaining on historical principles the stage that we have left, and that at which we shall ultimately arrive, it enables us to understand the character of the intermediate stage.

Popular dictatorship with freedom of speech. The solution of the problem consists in a new revolutionary government, adapted to the Positive phase of the Revolution, as the admirable institutions of the Convention were to its negative phase. The principle features of such a government would be perfect freedom of speech and discussion, and at the same time political preponderance of the central authority with proper guarantees for its purity. To secure perfect freedom of discussion, various measures would be taken. All penalties and fines which at present hamper its action would be abolished, the only check left being the obligation of signature. Again, all difficulties in the way of criticising the private character of public men, due to the disgraceful legislation of the psychologists, would be removed. Lastly, all official grants to theological and metaphysical institutions would be discontinued; for while these last, freedom of instruction in the true sense cannot be said to exist. With such substantial guarantees there will be little fear of reactionary tendencies on the part of the executive; and consequently no danger in allowing it to take that ascendency over the electoral body which, in the present state of mental and moral anarchy, is absolutely necessary for the maintenance of material order. On this plan the French assembly would be reduced to about two hundred members; and its only duty would be to vote the budget proposed by the finance committee of government, and to audit the accounts of the past year. All executive or legislative measures would come within the province of the central power; the only condition being that they should first be submitted to free discussion, whether by journals, public meetings, or individual thinkers, though such discussion should not bind the government legally. The progressive character of the government thus guaranteed, we have next to see that the men who compose it shall be such as are likely to carry out the provisional and purely practical purpose with which it is instituted. On Positive principles, it is to the working classes that we should look for the only statesmen worthy

of succeeding to the statesmen of the Convention. Three
of such men would be required for the central government. They would combine the functions of a ministry
with those of monarchy, one of them taking the direction
of Foreign affairs, another of Home affairs, the third of
Finance. They would convoke and dissolve the electoral
power on their own responsibility. Of this body the
majority would in a short time, without any law to that
effect, consist of the larger capitalists; for the office would
be gratuitous, and the duties would be of a kind for which
their ordinary avocations fitted them. Changes would
occasionally be necessary in the central government; but
since it would consist of three persons, its continuity might
be maintained, and the traditions of the previous generation, as well as the tendencies of the future, and the position actually existing, might all be represented.

Such a government, though of course retaining some
revolutionary features, would come as near to the normal
state as is at present practicable. For its province would
be entirely limited to material questions, and the only
anomaly of importance would be the fact of choosing
rulers from the working classes. Normally, this class is
excluded from political administration, which falls ultimately into the hands of capitalists. But the anomaly
is so obviously dependent simply on the present condition
of affairs, and will be so restricted in its application, that
the working classes are not likely to be seriously demoral-
ized by it. The primary object being to infuse morality
into practical life, it is clear that working men, whose
minds and hearts are peculiarly accessible to moral influence, are for the present best qualified for political power.
No check meantime is placed on the action of the capitalists; and this provisional policy prepares the way for their
ultimate accession to power, by convincing them of the

urgent need of private and public regeneration, without which they can never be worthy of it. By this course, too, it becomes easier to bring the consultative influence of a spiritual power to bear upon modern government. At first such influence can only be exercised spontaneously; but it will become more and more systematic with every new step in the great philosophical renovation on which the final reorganization of society is based.

The propriety of the provisional policy here recommended is further illustrated by the wide scope of its application. Although suggested by the difficulties peculiar to the position of France, it is equally adapted to other nations who are sufficiently advanced to take part in the great revolutionary crisis. Thus the second phase of the Revolution is at once distinguished from the first, by having an Occidental, as opposed to a purely National, character. And the fact of the executive government being composed of working men, points in the same direction; since of all classes working men are the most free from local prejudices, and have the strongest tendencies, both intellectually and morally, to universal union. Even should this form of government be limited for some years to France, it would be enough to remodel the old system of diplomacy throughout the West.

Such are the advantages which the second revolutionary government will derive from the possession of systematic principles; whereas the government of the Convention was left to its empirical instincts, and had nothing but its progressive instincts to guide it.

A special Report was published in 1848 by the Positivist Society, in which the subject of provisional government will be found discussed in greater detail.

Quiet at home and peace abroad being se- Positive Committee for cured, we shall be able, notwithstanding the Western Europe.

continuance of mental and moral anarchy, to proceed actively with the vast work of social regeneration, with the certainty of full liberty of thought and expression. For this purpose it will be desirable to institute the philosophical and political association to which I alluded in the last volume of my " Positive Philosophy" (published in 1842), under the title of "Positive Occidental Committee." Its sittings would usually be held in Paris, and it would consist, in the first place, of eight Frenchmen, seven Englishmen, six Germans, five Italians, and four Spaniards. This would be enough to represent fairly the principal divisions of each population. Germany, for instance, might send a Dutchman, a Prussian, a Swede, a Dane, a Bavarian, and an Austrian. So, too, the Italian members might come respectively from Piedmont, Lombardy, Tuscany, the Roman States, and the two Sicilies. Again, Catalonia, Castille, Andalusia, and Portugal would adequately represent the Spanish Peninsula.

Thus we should have a sort of permanent Council of the new Church. Each of the three elements of the moderating power should be admitted into it; and it might also contain such members of the governing class as were sufficiently regenerated to be of use in forwarding the general movement. There should be practical men in this council as well as philosophers. Here, as elsewhere, it will be principally from the working classes that such practical co-operation will come; but no support, if given sincerely, will be rejected, even should it emanate from the classes who are destined to extinction. It is also most important for the purposes of this Council that the third element of the moderating power, women, should be included in it, so as to represent the fundamental principle of the preponderance of the heart over the understanding. Six ladies should be chosen in addition to the thirty members above mentioned : of these, two would be French, and one from each of the other nations. Besides their ordinary sphere of influence, it will be their special duty to disseminate Positivism among our Southern brethren. It is an office that I had reserved for my saintly colleague, who, but for her premature death, would have rendered eminent service in such a Council.

While material order is maintained by national governments, the members of the Council, as pioneers of the final order of society, will be carrying on the European movement, and gradually terminating the spiritual interregnum which is now the sole obstacle to social regeneration. They will forward the development and diffusion of Positivism, and make practical application of its principles, in all ways that are honourably open to them. Instruction of all kinds, oral or written, popular or philosophic, will fall within their province ; but their chief aim will be to inaugurate the worship of Humanity so far as that is possible. And already a beginning is possible, so far at least as the system of commemoration is concerned. Politically they may give a direct proof of the international character of the Positive system, by bringing forward several measures, the utility of which has long been recognised, but which have been neglected for want of some central authority placed beyond the reach of national rivalry.

One of the most important of such measures would be the establishment of a Western naval force, with ·the twofold object of protecting the seas, and of assisting geographical and scientific discovery. It should be recruited and supported by all five branches of the Occidental family, and would thus be a good substitute for the admirable institution of maritime Chivalry which fell with Catholicism. On its flag the Positivist motto

Occidental navy.

would naturally be inscribed, and thus would be for the
first time publicly recognised.

International coinage. Another measure, conceived in the same
spirit, would soon follow, one which has been
long desired, but which, owing to the anarchy prevalent
throughout the West since the decline of Catholicism,
has never yet been carried out. A common monetary
standard will be established, with the consent of the
various governments, by which industrial transactions
will be greatly facilitated. Three spheres made respectively of gold, silver, and platinum, and each weighing
fifty grammes (772 grains), would differ sufficiently in
value for the purpose. The sphere should have a small
flattened base, and on the great circle parallel to it the
Positivist motto would be inscribed. At the pole would
be the image of the immortal Charlemagne, the founder
of the Western Republic, and round the image his name
would be engraved, in its Latin form, Carolus; that
name, respected as it is by all nations of Europe alike,
would be the common appellation of the universal monetary standard.

Occidental school. The adoption of such measures would soon
bring the Positivist Committee into favour.
Many others might be suggested, relating directly to its
fundamental purpose, which need not be specially mentioned here. I will only suggest the foundation, by voluntary effort, of an Occidental School, to serve as the nucleus
of a true philosophic class. The students would ultimately
enter the Positivist priesthood; they would in most instances come from the working class, without, however,
excluding real talent from whatever quarter. By their
agency the septennial course of Positive teaching might
be introduced in all places disposed to receive it. They
would besides supply voluntary missionaries, who would

preach the doctrine everywhere, even outside the limits of Western Europe, according to the plan hereafter to be explained. The travels of Positivist workmen, in the ordinary duties of their calling, would greatly facilitate this work.

A more detailed view of this provisional system of instruction will be found in the second edition of the " Report on the Subject of a Positive School," published by the Positivist Society in 1849.

There is another step which might be taken, relating not merely to the period of transition, but also to the normal state. A flag suitable to the Western Republic might be adopted, which, with slight alterations, would also be the flag for each nation. The want of such a symbol is already instinctively felt. What is wanted is a substitute for the old retrograde symbols, which yet shall avoid all subversive tendencies. It would be a suitable inauguration of the period of transition which we are now entering, if the colours and mottoes appropriate to the final state were adopted at its outset.

Flag for the Western Republic.

To speak first of the banner to be used in religious services. It should be painted on canvass. On one side the ground would be white ; on it would be the symbol of Humanity, personified by a woman of thirty years of age, bearing her son in her arms. The other side would bear the religious formula of Positivists : *Love is our Principle, Order is our Basis, Progress our End,* upon a ground of green, the colour of hope, and therefore most suitable for emblems of the future.

Green, too, would be the colour of the political flag, common to the whole West. As it is intended to float freely, it does not admit of painting ; but the carved image of Humanity might be placed at the banner-pole. The principal motto of Positivism will, in this case, be divided into two, both alike significant. One side of the flag will have the political and scientific motto, Order and Progress; the other, the moral and esthetic motto, Live for Others. The first will be preferred by men; the other is more specially adapted to women, who are thus invited to participate in these public manifestations of social feeling.

This point settled, the question of the various national flags becomes easy. In these the centre might be green, and the national colours might be displayed on the border. Thus, in France, where the innovation will be first introduced, the border would be tricolour, with the present arrangement of colours, except that more space should be given to the white, in honour of our old royal flag. In this way uniformity would be combined with variety; and, moreover, it would be shown that the new feeling of Occidentality is perfectly compatible with respect for the smallest nationalities. Each would retain the old signs in combination with the common symbol. The same principle would apply to all emblems of minor importance.

The question of these symbols, of which I have spoken during the last two years in my weekly courses of lectures, illustrates the most immediate of the functions to which the Positive Committee will be called. I mention it here, as a type of its general action upon European society.

Without setting any limits to the gradual increase of the Association, it is desirable that the central nucleus should always remain limited to the original number of thirty-six, with two additions, which will shortly be mentioned. Each member might institute a more numerous association in his own country, and this again might be the parent of others. Associations thus affiliated may be developed to an unlimited extent; and thus we shall be able to maintain the unity and homogeneity of the Positive Church, without impairing its coherence and vigour.

As soon as Positivism has gained in every country a suffi-cient number of voluntary adherents to constitute the pre-ponderating section of the community, the regeneration of society is secured.

The members assigned above for the different nations, only represent the order in which the advanced minds in each will co-operate in the movement. The order in which the great body of each nation will join it, will be, so far as we can judge from their antecedents, somewhat different. The difference is, that Italy here takes the second place, and Spain the third, while England descends to the last. The grounds for this important modification are indicated in the third edition of my " Positive Calen-dar." They will be discussed in detail in the fourth volume of this Treatise.*

From Europe the movement will spread ulti-mately to the whole race. But the first step in its progress will naturally be to the inhabi-tants of our colonies, who, though politically independent of Western Europe, still retain their filiation with it. Twelve colonial members may be added to the Council; four for each American Continent, two for India, two for the Dutch and Spanish possessions in the Indian Ocean.

Colonial and foreign Asso-ciates of the Committee, the action of which will ultimately extend to the whole human race.

This gives us forty-eight members. To these twelve foreign associates will gradually be added, to represent the populations whose growth has been retarded; and then the Council will have received its full complement. For every nation of the world is destined for the same ultimate conditions of social regeneration as ourselves, the only difference being that Western Europe, under the leadership of France, takes the initiative. It is of great

---

* The relative position here assigned to England and Germany is reversed in the 'fourth volume of the " Politique Positive."

importance not to attempt this final extension too soon, an error which would impair the precision and vigour of the renovating movement. At the same time it must never be forgotten that the existence of the Great Being remains incomplete until all its members are brought into harmonious co-operation. In ancient times social sympathy was restricted to the idea of Nationality; between this and the final conception of Humanity, the Middle Ages introduced the intermediate conception of Christendom, or Occidentality; the real bearing of which is at present but little appreciated. It will be our first political duty to revive that conception, and place it on a firmer basis, by terminating the anarchy consequent on the extinction of Catholic Feudalism. While occupied in this task, we shall become impressed with the conviction that the union of Western Europe is but a preliminary step to the union of Humanity; an instinctive presentiment of which has existed from the infancy of our race, but which, as long as theological belief and military life were predominant, could never be carried out even in thought. The primary laws of human development which form the philosophical basis of the Positive system, apply necessarily to all climates and races whatsoever, the only difference being in the rapidity with which evolution takes place. The inferiority of other nations in this respect is not inexplicable; and it will now be compensated by a growth of greater regularity than ours, and less interrupted by shocks and oscillations. Obviously in our case systematic guidance was impossible, since it is only now that our growth is complete that we can learn the general laws common to it and to other cases. Wise and generous intervention of the West on behalf of our sister nations who are less advanced, will form a noble field for Social Art, when based on sound scientific principles. Relative without being arbitrary, zealous and yet always temperate; such should be the spirit of this intervention; and thus conducted, it will form a system of moral and political action far nobler than the proselytism of theology or the extension of military empire. The time will come when it will engross the whole attention of the Positive Council; but for the present it must remain secondary to other subjects of greater urgency.

The first to join the Western movement will necessarily be the remaining portion of the White race: which in all its branches is superior to the other two races. There are two Monotheist nations, and one Polytheist, which will be successively incorporated. Taken together, the three represent the propagation of Positivism in the East.

The vast population of the Russian empire was left outside the pale of Catholic Feudalism. By virtue of its Christianity, however, notwithstanding its entire confusion of temporal and spiritual power, it holds the first place among the Monotheistic nations of the East. Its initiation into the Western movement will be conducted by two nations of intermediate position; Greece, connected with Russia by the tie of religion; and Poland, united with her politically. Though neither of these nations is homogeneous in structure with Russia, it would cause serious delay in the propagation of Positivism should the connection be altogether terminated.

The next step will be to Mohammedan Monotheism; first in Turkey, afterwards in Persia. Here Positivism will find points of sympathy of which Catholicism could not admit. Indeed these are already perceptible. Arab civilization transmitted Greek science to us: and this will always secure for it an honourable place among the essential elements of the mediæval system, regarded as a preparation for Positivism.

27

Lastly, we come to the Polytheists of India; and with them the incorporation of the White race will be complete. Already we see some spontaneous tendencies in this direction. Although from exceptional causes Theocracy has been preserved in India, there exist real points of contact with Positivism; and in this respect the assistance of Persia will be of service. It is the peculiar privilege of the Positive doctrine that, taking so complete a view of human development, it is always able to appreciate the most ancient forms of social life at their true worth.

In these three stages of Positivist propagation, the Council will have elected the first half of its foreign associates; admitting successively a Greek, a Russian, an Egyptian, a Turk, a Persian, and finally, a Hindoo.

The Yellow race has adhered firmly to Polytheism. But it has been considerably modified in all its branches by Monotheism, either in the Christian or Mohammedan form. To some extent, therefore, it is prepared for further change; and a sufficient number of adherents may soon be obtained for Tartary, China, Japan, and Malacca to be represented in the Council.

With one last addition the organization of the Council is complete. The Black race has yet to be included. It should send two representatives; one from Hayti, which had the energy to shake off the iniquitous yoke of slavery, and the other from central Africa, which has never yet been subjected to European influence. European pride has looked with contempt on these African tribes, and imagines them destined to hopeless stagnation. But the very fact of their having been left to themselves renders them better disposed to receive Positivism, the first system in which their Fetichistic faith has been appreciated, as the origin from which the historical evolution of society has proceeded.

It is probable that the Council will have reached its limit of sixty members, before the spiritual interregnum in the central region of Humanity has been terminated. But even if political reconstruction were to proceed so rapidly in Europe as to render all possible assistance to this vast movement, it is hardly conceivable that the five stages of which it consists can be thoroughly effected within a period of two centuries. But however this may be, the action of the Council will become increasingly valuable, not only for its direct influence on the less advanced nations, but also and more especially, because the proofs it will furnish of the universality of the new religion will strengthen its adherents in the Western family.

But the time when Positivism can be brought into direct contact with these preliminary phases is far distant, and we need not wait for it. The features of the system stand out already with sufficient clearness to enable us to begin at once the work of mental and social renovation for which our revolutionary predecessors so energetically prepared the way. They however were blinded to the Future by their hatred of the Past. With us, on the contrary, social sympathy rests upon the historical spirit, and at the same time strengthens it. Solidarity with our contemporaries is not enough for us, unless we combine it with the sense of Continuity with former times; and while we press on toward the Future, we lean upon the Past, every phase of which our religion holds in honour. So far from the energy of our progressive movement being hampered by such feelings, it is only by doing full justice to the Past, as no system but ours can do consistently, that we can attain perfect emancipation of thought; because we are thus saved from the necessity of making the slightest actual concession to systems which we regard as obsolete. Understanding their nature and

Conclusion. Perfection of the Positivist ideal.

their purpose better than the sectaries who still empirically adhere to them, we can see that each was in its time necessary as a preparatory step towards the final system, in which all their partial and imperfect services will be combined.

Comparing it especially with the last synthesis by which the Western family of nations has been directed, it is clear even from the indications given in this prefatory work, that the new synthesis is more real, more comprehensive, and more stable. All that we find to admire in the mediaeval system is developed and matured in Positivism. It is the only system which can induce the intellect to accept its due position of subordination to the heart. We recognise the piety and chivalry of our ancestors, who made a noble application of the best doctrine that was possible in their time. We believe that were they living now, they would be found in our ranks. They would acknowledge the decay of their provisional phase of thought, and would see that in its present degenerate state it is only a symbol of reaction, and a source of discord.

And now that the doctrine has been shown to rest on a central principle, a principle which appeals alike to instinct and to reason, we may carry our comparison a step further, and convince all clear-seeing and honest minds that it is as superior to former systems in its influence over the emotions and the imagination, as it is from the practical and intellectual aspect. Under it, Life, whether private or public, becomes in a still higher sense than under Polytheism, a continuous act of worship, performed under the inspiration of universal Love. All our thoughts, feelings, and actions flow spontaneously to a common centre in Humanity, our Supreme Being; a Being who is real, accessible, and sympathetic, because she is of the same nature as her worshippers, though far superior to any one of them. The very conception of Humanity is a condensation of the whole mental and social history of man. For it implies the irrevocable extinction of theology and of war; both of which are incompatible with uniformity of belief and with co-operation of all the energies of the race. The spontaneous morality of the emotions is restored to its due place; and Philosophy, Poetry, and Polity are thereby regenerated. Each is placed in its due relation to the others, and is consecrated to the study, the praise, and the service of Humanity, the most relative and the most perfectible of all beings. Science passes from the analytic to the synthetic state, being entrusted with the high mission of founding an objective basis for man's action on the laws of the external world and of man's nature; a basis which is indispensable to control the oscillation of our opinions, the versatility of our feelings, and the instability of our purposes. Poetry assumes at last its true social function, and will henceforth be preferred to all other studies. By idealizing Humanity under every aspect, it enables us to give fit expression to the gratitude we owe to her, both publicly and as individuals; and thus it becomes a source of the highest spiritual benefit.

But amidst the pleasures that spring from the study and the praise of Humanity, it must be remembered that Positivism is characterised always by reality and utility, and admits of no degeneration into asceticism or quietism. The Love by which it is inspired is no passive principle; while stimulating Reason and Imagination, it does so only to give a higher direction to our practical activity. It was in practical life that the Positive spirit first arose, extending thence to the sphere of thought, and ultimately to the moral sphere. The grand object of human existence is the constant improvement of the natural Order that surrounds us : of our material condition first ; subsequently of our physical, intellectual, and moral nature. And the highest of these objects is moral progress, whether in the individual, in the family, or in society. It is on this that human happiness, whether in private or public life, principally depends. Political art, then, when subordinated to morality, becomes the most essential of all arts. It consists in concentration of all human effort upon the service of Humanity, in accordance with the natural laws which regulate her existence.

The great merit of ancient systems of polity, of the Roman system especially, was that precedence was always given to public interests. Every citizen co-operated in the manner and degree suited to those early times. But there were no means of providing proper regulation for domestic life. In the Middle Ages, when Catholicism attempted to form a complete system of morality, private life was made the principal object. All our affections were subjected to a most beneficial course of discipline, in which the inmost springs of vice and virtue were reached. But owing to the inadequacy of the doctrines on which the system rested, the solution of the problem was incoherent. The method by which Catholicism controlled the selfish propensities was one which turned men away from public life, and concentrated them on interests which were at once chimerical and personal. The immediate value of this great effort was, that it brought about for the first time a separation between moral and political power, which in the systems of antiquity had always been confounded. But the separation was due rather to the force of circumstances than to any conscious efforts, and it could not be fully carried out, because it was incompatible with the spirit of the Catholic doctrine and with the military character of society. Woman sympathized with Catholicism, but the people never supported it with enthusiasm, and it soon sank under the encroachments of the temporal power, and the degeneracy of the priesthood.

Positivism is the only system which can renew this premature effort and bring it to a satisfactory issue. Combining the spirit of antiquity with that of Catholic Feudalism, it proposes to carry out the political programme put forward by the Convention.

Positive religion brings before us in a definite shape the noblest of human problems, the permanent preponderance of Social feeling over Self-love. As far as the exceeding imperfection of our nature enables us to solve it, it will be solved by calling our home affections into continuous action ; affections which stand half way between self-love and universal sympathy. In order to consolidate and develop this solution, Positivism lays down the philosophical and social principle of Separation of theoretical from practical power. Theoretical power is consultative ; it directs education, and supplies general principles. Practical power directs action by special and imperative rules. All the elements of society that are excluded from political goverment become guarantees for the preservation of this arrangement. The priests of Humanity, who are the systematic organs of the moderating power, will always find themselves supported, in their attempts to modify the governing power, by women and by the people. But to be so supported, they must be men who, in addition to the intellectual power necessary for their mission, have the moral qualities which are yet more necessary ; who combine, that is, the tenderness of women with the energy of the people. The first guarantee for the possession of such qualities is the sacrifice of political authority and even of wealth. Then we may at last hope to see the new

religion taking the place of the old, because it will fulfil
in a more perfect way the mental and social purposes for
which the old religion existed. Monotheism will lapse
like Polytheism and Fetichism, into the domain of history ; and will, like them, be incorporated into the system
of universal commemoration, in which Humanity will
render due homage to all her predecessors.

Corruption of   It is not, then, merely on the ground of
Monotheism.   speculative truth that Positivists would urge
all those who are still halting between two opinions, to
choose between the absolute and the relative, between the
fruitless search for Causes and the solid study of Laws,
between submission to arbitrary Wills and submission to
demonstrable Necessities.   It is for Feeling still more
than for Reason to make the decision ; for upon it depends
the establishment of a higher form of social life.

Monotheism in Western Europe is now as obsolete and
as injurious as Polytheism was fifteen centuries ago. The
discipline in which its moral value principally consisted
has long since decayed ; and consequently the sole effect
of its doctrine, which has been so extravagantly praised,
is to degrade the affections by unlimited desires, and to
weaken the character by servile terrors. It supplied no
field for the Imagination, and forced it back upon Polytheism and Fetichism, which, under Theology, form the
only possible foundation for poetry. The pursuits of practical life were never sincerely promoted by it, and they
advanced only by evading or resisting its influence. The
noblest of all practical pursuits, that of social regeneration, is at the present time in direct opposition to it. For
by its vague notion of Providence, it prevents men from
forming a true conception of Law, a conception necessary
for true prevision, on which all wise intervention must
be based.

Sincere believers in Christianity will soon cease to interfere with the management of a world, where they profess
themselves to be pilgrims and strangers. The new
Supreme Being is no less jealous than the old, and will
not accept the servants of two masters. But the truth
is, that the more zealous theological partizans, whether
royalists, aristocrats, or democrats, have now for a long
time been insincere. God to them is but the nominal
chief of a hypocritical conspiracy, a conspiracy which is
even more contemptible than it is odious. Their object
is to keep the people from all great social improvements
by assuring them that they will find compensation for
their miseries in an imaginary future life. The doctrine
is already falling into discredit among the working classes
everywhere throughout the West, especially in Paris. All
theological tendencies, whether Catholic, Protestant, or
Deist, really serve to prolong and aggravate our moral
anarchy, because they hinder the diffusion of that social
sympathy and breadth of view, without which we can
never attain fixity of principle and regularity of life.
Every subversive scheme now afloat has either originated
in Monotheism or has received its sanction. Even Catholicism has lost its power of controlling revolutionary extravagance in some of its own most distinguished members.

It is for the sake of Order therefore, even more than of
Progress, that we call on all those who desire to rise above
their present disastrous state of oscillation in feeling and
opinion, to make a distinct choice between Positivism and
Theology. For there are now but two camps: the camp
of reaction and anarchy, which acknowledges more or less
distinctly the direction of God: the camp of construction
and progress, which is wholly devoted to Humanity.

The Being upon whom all our thoughts are concentrated
is one whose existence is undoubted. We recognise that

existence not in the Present only, but in the Past, and even in the Future: and we find it always subject to one fundamental Law, by which we are enabled to conceive of it as a whole. Placing our highest happiness in universal Love, we live, as far as it is possible, for others; and this in public life as well as in private; for the two are closely linked together in our religion; a religion clothed in all the beauty of Art, and yet never inconsistent with Science. After having thus exercised our powers to the full, and having given a charm and sacredness to our temporary life, we shall at last be for ever incorporated into the Supreme Being, of whose life all noble natures are necessarily partakers. It is only through the worship of Humanity that we can feel the inward reality and inexpressible sweetness of this incorporation. It is unknown to those who being still involved in theological belief, have not been able to form a clear conception of the Future, and have never experienced the feeling of pure self-sacrifice.

THE END.

CPSIA information can be obtained at www.ICGtesting.com
Printed in the USA
BVOW082002211112

306208BV00001B/31/P